Recruiting, Retaining, and Promoting
Culturally Different Employees

Recruiting, Retaining, and Promoting Culturally Different Employees

Lionel Laroche, Ph.D.
Don Rutherford

Routledge
Taylor & Francis Group

LONDON AND NEW YORK

First published by Butterworth-Heinemann

This edition published 2012 by Routledge
2 Park Square, Milton Park, Abingdon, Oxon OX14 4RN
711 Third Avenue, New York, NY, 10017, USA

Routledge is an imprint of the Taylor & Francis Group, an informa business

Library of Congress Cataloging-in-Publication Data
Application submitted

British Library Cataloguing-in-Publication Data
A catalogue record for this book is available from the British Library.

ISBN 13: 978-0-7506-8240-4
ISBN 10: 0-7506-8240-X

Contents

Acknowledgments

We are indebted to those who came before us in the cross-cultural field for sharing both their research and their experience through books, seminars, collaborations, and conversations. These include Edward T. Hall, Geert Hofstede, Fons Trompenaars, Phil Harris, Robert Moran, George Renwick, Milton Bennett, Janet Bennett, Noel Kreicker, and Dianne Hofner Saphiere. We are very grateful to these people.

We thank our clients for having us assist their employees through our cross-cultural programs. We have learned much from them and their questions. Thank you to Bieny Pryor (BP Canada), Joanne Butler (TransAlta), Kathy Marasco (Precision Drilling), Laurel McLean (Enbridge), Lynn Robinson (EnCana), Steve Fieldgate (Talisman Energy), Shannon Brown (Petro-Canada), Sue Irwin (ConocoPhillips Canada), Tacita Lewars (Shell Canada), Vanita Haining (Husky Energy), and Vicki Reid (EnCana). Thank you also to Nicole Morgenstern (American Management Association), Penny Partridge, Christine Barwell, Jenny Deslauriers, Susan Ghavam, Meadow Larkins (PwC Canada), Kat Quinn (Deloitte Canada), Jennifer Robertson-Decker, Wendy Yule (Sun Life Canada), Wendy Molotkow (City of Toronto), Luis DeSousa (ATI), Marie Rocchi Dean (University of Toronto), Diana Spizzirri (Ontario College of Pharmacists), Pinoo Bindhani, Barbara Nowers (Career Bridge), Sandi Heath (Teekay Shipping), Alma Farias (Canadian Chamber of Commerce in Mexico), and Adam McEniry (Canada-Peru Chamber of Commerce), and many others.

Friends and clients were polled to give us suggestions for issues to address in this book. These helpful people, in addition to the people just named, were Bob Arbuthnott, Derek Parnell, Fariborz Birjandian, Jacques Gendron, James S. Frideres, Janis Houston, Kelly Sudsbury, Michele Stanners, Paul Tildsley, and Wilf Zerbe.

Thanks to Ellen James for all her suggestions on ways to improve the manuscript.

We are very thankful to our supportive families, who put up with us while we were spending so much time on this book.

Finally, Lionel wants to thank all the people in Canada and the United States (in particular, his wife's relatives), who have accepted him as one of theirs. He also wishes to thank his parents for giving him the desire to travel and the curiosity to meet other people and learn from all situations, and his wife for being so patient with him while he learned the North American system.

This book would not have been possible without the support of these people.

Prologue

The human experiment gets more interesting all the time. The ways of foreigners are becoming our ways and our ways are becoming the ways of foreigners to an extent never seen before. The migration of earthlings is bringing us face-to-face with more culturally different people than ever before. Alongside the trends of adaptation and integration, there exists the equally strong phenomenon of cultures holding their own while interacting with others. For the authors, this fusion, clashing, and coevolution of cultures is fascinating and important. The future of work and the workplace will be changed by it, as will all aspects of society.

As a chemical engineer, Dr. Lionel Laroche worked for Procter & Gamble for a number of years and then with Xerox. Lionel worked on numerous international projects with engineers and scientists from all over the world. Even though they were all competent technical professionals who spoke English fairly well, the projects often fell short of their objectives. Lionel found that in both companies, the same kinds of cross-cultural challenges often derailed the work. His personal interest in cross-cultural issues led him to work full time assisting organizations and individuals to function successfully across cultures. A cornerstone of Lionel's current work is helping to prepare recent immigrants to adjust to the business culture realities of North America in order to find jobs that make use of their experience, education, and expertise. In this way, they can integrate more successfully in North American organizations. The flip side is helping organizations (particularly human resources (HR) and management) prepare themselves so that they can make the most of their incoming new talent.

Don Rutherford studied sociology, race, and ethnic relations at university. His fascination with how something normal in one culture was considered bizarre or immoral in another kept him studying and started him on his world travels. Don has lived eight years outside of North America in Latin America, Africa, Asia, and Europe. He worked for 10 years in the IT industry. Since cofounding the intercultural firm Culture Connect in 1997, Don has helped hundreds of people to prepare either for life and work on expatriate assignment outside of North America or for life and work as inpatriates or immigrants to North America. Another theme in his cross-cultural work is assisting multicultural work groups become more effective.

Lionel and Don have come to realize the following.

- Most professionals vastly underestimate the impact of cultural differences in their work. Whether it be accountants, engineers, or doctors, the common belief is that the technical skills can be universally recognized and that these skills are what will "make or break" the professional equally in any country. This belief is common among both the recent immigrants looking for work and North American organizations recruiting employees.

- Professional recent immigrants are often passed over at some stage in the recruitment process, not because of a lack of technical skills, but rather because of cultural disconnects or misunderstandings. Organizations are cutting themselves off from an incredible talent pool because they are misinterpreting the behaviors they are seeing in résumés, interviews, and probation periods.

- By being coached on cultural difference, both the recruiting organizations and recent immigrant job seekers can make a number of minor changes to their approach that will allow them to connect successfully. This book intends to provide some of that coaching.

The examples Lionel and Don use and the bulk of their experience come from business organizations or corporations. Governmental, educational, and nonprofit organizations may still find value in the comments and suggestions. For example, many of the cross-cultural issues related to communication, managerial, and teamwork style differences apply to the governmental and nonprofit sectors with limited modifications. On the other hand, the recruitment and selection process used by government, universities, and government agencies differs at times more substantially from the corporate recruitment and selection process, so the material presented in this book may require some adaptation in order to be used in that context.

The purpose of this book is to help organizations take full advantage of the opportunity that immigrants represent to their workforces. Culture influences the way people seek a job and perform a job as well as how organizations evaluate a candidate and develop an employee.

This book will help people and organizations do the following:

- Modify their recruitment and selection process to avoid rejecting culturally different candidates for reasons that are unrelated to their ability to do the job.
- Develop and promote culturally diverse employees to ensure that they retain and capitalize on the ideas and skills these employees bring.

Annually, the United States and Canada welcome significant numbers of immigrant professionals with high levels of formal education (bachelor's degree, master's degree, and Ph.D.) as well as extensive work experience; yet many of these immigrants are unemployed or underemployed. This book attempts to address the imbalance by delving into the cultural differences that hinder immigrants and companies from making the connection that would benefit both.

It is not suggested that all recent immigrants will make great employees, just as not all potential local hires will make great employees. However, if you can understand something of the cultural differences at play in recruitment, then you will be in a better position to determine which of the new immigrants will make great employees and which will not. Today many employers cannot make the distinction and as a result simply stay away from the groups of people they feel they do not understand.

An even more likely recipe for disaster is when the recruiters have been given a directive to hire more "diversity" and the recruiters are not supportive of the plan or prepared for the differences they are about to experience. In such cases, the recruiter may, in resignation, simply hire a bunch of "diverse," people with the unstated expectation that they will fail. Here, the recruiter has neither the skills nor the motivation to distinguish the good from the poor candidates. Fortunately, this appears to represent only a tiny minority of organizations.

Some concerns organizations often mention regarding recruiting and retaining culturally different recruits include the following.

- We need access to more of them, but there are issues with immigration and work permits, not to mention the cultural barriers.
- The people who apply for the jobs posted on our company's website have no relevant experience.
- Their résumés look very different.

- They behave oddly in interviews.
- I'm not sure we are really communicating.
- Feedback from their coworkers, teams, and managers is negative.
- They can't seem to figure out the simple stuff.
- Why should I care whether or not my company employs culturally differ-
  ent employees?

This book addresses all the foregoing concerns except immigration and work permits. The material in this book may not cover every question you have on recruitment, retention, and promotion; however, our intention is to tackle most of the important questions that relate to culture. It will provide you with ideas, background, and techniques to help you make decisions based on greater understanding.

The material presented in this book has its origins in three primary sources.

1. The authors have drawn on experiences from their professional and personal lives. Their interactions with professionals from dozens of countries
   and their own personal experiences in dozens of countries provide many
   of the stories. Since many of the concepts presented in this book are more
   easily understood through stories or anecdotes, these are liberally included
   to make relevant points.
2. The authors have learned from the questions and discussions with
   many of the stakeholders (immigrants in North America, middle/senior
   managers, and HR professionals in North American organizations).
   In particular, they have coached hundreds of foreign assignees and
   immigrants working for the Big Four accounting firms in Canada and
   taught hundreds of professionals and managers through bridging
   programs.
3. The authors have also relied on the contributions of the giants in the
   cross-cultural management field. Some of these include Geert Hofstede,
   Fons Trompenaars, Edward Hall, Phil Harris, Robert Moran, and George
   Renwick.

On the one side, immigrants are blamed for being security risks, stealing jobs, diluting national culture, and burdening the social, health, and educational systems. On the other side, immigrants are said to be creating new jobs, making our societies more dynamic and prosperous, and paying more in taxes than they draw out of the system. While we tend to believe the latter statement, this debate is beyond the scope of this book.

We expect continued immigration, and perhaps rising immigration rates, to be a fact or a reality in North America for the foreseeable future.

Sixty-six percent of senior executives surveyed from 160 international companies around the world expect corporate boards of directors to become more diverse in nationality and gender over the next 10 years, while 84 percent anticipate greater diversity among the top 100 management positions at corporations. The study was done in 2002.[1]

As with boards, so will it be with the general employee population. Corporations acknowledge that greater diversity will simply be the reality in the future.

Immigrants are entering Canada and the United States at a rate not seen for over a hundred years. The numbers are large and appear to be growing (see Appendix). The primary reason for these increased immigration numbers is that North America needs more workers. Diverse employees are most often invited into an organization because of a basic need for more labor. Benefits corporations receive from integrating diverse employees into their workforce typically go beyond the original expectation.

In particular, the aging of baby boomers is likely to create major shifts in the demographics of most North American organizations. The increasing number of retiring baby boomers will create openings mostly in the higher levels of organizations. People will move up to fill these openings, either from inside or from outside the organization. This will lead to the creation of many openings at the lower levels, which will be filled by new labor market entrants. In both the United States and Canada, labor market entrants are very different from the people who are retiring: There is a much higher percentage of women, visible minorities, and aboriginal people among them than among retiring baby boomers, so the demographics of many North American organizations are likely to be quite different in 10 years from what they are today. For most large organizations and developed countries, finding ways to integrate culturally different people without losing their identity and purpose will be one of the major challenges of the 21st century.

This book and its examples are geared primarily to English-speaking audiences in the United States and Canada. Much of this material can be applied,

[1]http://www.kornferry.com/Library/Process.asp?P=Articles_Detail&CID=507&LID=1

with some modifications, to the case of French-speaking immigrants in Quebec. For simplicity, we combine the two countries under the term *North America*; our apologies to Mexico. Readers in other parts of the world (particularly in Australia, New Zealand, and the UK) will no doubt find value in the text as well.

> Eliminating age, gender, and cultural barriers could add 1.6 million Canadians to the workforce and increase personal incomes by $174 billion according to a new report from RBC Economics, entitled "The Diversity Advantage: A Case for Canada's 21st Century Economy."[2]

Some of the world most respected companies have the following to say about the value of diversity in the workplace:

> At Microsoft, we believe that diversity enriches our performance and products, the communities where we live and work, and the lives of our employees. As our workforce evolves to reflect the growing diversity of our communities and the global marketplace, our efforts to understand, value, and incorporate differences become increasingly important.[3]

> To best serve our global GE business customers, we will create and sustain a working environment at the Global Research Center that cultivates awareness of and respect for differences and provides support for everyone. Diversity is something we live and breathe each and every day at GE Global Research—over 40 countries are represented in our mix of individuals. We come from different walks of life and speak countless languages. . . . We proactively address diversity.[4]

> At the Coca-Cola Company, we are committed to cultivating a diverse, rewarding culture that encourages our people to develop to their fullest potential. . . . As we have expanded over the decades, our company has benefited from the various cultural insights and perspectives of the societies in which we do business. Much of our future success will depend on our ability to develop a worldwide team that is rich in its diversity of people, cultures, and ideas. We are determined to have a diverse culture, from top to bottom, that benefits from the perspectives of each individual.[5]

[2]http://www.rbc.com/newsroom/20051020diversity.html
[3]http://www.microsoft.com/citizenship/diversity/
[4]http://ge.com/research/grc_6_5.html
[5]http://www2.coca-cola.com/ourcompany/at_work.html

We believe that unlocking the power of diversity will enable RBC Financial Group (Canada) to be more competitive and our communities more dynamic. This belief guides us in developing our business strategies, products, and services. Having a diverse workforce is the first step to ensuring we can best serve an increasingly multiethnic client base. Wherever possible, our employees reflect the makeup of the communities they serve.[6]

We have written this book thinking first and foremost of the challenges faced by the following people:

- Human resources personnel responsible for recruitment and selection, staffing, training, and development, succession planning, organizational development, and diversity.
- Line or functional managers responsible for recruitment, selection, and development of employees.
- Culturally diverse employees who are trying to make sense out of their experience and/or further their careers in North America.
- Nonprofit organizations specializing in helping immigrants settle and find jobs in the United States and Canada.

Other people may find value in reading this book as well:

- Senior managers wanting to plan for the upcoming demographic changes.
- Search firm employees.
- Government employees responsible for administering immigration policies and immigrant settlement funding.
- Anyone interested in knowing more about this timely topic.

This book is laid out as follows.

- Chapter 1 provides an introduction to the topic and gives some definitions, including how we are using the terms *culture* and *national culture*. The implicit and explicit forms of culture are detailed. The link between culture and the recruitment and retention process is given. The chapter ends with a caution about stereotyping and how it can be avoided.

[6]http://www.rbc.com/community/rbc_community/community_reports/2005report/pdf/CRR_ENG_CAN_2005.pdf

- Chapter 2 examines the collection and assessment of résumés in the process of recruiting culturally different employees. The cultural basis of common differences in the content and style of reference letters is highlighted—such as how accomplishments are presented, candidates who have "jumped around," and the inclusion of unusual information. Reasons are given for potentially good candidates' résumés being set aside and what organizations might do both to reach these potential candidates and not to screen them out during the résumé review process.

- Chapter 3 explores the interview phase of recruitment. A few of the topics include body language, English as a second language, deference shown, and appropriate topics of discussion. Suggestions are given to minimize the risk of eliminating solid candidates in the interview stage solely due to a cultural difference.

- Chapter 4 offers job search advice for immigrants and nonprofit organizations that help them find employment in Canada and the United States. It discusses how immigrants need to network, create a clear and concise résumé, position themselves as specialists, and more, in order to be taken seriously in the North American job market.

- Chapter 5 examines how organizations can assist in the integration of their new employees by understanding what they are going through and by making small adjustments that all add up to a major difference in terms of retention rates. The various orientation programs and topics are mentioned, with greater detail provided on the business culture orientation. In addition, the topics of coaching, mentoring, and family support are introduced.

- Chapter 6 provides in greater detail the numerous cross-cultural communication challenges related to recruitment, retention, and promotion. This is the longest chapter, and it covers the issues where workplace relations typically first break down. Verbal and nonverbal differences are detailed, with each subsection containing advice on how to overcome or avoid the misunderstanding represented.

- Chapter 7 discusses manager–employee relations and how these are dramatically affected by the level of hierarchy a person is accustomed to in their home culture. Respect of position, decision making and delegating, and performance evaluation are a few of the topics covered. The chapter concludes with a section on how the interpretation of feedback varies by culture.

- Chapter 8 examines how the concept of teamwork varies across cultures and affects the workplace. A national comparison chart on individualism introduces the topic. Most newcomers to North America originate from more collective or group-oriented cultures. This has major implications for the way they work in teams. Risk tolerance is a second area explored in relation to teamwork.

- Chapter 9 tackles retention and promotion issues resulting from cultural differences. It examines the different motivations and approaches to career management around the world in order to explain why culturally different employees find it so difficult to move up in North American organizations. It contains suggestions for both individual employees and organizations to eliminate the "glass ceiling" that many culturally different employees experience.

- Chapter 10 presents a summary and offers conclusions. The opportunity that culturally diverse employees present to North American organizations is revisited.

This book looks at the situation faced by employers of immigrants from a concrete, pragmatic perspective. It is based on the idea that the labor market is indeed a market, ruled by the law of supply and demand. From this perspective, this book expects culturally different people to be hired or promoted based on performance. The goal of this book is to help level the playing field so that organizations can hire the best person for the job regardless of his or her country of origin and so that immigrants can achieve their full potential in their new country.

Some of the material contained in the later chapters of the book are revised and expanded versions of the corresponding chapters in Lionel Laroche's book entitled *Managing Cultural Diversity in Technical Professions*. The revisions make the material more relevant to recruitment, retention, and promotion and to HR and management professionals.

The purpose of cross-cultural understanding is not so that we can necessarily do things in the style of the other person. Rather, the purpose is to be able to choose, from a position of understanding, an approach for the particular situation that is more likely to help everyone involved reach his or her professional objectives. It aims at helping everyone interpret the actions, words, attitudes, and behaviors of people who come from different parts of the world based on what they mean, rather than based on what we would mean if we acted, spoke, or behaved in the same way.

This book focuses on the impact of cultural difference in the workplace and the challenges that immigrants and their employers experience as a result. Some of its content will be applicable to other groups (such as aboriginal people). This book does not examine gender/race/sexual orientation or other related differences that are covered in diversity discussions.

Most organizations acknowledge that the majority of their success depends on the quality of their employees. Hiring, keeping, and managing people well provides the finest competitive advantage. Having the finest workforce begins with the critically important step of recruiting the finest people. Time is well spent clarifying the technical and nontechnical skills of each position within the broader context of what you would like your workforce to look like in 5, 10, and 20 years.

Lionel Laroche, Ph.D.   **Don Rutherford**

1

Introduction: Culture and Recruitment

Spanish monarchs King Ferdinand and Queen Isabella were able to see beyond cultural differences to hire the upstart foreigner from Genoa, Christopher Columbus. Columbus proposed to navigate their ships across the Atlantic Ocean to Asia. He never reached Asia, but his discovery made Spain one of the most prosperous nations in the 16th century. Whether the message from this is that you can't trust foreigners or that foreigners are the source of a nation's innovation and growth might be debated. However, the voyages did change the world. Is a potential Columbus being passed over in your organization's recruitment and retention efforts?

How do you go about getting a job? If this is your native country and culture, you have a pretty good idea of how to make a good impression on a potential recruiter and company. You may have researched it or invested in professional help with your résumé on how best to present yourself. We know that being hired for a professional job, unless it is directly through a personal connection, requires a complex combination of education, work experience, interpersonal skills, networking, and motivation, all put together into a professional presentation.

Similarly, the newcomer wants to present him- or herself in the best light and typically relies on past experience and learning for guidance. For some, that may mean focusing entirely on the incredible university attended; for others, trying to build rapport and gaining the interviewer's trust; and for still others, first pointing out one's prestigious family background. These are the approaches the candidates have learned work from real-life experience in their own countries. What many have not figured out yet is that these are not the approaches that will work in North America.

Immigrants are attempting to achieve the same objectives as North Americans but going about it in a different way, in alignment with their cultural background. In most cases, immigrants were successful in their home countries and will naturally try to apply the same "success strategies" that have served them well up to this point in their lives. However, the strategies may not yield the desired results in Canada and the United States.

The recruiting process is particularly prone to cross-cultural misunderstanding because it involves interactions between people who have never met before and who therefore rely on their cultural programming to interpret the other's behavior.

This chapter begins with a definition of the term *culture*, followed by a description of *national culture*. The iceberg analogy is used to differentiate *explicit* (external, visible) from *implicit* (internal, invisible) culture. A more direct link between culture and business choices is illustrated in the next section, "Culture is About Making Choices."

A segment on generalizations and stereotypes gives a warning of the hazards inherent in this type of discussion. While the goal of this book is to assist people in bridging the cultural divide, if each cultural comment is considered a hard-and-fast rule for every person in a particular society, then stereotypes are created, and the overall effect is negative.

Strategies and techniques for dealing with these cultural differences are provided in the subsequent chapters. The general advice is to temporarily suspend judgment in order to collect more information when faced with a confusing cross-cultural situation. This idea will also be expanded upon in later chapters.

Culture Defined

When a Google search in May of 2006 turns up over 1.1 billion links for the word *culture*, you know it has become a popular term. There is the Department for Culture, postmodern culture, cannabis culture, Hellenic culture, intellectual culture, biological culture, and popular culture, to name a few uses of the word listed in the first 20 hits.

For our purposes, *culture* can be defined as the shared beliefs and values of a group of people, our learned way of living. It encompasses what we are taught to think, feel, and do in any given situation by the society in which we were raised. As well as providing content, our cultural conditioning directs how we are to think, feel, and behave.

Here are a few descriptions of culture:

- The collective programming of the mind, which distinguishes one group of people from another. (Geert Hofstede)
- The way we do things when nobody tells us how to do them. (Jack Kemp)
- Like water to a fish. A fish does not know that water exists until it jumps out of it.
- Our concept of culture is closely tied in to Albert Einstein's definition of *common sense*, which he describes as "the collection of prejudices acquired by age 18."

National Culture

Since the mid-1960s, a great deal of social science research has focused on the concept of *national culture*. Edward Hall, Geert Hofstede, Fons Trompenaars, and others carried on significant research projects that highlighted value and behavioral differences among countries. This research provides the antecedents for many of the concepts in this book.

Studies into cross-cultural values and behaviors found that as well as personal, regional, and other sources of difference, national culture is tremendously influential in determining one's worldview and the way one acts in the world and in business.

One of the great philosophical questions asks in what way each person on the planet is similar to all others and in which ways people are different from one another. Perhaps the first part of this question is the easiest to answer. Basic physical needs and experiences are universal, shared by all humans. This includes activities like eating, drinking, finding shelter, showing affection, and procreation. This universal level may be thought of as our hardware.

The ways in which we are different might, for simplicity's sake, be broken down into two broad categories (Figure 1.1). The first category we can term *culture*. This represents how groups of ever-ingenious and adaptable humans came to meet the universal needs of nourishment, protection, and child rearing based on their unique environment and experience. The differences as well as the similarities between cultures from opposite sides of the globe are quite astounding. Culture is like our software operating system.

On top of culture, comes the unique behavior and contribution of the individual. This uniqueness comes out of personality and the decisions one makes. The amount of freedom allowed to individuals to deviate from the cultural norms is also guided by the culture. In some countries, individual differences

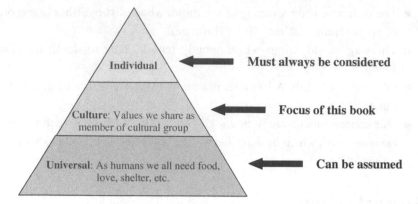

Figure 1.1 Universal, culture, individual.

are less pronounced, while in others individuals appear to behave very differently from one another.

> I considered myself an observant person and a quick learner until I went to Japan. Before arriving, I knew that I was to remove my shoes before I entered someone's home. The first time I entered a home with shoes I kicked myself, the second time I swore at myself, and the third time I began to question my intelligence, as I'm sure my hosts did. I did eventually get it, but it took far longer than I would have imagined. This is just one example of the dozens or hundreds of things I was doing wrong in Japan. It gave me a greater appreciation for the challenges people face who come from other cultures to live and work in North America. New ways of behavior are not adopted overnight.
>
> —A North American teacher in Japan

Changing an ingrained, habitual behavior is no small task, as anyone who has tried to keep a New Year's resolution is well aware or as anyone who has tried getting behind the wheel of a car in a country where they drive on the opposite side than he or she is used to has learned.

Here is a simple exercise to remind you of how tough this can be. For the next few people you converse with face-to-face, whether at home, in the office, or in public, change the amount of eye contact you make. Decide in advance whether you will give less eye contact or more eye contact in the conversations. Going either way will likely be very, very challenging for you, while the other person may end up questioning your mental stability or your general well-being.

This exercise gives us a small glimpse of what recent immigrants are going through when they try to change 10, 50, or 100 behaviors all at the same time. Some researchers say it takes three months of doing something continually the new way before it becomes the new habitual behavior.

In a wide range of situations, we know that we are supposed to do X and most Americans or Canadians would agree with us that X is the right thing to do in this situation. In the same situation, most French people know that they are supposed to do Y. The issue is not so much that there are two ways of handling the same situation, X and Y. The main issue is that, as far as most North Americans are concerned, X is the only option they can think of. Similarly, Y is the only option French people can think of. So when Americans or Canadians see French people do Y in a situation where they can only think of X, their first reaction is "Why?," then "It's weird," and then "It's wrong." The same is true in reverse: When French people see North Americans do X in a situation where they would do Y, they also go "Why?," then "It's weird," and finally "It's wrong."

One simple illustration of this issue occurs when people cross a street. Most Americans and Canadians have always lived in North America, so their first reflex is to look left first to see if a car is coming. When they go to the UK, Hong Kong, or Australia (or any other place in the world where people drive on the other side), most have the "near-death experience" of starting to cross the street and realizing almost too late that they should have looked the other way first. At that point, they realize that there is no law of physics that states that cars must come from the left, but that has been such a good approximation in their past experiences that it became a reflex. Most cultural differences follow a similar pattern: They are reflexes that made complete sense and helped people be more effective in one environment but become liabilities in another environment.

People who belong to different groups have derived different sets of unwritten rules. Within each group these rules are well understood, to the point that they are obvious. However, each group has different sets of rules, but few of the members of the various groups realize that there are differences between the various sets of unwritten rules.

For example, men and women operate according to different sets of unwritten rules. Among men, the male set of unwritten rules is clear and there is no need to explain it. The issues arise when men interpret the behavior of women according to the unwritten rules of men, since this leads to misunderstandings. The same is true when women interpret the behavior of men according to the female set of unwritten rules.

Iceberg Analogy

Culture is often represented as an iceberg. You may be aware that roughly 10 percent of an iceberg is above the water line while 90 percent is submerged. Like an iceberg, the much smaller, visible proportion of culture is made of the tangible or exterior manifestations, which we perceive through our five senses. In employee recruitment, retention, and promotion, tangible manifestations of a culture might include the following (Figure 1.2):

- Résumé content and style.
- Dress and appearance.
- Accent and use of English terms.
- Body language.
- Greetings.
- Reports, documents, presentations, etc.
- Organizational structure.
- Architecture of buildings and the layout of offices inside.

For example, when most North American professionals take a flight to Saudi Arabia and get off the plane in Riyadh, they know as soon as they step off the plane that they are not in Kansas anymore: The heat comes down on them (the outside temperature often exceeds 45°C/110°F), everyone is dressed differently, and the buildings have completely different architecture.

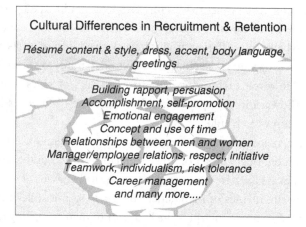

Figure 1.2 The visible and invisible parts of culture.

Similarly, many Japanese offices are set up quite differently from the way North American offices are set up. Many Japanese offices are set up like North American university lecture halls, with one desk facing rows of identical desks, chairs, and phones. In a Japanese office, the most senior manager sits at the front, facing everyone, and the hierarchy can be read in the room, since the people in the front row report directly to the most senior manager while people farther back are in lower positions. Those who are thought to be incompetent are often given a window office so they have something to do, namely, look outside.

> Our offices are set up in the same manner as those in our Japanese head office. This creates a real headache for me when we try to hire people: When American candidates walk into our offices (one big room with 120 desks), you can read the strong negative reaction they have on their faces. The lack of privacy turns many candidates away.
>
> —American HR professional working for the American subsidiary of a Japanese company

Because they are visible, these differences usually do not create the biggest challenges. For example, most Japanese coming to North America know, or learn quickly, that North Americans do not bow to introduce themselves. They shake hands instead. Initially, Japanese handshakes may be tentative and somewhat limp but they know that a handshake is what North Americans expect.

By contrast, invisible differences create far more issues for immigrants. The vast majority of a culture, like an iceberg, is invisible at first, below the surface. This is sometimes called *implicit* or *subjective* culture and consists of the values and thought patterns that each culture has created over time. It defines normal societal life and business customs. For example, culture provides parameters for the concept and use of time, motivators, and the meaning attributed to their existence. Since it cannot be directly observed, this part of culture needs to be inferred from what people say and do. In recruitment, retention, and promotion, the invisible part of the iceberg might include the following (among many more):

- Building rapport, persuasion.
- Accomplishment, self-promotion.
- Emotional engagement.
- Concept and use of time.
- Relationships between men and women.
- Manager/employee relations, respect, initiative.

- Teamwork, individualism, risk tolerance.
- Career management.

For example, the way people structure time is quite different in different parts of the world. One way to make this difference visible is to ask people when they would organize a half-day workshop for their teams. In North America, the answer tends to be on Tuesdays, Wednesdays, or Thursdays (North Americans avoid Mondays and Fridays, since they are too close to weekends—people may forget on Mondays and may not be altogether there on Fridays); mornings tend to be preferred to afternoons. By contrast, Mexicans will often schedule half-day workshops on Fridays, preferably in the afternoon, while Indians will schedule half-day workshops on Saturday mornings. Both options seem completely incongruous to most North Americans.

Invisible differences can create issues that are really difficult to unravel, as the following example illustrates.

I spent some time in the German plant of our company. After one reorganization, people in the German plant started to interact quite frequently with their counterparts in the Saudi plant. One of the really puzzling issues we encountered was the fact that Saudi secretaries would call the German plant and immediately hang up when someone started to answer the phone. It took us three months to understand where this issue was coming from and to deal with it by training or reassigning the people involved.

This issue stemmed from the fact that there are essentially no women (with the exception of a few female expatriates) in the Saudi workplace. As a result, all jobs are male jobs in Saudi Arabia—there is no such thing as female jobs there. As a result, if you call someone and you have a female voice on the phone, you have clearly reached someone at their private residence; if it was a corporation, your call would be answered by a man. In addition, a Saudi man is not supposed to talk to a woman he does not know. So the male Saudi secretaries would call the German plant to set up a conference call or something, hear a woman's voice (every secretary and receptionist in the German plant was female) that they did not recognize, think that they had the wrong number, and hang up immediately without talking to her.

—Canadian HR professional

Culture Is About Making Choices

Culture is about making choices—in most cases, instant choices between various options or choosing one option without really seeing any alternative. For example, think about the kind of manager you prefer. Do you like working for managers who give you space and freedom? Do you like managers who closely follow your progress? Alternatively, do you like managers who are somewhere in between? On the following scale, which position best represents the kind of manager that suits you best?

Question: I prefer that my manager:

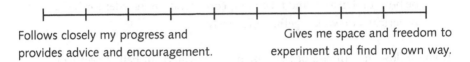

Follows closely my progress and
provides advice and encouragement.

Gives me space and freedom to
experiment and find my own way.

Figure 1.3 shows the responses to this question for a sampling of countries, namely, the United States, Canada, China, and India. For all four countries, the bell curve represents the normalized distribution of answers obtained by the authors from professionals from each country (*professional* is defined here as someone who needs at least a bachelor's degree in order to do his or her job—the sample population represented here includes engineers, IT professionals, scientists, accountants, pharmacists, CFOs, university professors, etc.).

Question: I prefer that my manager:

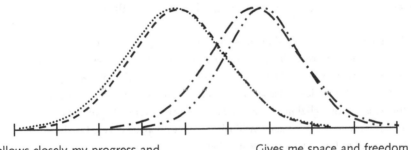

Follows closely my progress and
provides advice and encouragement.

Gives me space and freedom to
experiment and find my own way.

Figure 1.3 Normalized distribution of answers from professionals in:
United States: —■—; Canada: —■■—; India: ⋯⋯⋯⋯; China: ———.

Two important conclusions can be drawn from Figure 1.3.

1. As we might expect, people of the same country do not all answer the question in the same way. There is a natural bell curve distribution of responses. This tells us "we cannot judge a book by its cover." Knowing a

person is an American does not tell us how the person will answer this question. People from the same culture do not all prefer the same managerial style.

2. At the same time, Figure 1.3 shows that there are systematic differences between cultures. There are cultural tendencies. Most Indians expect clearer directions from their managers than the average American manager expects to give his or her reports. This difference in expectations needs to be both understood and taken into consideration in order for Indians and Americans to work together effectively.

If you follow the tail end of the Canadian or American bell curves to the left, you will see that they end further left on the continuum than the average "spike" on the Indian or Chinese curve. Not surprisingly, this suggests that you will find a few Canadians or Americans who like their work to be followed more closely by their managers, more so than the average Indian or Chinese.

Generalizations and Stereotypes

This book contains generalizations about cultures and the people within them. Generalizations, as described in the previous section, can be helpful when they give insight into people's behavior. They are unhelpful if we assume that the generalization applies to every individual from that culture.

> A director of international operations asked me to give an orientation to his work group, which was receiving an international employee. The new hire was an Algerian single woman. The director wanted to ensure that his work group did not offend her. We reviewed background on the country, the values of Algerians, and the tenets of the religion of Islam. I explained that some Muslims appreciate being able to pray in the workplace. A Muslim woman may be covered with clothing from head to foot, including most of her face.
>
> It was quite a shock for the work group when the Algerian woman arrived for her first day of work. She was not a practicing Muslim. She was not in the least bit reserved. Her clothes were stylish, modern, and revealing. In fact, someone from Human Resources had to explain to her what was acceptable attire not to offend modest North American office sensibilities.
>
> —A cross-cultural consultant

Differentiating generalizations from stereotypes can be done as shown in Table 1.1.

Table 1.1   Differentiating Generalizations from Stereotypes

Generalizations	Stereotypes
■ Are based on a large sample of a group ■ Provide general characteristics based on cultural and social factors ■ Assume that individuals within groups vary in their compliance ■ Inform rather than prescribe	■ Present a fixed and inflexible image of a group ■ Ignore exceptions and focus on behaviors that support the image they present ■ Are ethnocentric or racial
Examples: ■ Americans tend to be more individualistic than do the Japanese ■ The importance of one's family background in the interview situation tends to be valued more highly in South America than in North America	*Examples:* ■ All Japanese are group-oriented or collective-minded ■ All South Americans have their jobs because of their family background

Properly researched cultural generalizations help to give a heads up for the differences we "may" encounter when meeting someone of a particular culture. They also expose us to common cultural differences in order to reduce our shock when we first experience the difference. We become aware of areas that are likely to be sensitive and are to be handled with care.

There will be times when an employee will behave nothing like what this book says he or she might, based on his or her cultural background. Remember, this book does not say how an individual will act in any situation. It talks of tendencies and cultural generalizations. By understanding the extremes of cultural difference, you are in a better position to understand what is going on when you see that difference and are better able to react appropriately.

Definitions and Terms

Here are some terms commonly appearing in this book, along with their respective usage.

culture   Shared beliefs and values of a group of people.

national culture   The culture of a country. For example, the national culture of Japan differs from the national culture of the

	United States or Canada. Sample areas of focus include communication, relationships, and business culture.
culturally different employees	Employees born and raised outside the United States and Canada; recent immigrants. Immigrants.
values	Deeply held beliefs and preferences of outcome. A culture's preference or tendency to individualism, for example, over group orientation indicates that the value of individualism is greater than the value of group orientation in that culture.
diversity	In its broadest form, speaks to any way in which there is difference. For our purposes, it will usually refer to a difference of nationality or national culture.
North American	In this book, refers to the peoples of Canada and the United States; this includes English Canadians, French Canadians, Americans, as well as anyone born and raised in Canada or the United States (our apologies to Mexicans). While there are differences between English Canada, French Canada, and the United States, they are smaller compared to the cultural distance between North America and most other countries in the world.
Aboriginal	First Nations (in Canada), Native American (in the United States)
Indian	Person from India
company	Though we often refer to companies in this book, most of the material can equally apply to any organization: governmental, educational, not for profit, and so on.
recent immigrants	Immigrants who arrived in North America in the preceding five years.
international new hire	New employee who was recruited overseas and immigrated to North America to take a new position.

2

Screening Résumés

Job specifications or criteria are the central issue in screening résumés; i.e., comparing the requirements for the job with the skills of the potential candidate as described in the résumé or curriculum vitae (CV). This matching process becomes more complex when looking at the résumés of culturally different candidates. This chapter describes how résumés of recent immigrants may look different from those of mainstream North Americans. It will provide background to the differences and strategies needed to avoid eliminating great potential candidates because of unconventional résumés.

The recruitment and selection process brings together people who normally do not know one another. Throughout the process, candidates try to demonstrate to recruiters, through their behavior and words, that they have the skills and attributes required to perform well in the position for which they have applied. The recruiters try to evaluate which candidate is best suited for the position based on these behaviors and words. When candidates and recruiters come from different cultural backgrounds, they use different grids of interpretation, which can result in misunderstandings and lead to the rejection of candidates for reasons that are unrelated to their ability to do the job.

For example, the cover letters of Muslim candidates may contain statements like "I pray to God that you will consider my application." In Arabic, this statement makes complete sense, since, in Islam, only God controls the future, any statement that relates to something that will take place in the future is subordinated to God's will (which is why so many Arab statements end with "Insh'Allah—God willing." It is also simply protocol in many Muslim countries.

Translated into English, these statements do not fit the expectations of North American recruiters. In their minds, "God is not involved in our recruiting process," so they tend to downgrade or even eliminate candidates who have included such statements in their cover letters.

The same dynamic may be repeated at every step of the recruitment and selection process. Culturally different candidates behave or speak in ways that seem strange or wrong to the recruiters, who then pass them over for other candidates with whom they are more comfortable and whom they therefore consider better suited for the position. In the case of manual labor, it is relatively easy to test people to see if they can do the job properly. In the case of professional positions, the value of a candidate is in his or her ideas. If a candidate cannot get his or her ideas across, then he or she offers little value to the organization.

This chapter focuses on the dynamics that lead to the rejection of qualified candidates because of cross-cultural misinterpretations at the résumé-screening stage, while the next chapter looks at the interviewing stage. The main issue here is that what makes a good résumé in one part of the world may make a terrible résumé in another part of the world. Corporations look for different things in their employees in different parts of the world. As a result, recent immigrants who have put a lot of effort into creating a résumé that would be considered excellent by their home country's standards may not be considered in Canada or the United States because people interpret résumés very differently.

North American Recruitment and Selection Process

In many North American corporations, the job search process consists of the following.

- **Creating and distributing a job posting.** This can be done through several media:
  - ☐ **The Internet**, by posting openings on the company's website or on a job-posting website (such as Workopolis.com, HotJobs.com, and Monster.com).
  - ☐ **Word of mouth.** Corporations ask employees if anyone knows someone who could fill a given vacancy; when recruiting for specific skill sets is difficult, some organizations provide financial incentives to their employees.
  - ☐ **Programs designed to help specific categories of people** (people with disabilities, recent immigrants, First Nations, etc.) find employment.

☐ **Classifieds in newspapers.** This approach now tends to be limited to the recruitment of very senior people, who are difficult to reach through electronic media.

☐ **Search firms.**

■ **Collecting and screening résumés.** Some corporations do not accept applications other than through their website, in which case all the résumés they receive are collected in a candidate database and may be screened electronically. Many organizations, particularly if they are smaller, collect résumés through a variety of sources (fax, e-mail, post, etc.) and sort the pile of résumés manually. Note that the number of résumés can vary greatly, from one (in the case of word-of-mouth recruitment) to thousands (in the case of postings on job-posting websites). In most cases, this step is considered complete when the corporation has identified a short list of candidates, usually between three and eight people.

■ **Interviewing these candidates.** This step is often broken down into two, sometimes three, interviews:

☐ **A telephone interview and/or some screening tests.** For example, candidates may be asked to complete psychological assessment tools.

☐ **A video-conference interview** (this step is used primarily for out-of-town candidates).

☐ **One or more face-to-face interviews.** These interviews may include panel interviews (where the candidate is interviewed by several people at the same time), one, or several, one-on-one interviews, as well as a formal presentation of the candidate's past or proposed work. In total, interviews may last anywhere from 30 minutes to several days.

The issues created by cultural differences at the interview stage and ways to mitigate them are covered in detail in Chapter 3.

■ **Selecting a candidate, checking references, making an offer, and negotiating the offer.** Some corporations consider the recruitment and selection process to be complete when the selected candidate has signed the offer letter put forward by the organization.

■ **Getting the selected candidate through the probation period.** For the purpose of this book, we will consider that the recruitment and selection process is complete when the selected candidate has gone through the probation period, because many cross-cultural issues surface during the probation period. These issues, along with ways to mitigate them, are covered in Chapter 5.

Comparing North American Recruitment and Selection Processes with Other Regions

Understanding how people in other parts of the world recruit and select candidates helps us understand the mechanisms that lead to rejections, even when recruiters have no conscious bias against culturally different people. Most of the countries from which immigrants to North America come are both more *hierarchical* and more *collective* than North America. In such countries, the steps taken to recruit new employees are approximately the same (job creation and posting, résumé collection and screening, interviews, candidate selection, probation period), but each of these steps is conducted in a very different manner. The biggest difference is in the criteria used to evaluate whether or not a candidate is considered qualified for a position and in determining who is the best candidate.

- In many of the countries from which immigrants come, candidates are considered qualified when they meet a specific minimum educational requirement (for example, a specific position requires a bachelors degree in computer science or an MBA). Any candidate who meets this educational requirement is considered qualified, and the best candidate will be the one who has the broadest possible range of experience.
- In North America, people are qualified to do the job because they have already done it before. The ideal candidate in North America is usually someone who has done the same job in a competing organization for the preceding five years.

Organizations in other countries use very different criteria because they operate in a completely different environment. In many developing countries, there are far fewer candidates who have a high level of formal education, so corporations actively seek candidates who have the ability to move between positions and learn a new role quickly.

In South Africa, I was an HR generalist and my organization valued strongly my ability to switch from one role to another. In a country where 70 percent of the population was illiterate at the time, having a Bachelor's degree in anything puts you in a very small minority. Professionals need to be able to move from one role to another because there are so few professionals to go around. In a span of three years, I ended up moving from recruitment and selection to succession planning to executive compensation and benefits to training and development to diversity. When I talk to my Canadian colleagues about my experience, I get these glazed looks—they clearly don't understand how someone could move from one role to another in this manner.

—New Canadian HR professional

In hierarchical countries, corporations determine the potential and qualifications of people based on their degrees and the reputation of the university from which they graduated: The higher the degree a person has, the higher his or her potential and qualifications. Anyone who has a level of formal education that is higher than the minimum requirement set for a given position is considered qualified.

I was recruiting IT professionals for our insurance business. We did some recruiting in India through a recruiting agency. When I rejected a number of programmers' résumés, I would receive résumés back from the same people with revisions in the way they presented their material. This went on two or three times before I asked our agency partner what the heck was going on. Our contact explained that these programmers had graduated from the best university in the country and were surely the best candidates for our positions. They were simply trying to figure out what résumé style they would need to use to get our attention and realize finally that they were indeed the best candidates.

—Insurance company HR manager

In collective countries, corporations value the ability of employees to see the interactions between the various parts of the organization. In these countries, skills are considered far more transferable than in North America. This is particularly true in Canada, where competition with U.S. firms has led most Canadian corporations to follow a strategy of specialization (most Canadian organizations tend to be specialized in a niche market, and they expect their employees to be equally specialized). We come back to this point on several occasions in this chapter and the next, because this is one of the critical issues faced by immigrants when they come to North America—and one that neither they nor North American recruiters see as a cross-cultural issue.

Résumé Differences Across Cultures

Many recent immigrants find the whole recruitment and selection process in North America very confusing and frustrating, because it unfolds according to a logic that is completely foreign to them. Those who come from hierarchical cultures and who were at the top of their home country societies (for example, Indian graduates of the Indian Institutes of Technology) find the whole process challenging because they are expected to sell their skills in North America, whereas the issue they faced back home was simply choosing between competing offers made by various organizations.

This may be the first time they have ever had to go through the formal process of submitting a résumé for a job. Well-educated professionals in many countries will find their work through a network of family and friends, and many organizations will compete to hire them directly from a university, so the whole experience of trying to convince a recruiter that they are the best person for the job is quite foreign to them. While many adapt to this new requirement, some have a very hard time getting used to this new position.

"Jack of All Trades, Master of None"

The difference in organizational expectations leads to different behaviors throughout the recruitment and selection process.

- In the countries from which most culturally different candidates come, getting the job requires:
  - □ Demonstrating that one meets the educational requirements set for the position. As a result, most recent immigrant résumés start with education.
  - □ Demonstrating that one has as broad an experience as possible. As a result, the résumés of most recent immigrants try to list all the different things that they have done in as many areas as possible.
- In North America, by contrast, getting the job requires:
  - □ Demonstrating that one has the right attributes and experience for the job. As a result, most North Americans describe extensively their experiences, highlighting the match between their own experience and the experience required to do the job for which they applied, and they relegate their education to the end of their résumés.

☐ Demonstrating that one is the best at fulfilling the responsibilities expected of the successful candidates (we come back to that point a little later in this chapter).

When recent immigrants send their résumés to North American organizations, recruiters see candidates who have a little experience with a lot of things. They have breadth of experience, but they lack depth of experience. They are not experts in their fields—they are a "jack of all trades, master of none." Graphically, this issue can be represented as shown in Figure 2.1.

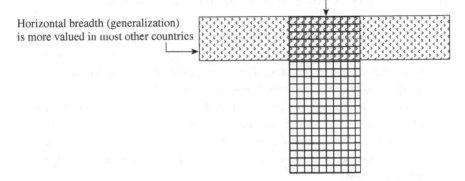

Figure 2.1 Graphical comparison of the experience of culturally different candidates as they attempt to describe it in their résumés (horizontal rectangle) and the experience required by North American corporations (vertical rectangle).

Recent immigrants tend to to portray their experience as being as broad as possible. Spreading this experience broadly makes it look shallow and lacking the depth that is expected of North American professionals. As a result, they are perceived as operating at levels below that at which they operated in their home countries. For example, Indian, Chinese, or Mexican engineers who describe their experiences as broad may be perceived as operating at the level of an engineering technician or technologist, because in North America this is the level at which people touch a little of everything. Engineers are expected to be technical experts in a specific area.

The cover letters of recent immigrant applicants may include statements like:

- I am an IT specialist; I can do anything with computers.
- I am a project manager; I can manage any kind of project.
- I can learn new subjects or job functions very quickly.

Such statements usually make North American recruiters think something like, "Yeah, right. Either you are fooling yourself or you are trying to fool me, but there is no way you can be good at everything. We are not looking for someone who can learn how to do the job; we are looking for someone who already knows how to do it." These résumés are invariably discarded.

Résumés will also start with very general objectives like "process engineering" or vague statements like "I want to have a career in a progressive organization that will give me the opportunity to apply my current skills and to learn new ones in order to become an important asset for this organization." Such statements or objectives are so vague that they could describe anybody and provide virtually no useful information to North American recruiters.

> I worked with an Indian engineer whose résumé started with the following statement: "Mechanical engineer with 12 years of experience in the paper product, tobacco and automotive industry." To me, it sounded like this guy had no specialization—this statement really made him a jack of all trades, master of none.
>
> I started asking him some questions in order to understand what he had done. He had arrived in Canada two years before and he had been employed most of these two years. I asked him what he had done in each of these sectors. It turned out that he was a statistical process control expert who had obtained a six sigma black belt in Japan.
>
> Since this expertise is very much in demand, I helped him change his approach. He started to think of himself as a specialist and obtained a job in three weeks.
>
> —Canadian career management counselor

The Ph.D. That Fits All Positions

The problem of breadth versus depth is particularly acute for culturally different candidates who have high levels of formal education (like a masters degree or a Ph.D.). In their home countries, having a Ph.D. can be compared to having a pass key. It opens almost any door, in that recruiters will consider someone who has a Ph.D. as being qualified for virtually any position in the country (since a Ph.D. exceeds the educational requirements of 99% of all positions). For example, if you have a Ph.D. in Nepal, you are considered qualified for almost every position. By contrast, a Ph.D. in North America can be seen as a bank safe deposit box key; it opens only one door, but what is behind that door is very valuable.

The issue for recent immigrant Ph.D.s is that, if you think you have a pass key, you try it on every door and quickly become frustrated. They may send their résumés to hundreds, sometimes thousands of positions posted on websites, thinking that they are qualified for these positions and could learn how to do these jobs very quickly. In most cases, they get no response at all. When they do receive a response, it usually states that they are overqualified.

Lack of Accomplishment

In order to determine that a given candidate is indeed a good candidate, North American recruiters look at the candidate's accomplishments. They look for descriptions of career accomplishments, particularly those that are quantified, since they can compare the numbers mentioned in the résumés to their own experiences and determine whether these numbers make sense or not.

The concept of accomplishment is highly cultural. It is primarily an Anglo-Saxon concept and does not exist in many other parts of the world. For example, there is no single word in the French language that carries all the meaning and importance of *accomplishment* for English Canadians and Americans. In Catholic and Far Eastern countries, people do not put themselves forward; others do it for them, and they are expected to downplay what they have done.

For example, during a job interview, a Chinese recruiter will notice that a candidate graduated from one of the best universities in the country and say something like, "Oh! I see you graduated from the University of Beijing." The implication of this statement is: "You are an excellent candidate, since this is one of the best universities in the country." The candidate will respond something like, "Yes, but that was a long time ago." In other words, the candidate is expected to downplay this accomplishment.

Because many recent immigrants do not know what an accomplishment is and because they are expected not to put themselves forward, their résumés tend to be void of any accomplishments. Their résumés list the various responsibilities they had but contain no information that would enable North American recruiters to determine whether or not they took care of those responsibilities well. Again, this leads to the rejection of many immigrant résumés. If there are enough qualified North American candidates, North American recruiters who are continuoually pressed for time will not short-list candidates who appear to be average.

Overemphasis on the Less Important

Immigrant candidates attempt to demonstrate how good they are by using points that do not register with North American recruiters. For example, they will emphasize the following.

- **Their education:** In hierarchical cultures, educational requirements are considered a minimum. Anyone who has more education than this minimum is considered as more qualified than someone who just meets the requirements of the job (for example, in Mexico, someone who has a master's degree in electrical engineering is considered more qualified than someone who has a bachelor's in electrical engineering, even if the experience of the holder of the master's degree is not as relevant as the experience of the holder of the bachelor's degree). So candidates who exceed the educational requirement will emphasize this point.
- **Their alma mater:** In hierarchical cultures, there is a hierarchy of universities that everybody knows and agrees on. Those who graduated from the best university will emphasize this point.
- **Their ranking at their university:** In hierarchical cultures, people are ranked. For example, French students at the École Polytechnique de Paris are not in the top 10 percent; they are number 57 or number 274. Candidates who had a high ranking will emphasize this point in their résumés.
- **Their titles:** In hierarchical cultures, titles are a direct reflection of a person's competencies. Being a "senior deputy manager" in India means the person has reached a high level in the organization and therefore will have a high level of skills. A fast progression in titles implies that the person is doing very well.
- **The number of people who report to them, directly or indirectly:** In hierarchical cultures, progress in organizations tends to be measured by the number of people reporting to them.
- **Other forms of praise:** For example, a Pakistani might mention that he or she received accolades from senior management in the first three years of working at the company. To a Pakistani recruiter, this is a clear signal that this person is exceptional, because it usually takes five years for Pakistani senior managers to praise someone in that way.

Most of these approaches fail to impress North American recruiters and they may even backfire.

- Candidates who exceed the educational requirements of the position are considered overqualified by North American recruiters.
- North American recruiters have no idea which university is best in Ghana or Chile, and they have no idea how this university compares

with universities in North America. The insistence of new immigrant candidates on this point (which is usually a matter of significant pride in their home countries, since it automatically implies that they would have brilliant careers) irritates North American recruiters, since it does not play nearly as big a role in people's careers in North America.

- Most North American recruiters are completely baffled by such rankings.
- Titles are far less important in North America than responsibilities. Responsibilities are to North Americans what titles are to Indians.
- The number of reports is not critical in North America. What really matters is what someone accomplished by coordinating and managing the activities of all these people.
- Most other forms of praise will be unnoticed or perceived negatively. Most North American recruiters will react to the statement "received accolades from senior management in the first three years" by thinking "What took this candidate so long?"

Inappropriate Information

In most of North America, it is against human rights laws to ask an applicant's age, sex, place of origin, marital status, or number of dependents, and résumés are expected not to include such information. In other parts of the world, candidates will be asked for this information. For example, French résumés will routinely include age, marital status, citizenship, number of dependents, and a photo of the candidate. Such résumés will often be rejected in North America, whether the candidate is able to perform the job or not.

Peculiar Cover Letters

Cover letters may include salutations or wording that sounds good in other languages or in English used in other countries but not in North America. For example, a letter from a Pakistani that begins with "your Excellency" or closes from the Kenyan with "from your humble servant" are likely to be ill-viewed. As mentioned earlier in this chapter, cover letters from Muslim candidates often include statements such as "I pray to God that you will consider my application." These may turn off recruiters.

Candidates Who Have "Jumped Around"

The résumés of new immigrants often give an impression of instability. Right after they immigrated, they often end up going through several employers over a short period of time. This "jumping around" also happens, in many cases, for a few years before they leave their home country and emigrate to North America. North American recruiters often discard these résumés because they interpret this "jumping around" as a result of instability. They see it as a personality trait of someone who may leave the organization shortly after having been offered the position, thereby forcing them to go through the same recruitment and selection process soon after they hire someone.

In most cases, this instability is not the result of choice by the individual, but the result of his or her situation. In the countries from which most immigrants to North America come, loyalty is highly valued by employers (for example, over 85 percent of Arab executives value loyalty over efficiency, compared to less then 10 percent in North America). As a result, when employees tell their employers that they plan to go and live in North America, employers cut ties and ask them to leave or fire them. In that case, they end up going from short-term position to short-term position, waiting all the while to receive their papers to go and work in Canada or the United States.

Once they have received these papers, they experience difficulties finding work that is in line with their experience, for the reasons already described. As a result, they end up going again from short-term position to short-term position, because this is the best they can find. Yet they may highly value loyalty to their employers and their professional objective is often to obtain a permanent position in a stable organization. Once they find permanent employment, they often demonstrate loyalty to their organization beyond the loyalty of most North Americans.

I once interviewed an Egyptian telecom engineer for a position in our organization. He had the right qualifications for the job, but I was really uneasy about the fact that he had worked for seven different organizations in five years. When I asked him questions about why he had changed positions so often, he explained to me what happened in each position. One company closed, another laid him off because there was not enough work, many were short-term contracts that were not renewed, etc. Eventually, I realized that this was not at all his idea of fun. Before deciding to emigrate to Canada, he had worked for the Egyptian Corps of Engineers for 15 years. When he announced that he had decided to leave the country, they asked him to resign.

—Canadian recruiter

Assessing Correctly the Qualifications and Experience of Culturally Different Candidates

Determining from their résumés the level at which candidates operated can be tricky at best. When dealing with new immigrant résumés, issues such as the lack of accomplishments are compounded by the fact that the same degree or title may mean quite different things in different countries. For example, a diploma in Eastern Europe is closer to the master's degree in North America. By contrast, the bachelor's degrees granted by several Filipino universities are typically closer to a three-year community college diploma in North America than to a North American bachelor's degree.

For recruiters, it is both helpful and quite difficult to know the different quality of the degrees granted by different universities within the same country. People in Japan, for example, know that if you graduate from Tokyo University, you have it made—you are automatically considered one of the best minds in the country. Similarly, graduates of any of the eight Indian Institutes of Technology will be offered at least five different positions by the time they complete their degrees, because they are expected to surpass vastly their counterparts in terms of knowledge, expertise, and intelligence.

The terms used by immigrants in their résumés can trip them up. In North America, certain words imply automatically that you operated at a certain level. For example, if your résumé says that you "drafted" plans, then you will be considered an engineering technician; by contrast, if your résumé says that you "designed" plans, then you will be considered an engineer. Similarly, people who state in their résumés that they prepared "marketing brochures" will likely be considered marketing assistants, while people who prepared "marketing collateral material" are more likely to be considered marketing managers. These small differences in the wording used in their résumés can pigeonhole new immigrants in positions that are not in line with their actual experience.

This issue is particularly acute in the case of immigrants who speak limited English, since they may look up words in dictionaries and end up using words that are unknown in North America. For example, a Mexican electrical engineer who worked for large Mexican port facilities repeatedly used the expression *stevedore companies* in his résumé and during job interviews, creating massive confusion, since none of the people who reviewed his résumé or interviewed him knew what this expression meant (*stevedore* is a rarely used British word that means "longshoreman").

Similarly, North American recruiters experience difficulties assessing the level of experience and responsibilities that many recent immigrant candidates had in their home countries because the titles they had and organizations for which they worked are unknown to the recruiters. North American recruiters have no sense of the organizations in which recent immigrant candidates worked, their structures, their work procedures, or how similar or different these might be from the organizations for which they are interviewed. For example, few people in North America know the names of the companies that are the equivalents of IBM in China, Maytag in Mexico, or Ford in Russia.

Spelling or Grammatical Errors

Recent immigrant candidates are sometimes rejected because of typographical or grammatical errors in their résumés. Candidates who come from countries where English is not one of the languages commonly spoken often experience this. Many HR professionals, who have communication or English literature training, tend to focus quite heavily on the ability of candidates to write a résumé and a cover letter without typos or spelling mistakes. While this is indeed critical in positions like sales, communication, and HR, it may be a lot less relevant for programming positions and may lead to the rejection of candidates for reasons unrelated to their ability to perform in the position.

Why Culturally Different Résumés Do Not Reach Their Target Audience

Compounding all the issues that North American recruiters face when reading the résumés of recent immigrants is the fact that, in many cases, these résumés do not reach their intended audiences, for a variety of reasons.

Website Access

Résumés are often requested to be sent via e-mail or through a website. This puts people and cultures that have less access to the Internet and computer technology at a significant disadvantage. Immigrants, refugees, and people on social assistance end up being handicapped, since they cannot afford to buy a computer and pay for Internet access at home. They have to use publicly accessible computers, where usage time is limited. This hindrance applies not only to international candidates, but also to certain disadvantaged domestic groups as well, such as Native Americans.

Keyword Screening

The process of keyword screening looks for specific words in a résumé that will indicate training or experience in the areas required. For example, résumés may be screened for terms like *MCSE*, *CCNA*, or *photonics*, depending on what the company wants. Immigrants may use different words to describe the same area of study, job function, or work experience.

When résumés are screened automatically by programs that look for specific words, culturally different candidates are more often eliminated from the competition, either because these are not words typically used in their home countries to talk about the same things or because they tried to describe their professional experiences too broadly.

Manual screening of résumés often yields the same results, since recruiters usually do a first pass (during which they allocate a very short amount of time to each résumé—Manpower professionals estimate that most recruiters spend approximately 7 seconds per résumé at this point) that eliminated all résumés that do not have the right key words in the first half of the first page. Since many recent immigrants start their résumés with some general statements and their educational backgrounds, their résumés often do not make it to the second pass, during which recruiters spend a bit more time (30 seconds to 2 minutes) per résumé.

Résumé Sent to the Wrong Person

People who come from hierarchical cultures will tend to send their résumé to the person as high in the organization as possible. The expectation is that the senior manager who has received their résumé will realize how good this candidate looks and will recommend him or her to the appropriate people. In North America, this approach usually leads nowhere, since the résumés sent to the VP of HR or the CEO are far more likely to go directly into the garbage than to be cascaded down the organization.

One of my clients, a Bangladeshi marketing manager who studied in Japan and worked for Japanese corporations for 10 years, experienced tremendous frustration when he looked for a job in the Canadian subsidiaries of Japanese companies. Because he spoke Japanese fluently, he was able to reach, talk to, and meet the CEOs of these companies, who were invariably Japanese expatriates. These CEOs would notice his experience and his education and immediately pass on his résumé to HR, where it would languish for months because there were no suitable positions, given his experience. In the minds of the Japanese CEOs, HR should have created a position for this person. In the minds of HR, this person would be bored to tears with the level of responsibilities they could give him and he would leave the organization in a matter of months.

—Canadian counselor

Action Steps for the Organization

Some recruiters maintain that unless candidates have done enough preparation to figure out how to submit a great résumé in the eyes of the organization, the candidates are unworthy. The recommendations in the box below include ways to set clear expectations for those submitting résumés. If an organization is hoping to broaden its pool of potential candidates, the ideas below are places where some flexibility will yield the best results.

For Career Counselors and Culturally Diverse Candidates

When screening résumés, most HR professionals and line managers need to reduce hundreds or thousands of résumés to a list of three to eight people. Because of the sheer number of candidates, automatic screening programs or rapid manual screening is an absolute necessity (it takes four days to screen 2,000 résumés if you spend just one minute per résumé). As a result, any work aimed at reducing the unemployment or underemployment of culturally different employees by helping them get through the résumé-screening stage needs to be focused primarily on the candidate side, because it is impractical to expect corporations to increase substantially the amount of time they spend screening résumés by devoting more time to each résumé. Chapter 4 presents suggestions for career counselors aiming to help culturally different people find employment in North America.

The following steps will likely help level the playing field.

- **Include on the recruitment and selection team people who are not part of the mainstream.** They are more likely to differentiate between culturally determined behaviors and competencies. In the Faculty of Science of one Canadian university, including one woman in the recruitment and selection team significantly increased the number of diverse candidates who were short-listed and contributed significantly to the hiring of one female, Chinese professor.

- **Don't reject résumés because they only describe responsibilities.** Just because accomplishments are not mentioned does not mean the person hasn't accomplished anything. If the described responsibilities are in line with your job opening, then the candidate may be a valid one who has no idea what an accomplishment is but may well be the best for this position.
- **Overlook frequent changes of positions after and immediately before the time they immigrated.** In most cases, this is not the result of some personality flaw; it is the consequence of circumstance.
- **Focus on progression of culturally different employees in the United States or Canada, not on their current level** (see Chapter 10 for more details on this point). Most immigrants experience a significant drop in level of responsibilities. The level at which they are now may not represent their capability. If recent job experience doesn't fit, it doesn't necessarily mean the person cannot do the job—look at the positions they had in their home countries and at how quickly they were moving up within their new home country.
- **Look and ask for evaluations of academic credentials by organizations that specialize in comparing education standards around the world.** For example, World Education Services and many universities can help assess the equivalency of the degrees of recent immigrants with North American degrees.
- **Explain in detail the recruiting process used in your organization.** This can be done by posting on the website of your organization:
  - ☐ A description of the steps involved.
  - ☐ Sample résumés outlining the preferred format.
- **Check for actual communication skill requirements of the job.** How important for this position is the ability to write English well (without spelling mistakes or typos) or to express oneself well? This varies significantly from programming positions (where it does not matter as much) to public relations positions (where this is one of the key requirements). Once you have determined these requirements, check for typos and fluency in résumés according to the level of communication skills you consider to be needed for the position.
- **Create clear and specific position descriptions** by identifying, listing, and clearly differentiating "must have" and "nice to have" skills. Many North

American job postings contain lists of 20 different characteristics that the successful candidate needs to have. While these characteristics may appear equally weighted, the reality is often different. In most cases, a few of these characteristics are "must haves," while the others are "nice to haves." Clearly differentiating between the two helps culturally different candidates determine whether they should apply or not, thereby reducing the number of irrelevant résumés that corporations need to sort through to create short lists.

At the risk of sounding too clinical, we can state that the key to successful recruitment is in clearly setting out the "technical" requirements of a position and targeting your recruitment to candidates who meet those minimum requirements. In our experience, a candidate can only hope to be successful by being able to deliver "on the job," as it were. Minor gaps in the base technical requirements can often be remedied quite easily, but candidates who are severely lacking in the job's critical competencies will most likely fail—regardless of where they're from.

—North American recruiter of international employees

As organizations become more culturally diverse, it is worth asking all new recruits, including recent immigrants, about their interest and skill in working with people of other cultures. Cultural adaptivity as well as interpersonal and cognitive flexibility will be important for all employees.

3

Interviewing Candidates

When recruiters have narrowed down the stack of résumés to a manageable short list of a few candidates, they move on to the interview stage. Because interviews involve interactions and communication between people who do not know one another, they can easily be derailed by cultural differences. Indeed, culturally different candidates attempt to demonstrate that they are the best person for the job by behaving in ways that, in their home countries, demonstrate that they have the right attributes and skills for the position. The way these candidates behave and the words they use are interpreted differently by North American recruiters. In most cases, the interpretations are negative, and these candidates do not get the job, for reasons that are unrelated to their ability to perform the job.

For example, if a culturally different candidate avoids eye contact (by looking at the floor, at the ceiling, or at the walls) throughout a face-to-face interview, most North American recruiters will interpret this behavior as implying that:

- This candidate is not interested in the position or the corporation.
- This candidate lacks self-confidence.
- This candidate is not trustworthy, since avoiding eye contact implies to mainstream North Americans that one is hiding something.

If this candidate comes from certain parts of the Middle East or Far East, where making eye contact is highly disrespectful, the correct interpretation of this behavior is that he or she is trying to show respect for the recruiter.

Unless they have a lot of interviewing experience or some related training, most line managers and many HR professionals involved in the recruitment and selection process will score this eye contact avoidance negatively (as a point against the candidate), because in their mind it implies a lack of interest, of self-confidence, or of trustworthiness. They will not interpret it as it is meant, i.e., as trying to show respect.

This chapter makes extensive use of the information on the pitfalls of cross-cultural communication provided in Chapter 6. Readers who want to understand in detail the communication dynamics at play during job interviews may consider reading Chapter 6 before proceeding.

Telephone Interviews

Many corporations interview short-listed candidates by telephone before bringing them for face-to-face interviews. Several factors combine to make the rejection rate of immigrants at this stage much higher than the rejection rate of mainstream candidates.

- Those who speak English as a second language (ESL) are often eliminated at this stage if they have a strong accent, because recruiters have difficulty understanding what these candidates are saying.
- When ESL candidates speak English during telephone interviews, they often stumble and look for appropriate words. This is particularly true for a candidate who is called at home. Though they may speak English at work, they may speak a language other than English at home. When they take a call from a recruiter, their minds need to switch from their native language to English. If they are not fluent in English, they may not sound nearly as intelligent or qualified on the telephone as they actually are. Again, they are far more likely to be rejected at this stage because recruiters interpret their hesitation and stumbling as a lack of skills rather than as a limitation in their ability to communicate the North American way.
- Telephone interviews prevent reading lips and seeing facial expressions as aids to communication. They also limit the ability of recruiters to see the physical responses of candidates and to realize that some candidates really understand the questions asked by recruiters but are struggling for the right words in their response.

I have done a lot of interviews and I find that telephone interviews are not always a good indicator of a candidate's ability to communicate in English, compared to a face-to-face conversation. When a candidate can hardly speak English, forget it. However, I have been surprised at how much better many immigrants can communicate in person, compared with by telephone. Some of the candidates who were quite painful to deal with by telephone turned out to be able to communicate fairly well in person.

—North American recruiter

Face-to-Face Interviews

Most of the cross-cultural communication issues described in Chapter 6 and many of the issues at play during the résumé-screening stage come into play during face-to-face interviews.

Getting There

Being on time means different things in different countries. In much of Latin America, it is common for people to arrive at meetings 20 minutes after the scheduled meeting time and not to apologize because, by their standards, they are on time (people in Latin America may consider themselves late only if they are more than 30–45 minutes late). While Latin Americans are likely to arrive closer to the appointed time for an interview than for regular meetings, being 5 or 10 minutes late for an interview may not seem like an issue to them, whereas it is usually considered a terminal mistake by many North American recruiters and a significant negative by others.

The date and/or time of the interview may be a challenge for some candidates. Muslim candidates may try to avoid scheduling interviews on Friday afternoon, since this is the time of their weekly prayers (the equivalent of Sunday morning for Christians). Jewish candidates may want to avoid scheduling interviews on holidays that are meaningful to them but not to the rest of the population. Some recruiters may unconsciously downgrade such candidates because of their lack of availability.

Greetings

Interviews may derail right from the start with greetings that do not match recruiters' expectations. The handshake is not a universal greeting ritual, nor is the manner in which it is executed. For example, people from East Asia may have a gentle handshake, which would be perceived as weak in North America. Since many recruiters interpret a firm handshake as a sign of trustworthiness, they may downgrade East Asian candidates right from the start.

Male candidates who come from Muslim countries may not shake hands with female recruiters, or vice versa. Bypassing the handshake may put off the recruiter and start the interview on the wrong foot, since North Americans are likely to interpret this as a snub. Female recruiters may be particularly unimpressed with Muslim male candidates who do not shake their hands, for the interpretation may be that these candidates will have difficulty taking direction from female managers, whereas this gesture may indicate respect in the minds of such candidates.

North American recruiters are also likely to be put off by the handshakes of First Nations/Native Americans (who often move their hands up and down only once, instead of a few times as is more common among mainstream Canadians and Americans) and the close and extensive handshakes of Latin American candidates (who are likely to shake hands for a longer period of time and at closer range than North Americans).

Personal Space

The vast majority of immigrants to North America come from countries with much higher population densities than in North America and have a smaller personal space than North Americans. This creates numerous issues during job interviews. When candidates meet recruiters, candidates attempt to position themselves relative to the recruiter at a distance that feels right (to them). When their personal space is smaller than the personal space of North American recruiters, they are at the right distance by their standards but too close by the recruiters' standards—they are in the recruiters' personal space.

Two things may happen at that point.

- Some recruiters move back in order to recreate the space they need to be able to carry on the conversation. Some candidates interpret this reaction as implying that something is wrong with them and that recruiters dislike them, which starts the interview on a negative note.
- A significant number of recruiters (higher in Canada than in the United States) do not object but let candidates stay in their space throughout the interview. They go through the whole interview feeling extremely uncomfortable. They hear the words of the candidate but retain nothing of what is said. They can't wait for the interview to be over. In virtually all such cases, these candidates are immediately taken off the list of potential new hires.

In the following senario an American professional lost a position because of the misuse of personal space.

> I went for an interview at the London headquarters of a global media firm. The room in which the interview took place had two desks placed side by side and a chair in the middle. The chair was facing the two desks; there were more than two meters (7 feet) between the two desks and the chair. I walked into the room, picked up the chair, and moved it about one meter (3 feet) forward. Both English recruiters had a visible reaction, almost like a gasp. They were not amused. I had the feeling that I lost the job right there and then.

Some candidates will leave extra distance between them and recruiters as a way to show deference and respect. For example, Indian male candidates may do this with female recruiters. However, it is often interpreted by female North American recruiters as implying the opposite, namely, a lack of respect and a sense of superiority.

Gestures and Body Language

Confusion may arise during interviews (particularly at the beginning) as a result of gestures or body language that mean different things to the recruiter and to the candidate. Here are the gestures and body language most likely to create confusion.

- **The gestures used to beckon someone** (the gesture used in East Asia to ask someone to come here is often misunderstood by Westerners as implying "get lost").
- **The gestures used to signal that something is really good** (for example, the "thumbs-up" used in North America is the equivalent of giving someone the finger in Iran).
- **The gestures used to count on one's fingers.** Chinese count from 1 to 10 on their fingers using one hand. Westerners are lost past five (the gesture used by Chinese to indicate 6 is interpreted in North America as "talking on the phone").
- **Smiles.** These can create confusion, since a smile usually implies friendliness in North America, whereas it may indicate embarrassment in East Asia. Candidates are expected to smile throughout interviews in North America (particularly in the United States), so candidates who

come from cultures where people smile only "when there is something to smile about" (as Germans often say) are often perceived as unfriendly or aloof.

- **Body language that indicates agreement** (such as nods in North America) **or disagreement.** This is not the same the world over. People in eastern Greece and Bulgaria move their head down in one quick move to indicate agreement—this is usually mistaken for disagreement in North America. Indians will roll their heads from side to side to indicate that they agree with what is being said—again, this is more likely to be interpreted by North American recruiters as disagreement than as agreement.

- **Eye contact or lack thereof.** While making eye contact on a regular basis is interpreted as a sign of trustworthiness and respect in North America, making eye contact with people who are in higher social positions is considered very disrespectful in other parts of the world (for example, in parts of East Asia and the Middle East). As a result, candidates who come from such cultures will make a point of avoiding the eyes of recruiters and look continually at the ceiling, the floor or, the walls but not at the recruiter's eyes. Many recruiters interpret this behavior as a lack of self-confidence, interest in the position, or trustworthiness. In all cases, they are tempted to write off these candidates. By contrast, candidates who come from cultures where continual eye contact is the norm (like Italy or Mexico) may be considered as prying or challenging recruiters—again, not the kind of person recruiters want in their organizations.

Chitchat

Many interviews start with a little bit of chitchat between recruiters and candidates. What people consider good chitchat topics in one part of the world may in another be reserved for conversations with very close friends. For example, many people in Latin Europe will chitchat about family and politics, while Canadians will talk about the weather, traffic, and hockey and Americans will chitchat about traffic, football, and baseball. In both Canada and the United States, starting interviews by asking recruiters about their families (such as "Are you married?" or "Do you have children?") or about their political opinions (such as "What do you think of [the latest political statements made by the President or the Prime Minister]?") is likely to make recruiters defensive.

First Impressions

As the saying goes, you only have one chance to make a good first impression. During job interviews, first impressions weigh quite heavily in the final outcome, because most recruiters make their hire/no-hire decision in the first seven minutes and use the rest of the time allocated to the interview to gather data that will support their decision or recommendation to their manager or peers. In the case of culturally different candidates, their efforts to make a positive first impression often backfire and have the opposite effect on North American recruiters, because of greetings, personal space, gestures/body language, and chitchat topics.

Smells and odors will also contribute to this first impression. The North American workplace is expected to be odor free. Many buildings and conferences have become "perfume free," and North Americans spend a lot of money on deodorants, increasingly odor free. By contrast, people may make extensive use of perfumes in other cultures (for example, France and Iran). Candidates who come from those parts of the world may turn off North American recruiters completely with strong smells of perfume or cologne. Other odors, such as smoke, cooking smells (for example, the smell of garlic or spices), or body odor, are also likely to lead North American recruiters to cross a candidate mentally from their lists at first glance.

The combination of all these issues can result in the almost-immediate rejection of qualified candidates. For example, some Mexican candidates turn off North American recruiters completely in the first 30 seconds of their interviews because they:

- May be a few minutes late.
- May be using a strong cologne.
- Start by looking the recruiter over from head to toe, then toe to head when they are about 1 meter/3 feet apart. This gesture is meant to gauge the recruiter's mood and get a sense of who he or she is. It is often interpreted by recruiters as a review (as a general reviewing troops would do) and therefore feels uncomfortable.
- Shake hands at closer range and for a longer time than most North Americans do. They also often place their left hands on the right elbow of the recruiter to show how glad they are to meet and see this person. All the recruiter can think of during that time is how uncomfortable he or she is.

- Make continual eye contact with the recruiter, which makes recruiters uncomfortable.
- Engage recruiters on topics such as their family and/or politics, which are both out of bounds in North America.

Showing Too Much or Too Little Emotion

In order to be considered the right person for the job, candidates in North America need to show they are interested in the position by exhibiting enthusiasm and excitement—but not too much emotion. As is discussed in more depth in Chapter 6, the range of emotions that people can safely show in the workplace varies greatly from culture to culture, leading to significant misunderstandings.

- People who come from cultures where one typically displays significantly more emotion in the workplace than in North America (for example, Latin Americans, Latin Europeans, and Arabs) may be perceived by North American recruiters as being out of control and/or aggressive. As a result, they often do not get the job, because recruiters have concerns about their emotional stability.
- People who come from cultures where one typically displays significantly less emotion in the workplace than in North America (for example, East Asians) may be perceived as not being very interested in the position, because recruiters are not able to read their excitement and interest.

The end result is the same in both cases: Such candidates are passed over in favor of candidates who show the appropriate level of interest.

English as a Second Language

One important goal of face-to-face interviews is to assess a candidate's technical knowledge. Candidates who speak English as a second language may sound as if they know little about a subject, for several reasons.

- They may be translating back and forth in their minds between English and their first language. When they stumble on technical words, North American recruiters tend to interpret this as implying that they do not know their stuff, whereas actually they may not be able to find the precise words.

- The conversation proceeds more slowly than usual and recruiters are frustrated by the pace. Since time is considered one of the most precious resources in North America and interviews are normally time-compressed events, slow conversations cause these candidates to be discounted.
- Accents may also make the conversation more difficult than usual, resulting again in frustration for recruiters.

Excessive Deference

Most immigrants to North America come from cultures that are significantly more hierarchical than Canada or the United States. During interviews, they usually (but not always) see themselves in the subordinate position relative to recruiters. As a result, they try to show deference to recruiters in many ways that North American recruiters usually either do not notice, notice but ignore, or find annoying or inappropriate. For example, culturally different candidates may:

- Keep calling recruiters "Sir" or "Madam" even after recruiters have asked them to use their first names.
- Stand until they are told explicitly to sit down.
- Insist on letting recruiters go through doors first.
- Offer to carry things for recruiters (if recruiters have things in their hands when they meet).
- Refer to the people who are interviewing them by their titles rather than by their names. For example, if they mention to one recruiter the discussion they had with another recruiter, they may refer to that other person by his or her title rather than by his or her first name. Instead of saying something like, "As I was saying to Sally . . . ," they might say, "As I was saying to your vice president . . ."

This sense of hierarchy creates issues for culturally different candidates during panel interviews. In their home countries, the proper protocol consists of, first, identifying who the highest-ranking person in the room is and, second, focusing all or most of one's attention on that person. There, this is the approach that is most likely to result in a job offer, since everyone understands and agrees that people should focus their attention on the most senior people in the organization, for two reasons: this demonstrates respect for hierarchy, and the most senior manager's opinion is likely to have the most weight in the final hiring decision.

By contrast, this behavior is often perceived by North American recruiters as "sucking up" to senior people, something that often backfires. The people overlooked by the candidate during the interview usually cross this candidate off their list. The most senior person in the room may not have the most say in the final decision. In North America, in many cases, the line manager to whom the new recruit will report upon hiring is the person who has the most weight in the final hiring decision, since he or she will work the most closely with this person initially.

Downplayed Accomplishments

Candidates who come from cultures where the concept of accomplishment does not exist are at a significant disadvantage during job interviews, since they often do not know how to convince recruiters that they have the right skills for the job. In many cases, they were taught to downplay their accomplishments, which usually makes them look like second-rate candidates in North America—not the kind of person North American corporations want to hire.

> I was interviewing a Chinese analytical chemist. I saw on her résumé that she had done the first-ever analysis of the sexual secretions of panda bears, so I asked her about this work of hers. It sounded interesting and I thought it would give me a good idea of what she was capable of. Her first comment was that it was no big deal—after all, chemists in other countries could not gain access to panda bears as easily as she did! The same applied to all her work. She continually downplayed her accomplishments and made it sound like what she had done was no big deal.
>
> —North American recruiter

By contrast, some candidates may be perceived as boasting of accomplishments that are not realistic. For example, when American candidates come for interviews in Canada, they are often perceived as overselling themselves. This also results in the rejection of some American candidates in Canada.

> When I interview American candidates for positions that report directly to me, I have a hard time figuring out what they really did. Many of them sound like they could do my job better than me, even though they have three years of experience and I have 15. They can't be serious.
>
> —Canadian IT manager

This issue, which is a problem at the résumé-screening stage, becomes even more of a problem at the interview stage. Candidates need to display the right level of self-promotion. Too little makes them sound as if they can't do the job, while too much makes them sound like they are boasting of unrealistic accomplishments.

No Personal Accomplishments

Candidates who come from very collective cultures (such as Asian candidates) usually work in tightly knit groups where there is little or no separation between people's responsibilities. In China or India, for example, team members do not divide team objectives into individual roles and responsibilities—the whole team is responsible, and there is no division of roles and responsibilities within a Chinese team. The interviews of such candidates often sound like this:

> North American recruiter: I see in your résumé that you worked on a [. . .] project. What did you do?
>
> Chinese candidate: As a team, we were responsible for . . .
>
> North American recruiter: OK, I understand what the team did. What did you do personally? What was your role on this team?
>
> Chinese candidate: Well . . .

A difficult silence often follows. In China, people do not define who is responsible for what. In addition, even in the unlikely event that someone does something on his or her own in China or India, this person would still describe this work as a team effort, because candidates who say "I" in China or India will be considered by Chinese or Indian recruiters as poor team players and may be immediately eliminated from the running for the position. Contrast this with the situation in North America, where anyone saying "we" during job interviews is perceived by recruiters as hiding behind the team because he or she did not contribute much!

"Jack of All Trades, Master of None"

This issue, which leads to the rejection of many culturally different candidates at the résumé-screening stage, also creates havoc during job interviews. Candidates who come from cultures where generalists are preferred to specialists are often perceived by North American recruiters as being a "jack of all trades, master of none," lacking the expertise and depth of experience the position requires. They are often passed over in favor of candidates who have learned to present their experience in a specialized manner.

Emphasis on Points of Limited Importance to North American Recruiters

During interviews, candidates put forward points that they expect will demonstrate that they have the necessary qualifications, skills, and experience for the position. Since North American recruiters are looking to match the experience and accomplishments of candidates and the requirements of the position, North American candidates emphasize the connection in order to put themselves in the best possible light.

Candidates from other cultural backgrounds may emphasize points that matter most to recruiters in their home countries but do not mean much to North American recruiters. For example, they may emphasize the university from which they graduated and tell recruiters what the ranking of this university is in their country ("I graduated from the University of [. . .], which is the best in the country") as well as their own ranking within this university ("I was ranked seventh in my class"). This usually fails to impress North American recruiters, for two reasons:

- Degrees tend to have a five-year shelf life in North America. After that, a degree does not carry much weight. What matters is what people have done with their degrees. This point impacts not only immigrants; women who have stopped work for several years also face this issue, since they often have to reenter the workforce at a significantly lower level than when they left. Culturally different candidates who take pride in having graduated from a well-known university in their home country 10 or 12 years ago are usually perceived as being out of touch with reality in North America.
- The universities from which they graduated are often unknown to North American recruiters. In that case, recruiters fail to give full credit to candidates for their education. This is particularly true in the United States, where degrees obtained outside of the United States are often perceived as of lower caliber than degrees obtained within the United States.

Candidates may also emphasize the following:

- Their family connections or backgrounds.
- Their loyalty to the organization, which is very important in collective cultures but has limited value in North America.
- Their titles or the number of people who reported to them. These two points are important in hierarchical cultures but have limited value per se in North America—the key is what candidates accomplished by managing these people.
- Other forms of praise that do not mean much to North American recruiters, as in the case of Pakistani professionals who mention that they received accolades from senior management within three years of joining the organization.

In most cases, these points will miss the mark with North American recruiters.

Inappropriate Responses

Interviews in most countries tend to be scripted dialogues, in the sense that recruiters ask specific questions to obtain information related to specific skills or experiences of candidates, while candidates prepare certain kinds of answers. The challenge is that the script is quite different in different countries. Culturally different candidates learn to answer different questions (in which case they have difficulty answering the questions asked by North American recruiters) or to answer the same questions differently. For example, one of the most common questions to start interviews in North America is "Tell me about yourself." To a North American candidate, this clearly invites a short answer (maybe 10–15 seconds) during which they have the opportunity to highlight the match between their experience and the requirements of the position.

In the Middle East, "Tell me about yourself" is an invitation to give a full description of one's background. Middle Eastern candidates will often answer by describing their family, educational, and professional background in detail. Their answers are usually much longer than what North American recruiters expect. This may turn off the recruiter from the very start.

Similarly, candidates may volunteer information that is considered inappropriate to share during interviews (such as the number and age of their children). In a land where time is money, answers that contain what is perceived by recruiters as irrelevant details are rated more negatively.

In North America, the main communication principle is the KISS principle: Keep it simple, stupid! In many other parts of the world, candidates for professional positions are expected to show that they can master complex subjects by using complex vocabulary and sentence structures, something that does not translate well into North American English.

Behavioral interviews are also a source of confusion, since this style of interview is not common in many other parts of the world. Candidates who come from risk-averse cultures (such as France), where theory trumps practice, tend to answer questions like "Tell me of a time when you had to deal with a difficult customer" by describing what they would do if they had to deal with a difficult customer, rather than giving an example of a past situation where they dealt with an actual customer. This may be interpreted as if these candidates had never experienced this situation, when in fact they may have but they understood the question as trying to get to the theory rather than focusing on the practice.

The last question asked of candidates in North American interviews tends to be "Do you have any questions for us?" This creates a lot of stress in candidates who come from hierarchical cultures, since they have never had to deal with this situation. In their home countries, since they are in the subordinate position during interviews, they are usually not given the chance to ask questions. Asking a question like "Who would I report to if I am offered this position?" or "What managerial style is preferred in your organization?" is completely out of bounds in their home countries, so they end up asking questions about benefits or other noncritical topics. These are safe questions back home, but they reflect poorly here, since corporations do not want to hire people who are focused on the benefits offered by their organizations.

Lack of Knowledge of the American/Canadian System

Some positions require detailed knowledge of rules, laws, codes, or regulations that are specific to the North American jurisdiction (at the federal, state/provincial, or county/municipal level). For example, building codes and environmental regulations vary significantly from one part of North America to the next, let alone from one part of the world to the next. This creates confusion for culturally different candidates who are unfamiliar with North American codes, laws, rules, and regulations and who have difficulty understanding the division of roles and responsibilities between the various levels of government (in hierarchical cultures, a significantly higher percentage of administrative power is concentrated in the hands of the country's equivalent of the federal government).

I was part of a team that interviewed candidates for a planning position within a not-for-profit agency responsible for the environmental conservation of waterways. One of the questions we had created for the interview was quite simple: We asked candidates to look at a map that described several proposed routes for a sewer line that was going to be built in the coming years. All the proposed routes started from the same point and ended at the same point. One went straight, while a couple would go south then east (we called them the "southern routes"), and the rest were going east then south (the "northern routes"). Each candidate was given about two minutes to read the map, tell us what environmentally sensitive features he or she noticed on the map, and suggest the route most likely to be preferred based on this (very) crude preliminary analysis. We had eight candidates in total: Six were born and raised in Canada, one came from Pakistan, and one from Slovakia. All six Canadian candidates chose northern routes, while the Pakistani candidate chose one of the southern routes, and the Slovak candidate chose the straight route. They were all trying to help the environment, but they were going about it in very different ways.

—Canadian HR professional

Speaking Up

Another major issue for many culturally different candidates is that of silence: How much of a pause is needed between two people having a conversation? People in Latin America, Latin Europe, the Middle East, and South Asia often all speak at the same time, because the social norm states that people should start to speak as soon as they have understood where their counterpart is trying to lead them (this shows interest and engagement). In North America, this communication style is perceived by recruiters as rude and as demonstrating poor listening skills, since these candidates continually interrupt.

By contrast, people in East Asia are taught to leave pauses between speakers during a conversation. These pauses indicate that the person said something interesting and important that deserves to be pondered carefully before formulating an answer. During interviews, East Asian candidates may leave pauses that make it appear to North American recruiters as if they don't understand the questions being asked. Many recruiters react by restating their questions or by starting to answer partially, as a way to prime candidates, but East Asian candidates perceive this reaction as an extension of their previous question (they have not stopped talking), so they wait again for a long pause—long enough by their standards. However, North American recruiters become very uncomfortable with this much silence and start to speak before the pause gets to be long enough, so interviews turn into monologues by North American recruiters. In the end, these candidates are rejected because recruiters perceive them as incompetent, whereas the candidates feel they never had a chance to say their piece during the interview!

Finally, many North American recruiters consider extroversion a positive trait. By contrast, extroversion is viewed quite negatively in East Asia, so East Asian candidates rarely display this trait.

Testing

Many corporations and search firms use assessment tests that tend to eliminate a higher ratio of culturally different candidates than mainstream candidates. In most cases, North American culture and values are embedded in these tests through the vocabulary, situations, and expectations they put in front of candidates.

The easiest way to appreciate this point is to put the shoe on the other foot and look at situations where North American candidates are rejected because of tests that are considered valid in other parts of the world but not in North America. For example, many French corporations use graphological analysis (analysis of the candidate's handwriting) as a way to determine which candidates are best suited for a specific position, whereas such tests are considered meaningless by many North American recruitment specialists. They have far more meaning in France than in North America because French students write a lot more by hand throughout their studies than North American students, so their handwriting is far more individualized and developed (for example, French signatures are often quite ornate and complex as compared with the straight writing of names used by many North Americans). When North Americans have their handwriting analysis done by French recruiters, they usually come up short as compared with French candidates.

Action Steps That Organizations Can Take to Minimize These Issues

Between the résumé and interview stages, many culturally different candidates are passed over due to superficial misunderstandings. Corporations that want to hire the best person for the job regardless of cultural background may consider implementing the following action steps.

- Be prepared for surprises when interviewing culturally different people. Don't be put off by the unexpected. Try to suspend negative judgment until you have collected more information. Go with the situation.

- Give the benefit of the doubt to ESL candidates during telephone interviews, since these interviews may not provide an accurate representation of these candidates' ability to communicate face-to-face. Obviously, if communicating by telephone is an important part of the job, this would be a criterion in the selection process. It may not be relevant in positions that do not require many telephone interactions.

- Include HR professionals and/or diverse people in recruiting teams. While this may sound obvious, it is often not followed, particularly in smaller organizations. In some cases, the human resources department is actually the last one to know that there's an opening. The department with the open position may create its short list and hire someone without HR's involvement until it is time to write the actual offer letter. A culturally different employee will be helpful in identifying cultural differences that may put off other recruiters and in locating potential "diamond in the rough" candidates that may otherwise be rejected.

- Provide training to people involved in the recruitment and selection process on a regular basis so that they know how to identify and overlook culturally determined behaviors likely to lead to the rejection of candidates for cultural reasons. Such training will help recruiters adjust their communication style to accommodate culturally different candidates and help them find ways to obtain the information they need to assess accurately the skills of these candidates by learning how to ask follow-up questions in different ways.

- Focus on transferable skills. Some culturally different candidates may have worked in industries that require the same technical skills even though they appear to be quite different. For example, a Pakistani mechanical engineer who specialized in the production of ballistic missiles was able to find a job when recruiters realized that his expertise lay in the fabrication of the outside casing (see Chapter 4 for more details on this situation).

- Consider hiring culturally different candidates with strong potential but who need to learn more about the American/Canadian system at the low end of the pay scale, and put them in developmental positions with managers who know how to develop people. Note that this will only work if the new hire is directed by a suitable mentor who has the patience and time to guide the new hire through the differences that he or she has to overcome.

- Create tests to evaluate candidates in real-life situations. For example, one search firm created the following test to evaluate how candidates handled pressure: Candidates were asked to complete a multiple-choice questionnaire that contained many questions and were told to complete this questionnaire in a room in an amount of time that was clearly tight. While candidates were working on their tests, someone would come and ask them a question about their backgrounds. The real test was how gracefully they answered this request.
- Use short-term contracts (whenever possible) to reduce the risk of hiring the wrong person.
- Use volunteer and/or shadow positions to evaluate the potential of culturally different candidates who show potential.
- Use the graduates of special programs designed to help immigrants find positions that make use of their skills in order to recruit people who have been given training to adapt to the North American workplace.
- Describe on your website the recruiting process used by your organization, including sample interview questions and answers. This kind of detail can help every candidate show their true abilities, especially culturally different candidates.
- E-mail questions to candidates 48 hours before the interview, and ask them to respond in writing by e-mail. This gives the candidates a chance to look up words and to figure out how they are going to present more complex concepts. Giving recruiters a chance to read candidates' responses to the first set of questions also allows them to cover more ground in a limited-time interview by asking follow-up questions.
- Determine up-front specific candidate-ranking criteria. Otherwise, culturally different candidates often end up being second best on everyone's list, for a variety of reasons.
- Define up-front the English-language skill level required for the position. Be prepared to test for language proficiency rather than assume the person's skill level.

These steps take time and effort and will usually be implemented thoroughly only if there is a strong need for the organization to recruit outside of the more traditional talent pool. This usually occurs either when there is temporary shortage of qualified workers in a specific field (as in the case of audit accountants, who are in short supply globally since the U.S. Congress passed the Sarbanes–Oxley Act) or when organizations are under pressure to bring in people from specific cultural groups (as a result of legislation like Affimative Action in the United States and Employment Equity in Canada).

Helping Immigrants Find Jobs

Finding a job in North America is not difficult in theory: It requires finding the answer to the following four questions.

1. What problems are you good at solving?
2. Who has these problems and is willing to pay money to have them solved?
3. How do you make sure these people know you exist?
4. How do you convince them that you are the best at solving these problems for them?

If you can find the answers to these four questions in your particular case, you have found yourself a job. Here, the devil is in the details. The answers to these questions are specific to each person. Finding the answers in your personal case is much harder than asking the questions.

As discussed in the previous two chapters, the way one looks for a job in North America is very different from the way one looks for a job in other parts of the world (even other G7 countries), so immigrants often experience major difficulties when they look for their first job in North America. There are many nonprofit organizations, governmental programs, as well as private companies dedicated to helping immigrants integrate into the North American workforce. This chapter is designed to help the career counselors in these programs so that they can, in turn, help their clients more effectively.

Who Are You and How Can You Possibly Help Me?

One of the common challenges faced by social workers who help recent immigrants find employment in North America is that their clients perceive the workers as being lower on the social ladder and have difficulty understanding how this person can help them. For example, a 50-year-old male Middle Eastern statistician who has a Ph.D. may perceive the 30-year-old female counselor who has a bachelor's degree in communication and who is counseling him on how to find suitable employment as unqualified to do so. Differences in gender, age, and educational level all make him consider this counselor as lacking the experience needed to teach him how to find a job. He may think things like: "She has never had a job at the Ph.D. level, so how can she tell me how to find one?"

Overcoming this perception is critical to the success of the counselor's intervention, since the client is unlikely to change his approach if he does not accept her advice and will likely repeat the mistakes (by North American standards) that so many immigrants have made by looking for a job in North America in the same manner as they would in their home countries.

Because most immigrants to North America come from cultures that are significantly more hierarchical than Canada and the United States, counselors may consider showing their clients parts of this book at the appropriate time. Indeed, hierarchical people give a lot of weight to what is said by people considered experts in their field: "It is has been published, therefore it must come from experts and I will pay attention to what it says."

As cross-cultural trainers, we have often made presentations to audiences of immigrants who are looking for a job. While the message we communicate is often the same one provided by counselors, the fact that it comes from an external source with a high level of formal education who is recognized as a subject-matter expert lends more credibility to the message and often contributes to significant changes in job seekers' approaches.

The Résumé Is Not the First Step in the Process

When they look for jobs in North America many immigrants start by creating a generic résumé, edit it numerous times until the English grammar, syntax, and vocabulary are good, and then post it on Internet job-search websites for which they consider themselves qualified. In their minds, the first step in the job-search process is the creation of a good generic résumé.

In North America, as all career counselors know and tell their clients, creating a good generic résumé is not the first step in the process; it is somewhere in the middle. In terms of the four questions listed at the beginning of this chapter, a résumé is useful when you get to the third question—it helps in making sure people know a candidate exists. Before job seekers can start to write the first draft of their résumé, they need to analyze three things:

- Their experience and expertise.
- Their constraints.
- The labor market in their specific field.

Conducting these analyses thoroughly is critical to the success of a job search. When these analyses are not performed properly, job seekers end up contacting hundreds, sometimes thousands, of organizations without receiving a single response.

Analyzing the Experience and Expertise of Immigrants

Many career counselors use the situation/problem/action/results method to guide immigrants in the analysis of the projects they have worked on in the past. This approach tends to be particularly powerful in the case of nonnative English speakers who work in fields where the use of specialized vocabulary is expected. In these cases, it is important that job seekers write down the full story of the projects they have worked on (even if this results in a 20- or 30-page document) because:

- This exercise forces them to look up the words they will need during job interviews.
- It enables counselors to understand more quickly the qualifications of job seekers. In particular, it becomes much easier to answer the question "What problem are you good at solving?" by looking for patterns and common themes in the various projects of job seekers.
- It helps job seekers learn how to describe their experience in a sequence that is familiar to North American interviewers, thereby making interviews smoother.

Once counselors have identified the themes and patterns of job seekers' projects they can move on to the next question: "Who has these problems and is willing to pay money to have them solved?"

One of the important points to consider is whether the experience and expertise of the immigrant is transferable to North America. In other words, when they describe to a North American interviewer what they did, will they be considered as serious contenders or will they be eliminated immediately, either because they will not be considered as credible, or because their experience is considered irrelevant in the North American context? While it is difficult to answer this question in a general sense, there are some key areas to watch out for.

- **Lack of recent experience:** Because degrees and experience have a shelf life of approximately five years in North America, immigrants who have degrees in one field but have not worked in that field for the last five years will be considered, for all practical purposes, as having lost that degree. For example, a Guyanese engineer who obtained a bachelor's degree in aerospace engineering at a British university and who worked in a sugar refinery for nine years following graduation was unable to find a position in aerospace engineering when he immigrated to Canada. He was, however, able to find a position in an engineering consulting firm that designed food-processing facilities and equipment.
- **Nontransferable experience:** People coming from developing countries may have been working on problems that have been solved or would be described or approached in very different ways in North America. For example, a Nepali environmental scientist spent many years in Nepal designing and building composting equipment on a small-town scale so that this equipment could be operated by local people. This composting equipment enabled the town to get rid of much organic waste (usually left over when the town market closed) in a way that reduced pollution and provided some energy to the town (the methane produced by fermentation was captured and used as a source of heat). While this was a great accomplishment, this experience is not transferable to North America because here the same problem is handled completely differently—organic waste is collected in a centralized manner and moved to large-scale composting facilities (where these facilities exist) or dumped in a landfill. With the help of a career counselor, she was able to start her own gardening business.
- **Level of experience:** In hierarchical cultures, people who have good technical skills move up in the organization and end up managing people—quite often, large numbers of people. When they immigrate to North America, they often end up being completely stuck. They cannot obtain a managerial position because North Americans know (or can see from the soft skills of candidates) that being a good manager in India or China is very different from being a good manager in North America. They also

cannot obtain positions at the individual contributor level because they have been too far from that level for a while. People who were managing plants or mines in developing countries often have to go back to the basic level of their profession by becoming technicians.

Counselors often have to use creativity to help recent immigrants, particularly those who come with a high level of skills and education, because their specialization rarely applies directly in the North American workplace, as the following example illustrates.

I worked with a Pakistani mechanical engineer who immigrated to Canada. He obtained a master's degree in mechanical engineering from a Canadian university and ended up working as a convenience store clerk at minimum wage because he could not find work as an engineer. I worked with him to analyze what problems he was good at solving. He told me that he had spent his whole career in Pakistan building missiles. I figured that his chances of finding a job in his field were exactly zero, since Canada does not build a lot of missiles and whatever it builds will require security clearance that he will not be able to get for a long time (if ever).

So we discussed in more detail what he did. It turned out that he was specialized in making the casing for Pakistani missiles. His expertise consisted of taking flat pieces of thick steel, rolling them into cylinders, welding them on the edge, and making sure the welding was done properly. I talked to some engineers in order to find where this expertise could be applied. One of them answered that this is the same process used to make tank trucks, tank cars, boilers, and pressure vessels. We refocused his job search in that direction and he found a job as a welding engineer.

—Canadian employment counselor

It is really important here to go into the details of immigrants' experiences in order to understand what their specialization is. As discussed in the previous two chapters, statements like "I am an IT professional, I can do anything with computers" will not get them anywhere. So counselors need to work with people who make such statements until their specialization becomes clear. One way to do this is to ask them what kind of projects they have worked on (usually, the initial answer to this question is something like "a wide range") and to classify these projects by category to get a sense of the categories that are most represented. Here is an example of this approach.

I worked with an Iranian civil engineer who immigrated to Canada. When I first met him, he introduced himself as a civil engineer who can design anything.

"Right!" I thought. Then I asked him: "What kind of projects have you worked on?" He responded that he had worked on tunnels, roads, high-rise buildings, bridges, and dams. So he did have a broad range of experience. Then I asked him to put back to back all the projects he had worked on that were related to each category and to tell me how many years of experience he had in each category. He answered:

- One year of experience on high-rise buildings.
- One year of experience on bridges.
- One year of experience on tunnels.
- Two years of experience on roads.
- Twenty years of experience on dams.

My mouth dropped. Clearly, he was specialized in dams! I asked him some more questions to understand specifically what he had done. He was a specialist on the instrumentation and monitoring of dams. We refocused his job search in that direction and he found a job at a hydro company.

—Canadian employment counselor

Analyzing the Constraints of Immigrants

In some cases, job seekers have or place constraints on their job search. These constraints may come from their family situation; for example, one of their children may have special needs, or their spouse may have a job he or she does not want to lose. These constraints are external and need to be considered as hard facts.

In many other cases, the constraints are self-imposed; for instance, immigrants do not want to go to a small town because in their mind this would imply a step down (this is often related to their strong hierarchy—see Chapter 7 for more details). Perhaps they do not want to leave a city because there are many people there who come from the same part of the world (this is often related to their strong sense of collectivism—see Chapter 8 for more details). For example, they may not want to go to Fort McMurray in Alberta because they fear they will be completely isolated from other immigrants coming from the same part of the world or that their relatives back home will look down at them for having left a world-class city for a small town that they have never heard of.

Self-imposed constraints can decrease significantly the chances of success, as the following story indicates.

As a chemical engineer, I studied distillation for my Ph.D. Since the oil and gas industry is the industrial sector that employs the largest number of distillation engineers, it was very clear to my North American counterparts that, when I looked for a job in Canada, I should look in Alberta. There was no alternative in their minds.

I approached the problem in a completely different manner. I projected onto Canada the structure of French society. The structure of French society says that, if you want to have a good career, you have to go to Paris. There is no alternative in the minds of French people. So I looked for a job in the Canadian equivalents of Paris. In my mind, that was Montreal, Toronto, and Vancouver—Ottawa is the political equivalent of Paris in Canada but not its economic equivalent.

I did not consider looking for a job in Alberta. When my wife told me that she may have a job opportunity in Calgary, my reaction was something along the lines of "Over my dead body will we go to Calgary." To my mind, going to Calgary would shut down all my career opportunities. The reality was the opposite: Not going to Calgary shut down the opportunities I had to use my knowledge of distillation. I have learned in the 15 years I have been in Canada that there were only two organizations that were interested in my knowledge of distillation, and both were located in Calgary. I found jobs in Toronto and Montreal where my Ph.D. was valued but not my knowledge of distillation.

—French chemical engineer in Canada

For this reason, it is critical to determine with job seekers whether the constraints they have are external or self-imposed. In Canada, at the moment, the majority of jobs are created in Alberta and outside of big cities. Immigrants who limit their job search to the Greater Toronto Area (GTA) are often severely limiting their chances of success, since the GTA is full of job seekers (many of them immigrants).

Another major limitation is the amount of time they can invest in their job search. Looking for a job is a full-time job, so doing a full-time job in parallel with a job search is a very tall order for someone learning the structure of North American societies who has a very limited network. Counselors need to make job seekers aware of the significant decrease in the probability of success that results from a limited geographical reach and/or limited time investment.

Analyzing the Labor Market

This step is usually very difficult for many immigrants, since the concepts of market and labor market may not be clear in their minds, particularly if they come from cultures where the economy and the job market are run by the state. They usually need guidance to avoid being discouraged by the magnitude of the task. It often takes 200–300 hours to conduct a comprehensive labor market analysis for someone who has 10–15 years of experience in a particular field (in other words, 5–8 weeks of full-time work).

Many people focus their labor market analysis on the organizations that might employ them. While this is clearly a critical part of the labor market analysis, a number of other areas need to be examined in detail in such an analysis. The idea behind the search in these other areas is to gain knowledge about the organizations and the field that job seekers target so that they sound like they belong there.

A comprehensive labor market analysis performed at the individual level is performed in two stages:

1. Gather information on targets, i.e., organizations that may employ you or sources of information that will help you understand how these organizations operate
2. Digest all this information and talk to people within your field to create a picture of this field so that you can determine where you fit in this picture

Gathering Information

The first phase of the labor market analysis consists in gathering information on your potential employment targets, i.e., organizations that have the problem you are good at solving. This phase aims at comprehensiveness (finding all related items) rather than relevance (prioritization comes later, when the labor market analysis has been completed) and at finding the following:

- Professional associations that job seekers could join.
- Conferences, events, and presentations they could attend.
- Trade magazines they could read.
- Search firms to which they could send their résumés.
- Job postings to which they could respond.
- Nonprofit organizations where they could volunteer to demonstrate their skills.
- Salary surveys that indicate the range of salaries they might expect.
- Organizations to which they could apply.

Professional Associations. Networking is one of the most effective ways to find a job in North America. Studies conducted by outplacement companies show that anywhere between 65 percent and 85 percent of North American positions are filled by networking, as opposed to less than 15 percent that are filled through a job posting. The following anecdote illustrates the importance of networking for immigrants.

> I had been doing chemical engineering research for several years. To speed up the pace of my projects, I wanted to have a technician but did not have the budget for that, so I contacted a nonprofit agency that helped immigrants find jobs and asked them to send me candidates. The deal was fairly simple: They would work for me for free for two months (their salary was paid by the federal government) and I would help them find a job through my network. I have had 13 interns work for me, and seven of them have found jobs as chemical technicians.
>
> Three of them found jobs in our research center. In all three cases, what happened was that the pilot plant manager came to me and asked if any of the interns who had worked for me were good or not, because he needed to hire a new technician for an upcoming project that was about to start in a few weeks. In all three cases, I was able to recommend someone. He asked me to arrange an interview with the people I recommended. The three people I recommended got the job; to the best of my knowledge, he did not interview any other candidates.
>
> —Canadian research engineer

One of the most important means to network in North America (see Chapter 9 for more details on this point) is professional associations. Joining and becoming active in professional associations yields several major benefits for recent immigrants.

- They interact with people in their field, who can give them advice and offer perspective on the trends in their field (technical, business, or employment trends). These contacts can review the résumés of immigrants to make sure the technical terms they use will be understood as they intend them and perhaps suggest alternatives.
- They have a chance to create North American references. In the case of immigrants who become actively involved in the organization of an event or the management of a local chapter, they have a chance to demonstrate their effectiveness and give something to others, which usually makes them more open to give back in the form of leads for potential positions or knowledge of the sector.

- They have a chance to demonstrate their knowledge by making a presentation at one of the association's events or by writing an article in the association's newsletter.

One critical point is to select carefully the professional associations that one joins. Most North American professionals could join anywhere between 10 and 20 professional associations, but doing so would dilute their efforts and cost a lot of money in fees. It is usually most cost effective to join two, maybe three associations and to be really active in one. Counselors can recommend to their clients that, before deciding on one particular association, they shop around by calling the executives and attending one event (most associations have events that are open to the public) to determine what kind of people they will meet if they join a particular association.

Professional associations can be found by combining several searches:

- **Internet search:** By entering keywords like "association" and "society" along with words that typically correspond to one's field. This step requires a bit of creativity to ensure that one does not overlook possibly important associations.
- **Directories:** Directories of professional associations can be found in public libraries.
- **Other professionals:** One of the best ways to figure out which professional association to join is to ask people who do the job one wants to have what association they belong to.

This analysis is complete when job seekers have created a table or spreadsheet containing a comprehensive list of organizations that may be potential target employers. This list is meant to contain all the organizations that have the problem the job seekers are good at solving, whether or not they are ready/able to pay to have these problems solved.

Conferences, Events, and Presentations. Immigrants need to attend the conferences, events, and presentations where they are likely to meet people who do the kind of work they are looking for. From this perspective, they need to look for events through the Internet. As well, since many professional associations have websites that quickly become out of date, it is often useful to contact the association directly to find out when and where their next events will take place. The determining factor for attendance should be the topic of the event and the type of people who are likely to attend.

- If the topic is related to the type of problems that immigrants worked on in the past, they should attend this event in order to find out how North Americans solve these problems and to network with people who have the same professional interests.
- If the people who are likely to attend have similar specializations, then it is worth attending to listen to conversations and gather information that can be used to direct one's job search.

While cost should not be considered as a major factor in the go/no-go decision, it sometimes is—registration in some events can cost up to several thousand dollars. Some immigrants cannot afford such registration fees. In that case, they can try several approaches.

- Many events offer discounts to students and retired association members. Some offer discounts to unemployed members—if an association does not, it is sometimes possible to negotiate such a discount with the event organizers.
- Some immigrants have negotiated the right to attend a conference by volunteering for the organizing committee. An example is an unemployed Filipina specializing in the telecom industry who obtained access to a conference where registration fees were close to $2,000 by volunteering on behalf of the organizing committee by calling prospective participants.

Conferences, events, and presentations can be found by combining several searches:

- **Internet search:** By entering keywords like "conference" and "presentation" along with keywords that typically correspond to one's field. This step requires a bit of creativity to ensure that one does not overlook possibly important events.
- **Other professionals:** One of the best ways to determine which meetings to attend is to ask people who do the job one wants to have what meetings they will attend.
- **Trade magazines:** Many trade magazines include sections that list upcoming meetings that may be of interest to their readers.
- **Universities:** Some of the presentations at universities can be of interest to job seekers who want to refresh their knowledge in a particular area.
- **Networking associations:** A number of organizations are designed specifically to help immigrants network.

This analysis is complete when job seekers have created a table or spreadsheet containing a comprehensive list of conferences, events, and presentations they are considering attending. They will determine at a later stage whether or not they actually attend these events.

Trade Magazines. There are thousands of trade magazines in North America, from *Chemical News* to *Chemical Engineering Progress* and from *HR Professional* to *HR Magazine*. Immigrants need to locate and identify and read carefully the trade magazines that are most relevant to their field. The parts that are usually the most helpful to them are:

- **Articles that describe trends in their industry or sector.** These may be technical, business, or employment trends—being aware of these trends helps immigrants determine where they fit within their industry or sector.
- **Articles that provide job search advice or discuss soft skill development.**
- **News clips that examine new developments in their industry or sector.** Knowing that a given corporation is expanding or building a new plant suggests that it is likely to hire some people. If the positions happen to be in the right area, this may be very useful information. On the other hand, knowing that one organization is downsizing suggests that this is probably not one of the best employment prospects.
- **Ads that profile services or products that require skills that immigrants have.** This helps build a database of potential employment targets.
- **Notices of future events/conferences/presentations.**
- **Job postings,** when they exist.

Since subscribing to the many magazines that may be relevant to each professional in North America is beyond most immigrants' budget, it is important for them to find a place where they can access these magazines at a low cost. Public and university libraries are often a good place to start; even though trade magazines cannot be borrowed, it is usually possible to read them on-site.

Trade magazines can be found by combining several searches:

- **Internet search:** Enter keywords that typically correspond to one's field, and then follow the links. Many professional associations have one or more publications, so it is possible to find a number of trade magazines online by starting from the websites of professional associations. There are also websites that contain links to many magazines.

- **Other professionals:** One of the best ways to determine which trade magazines to read is to ask people who do the job one wants to have what magazines they recommend.

This analysis is complete when job seekers have created a table or spreadsheet containing a comprehensive list of magazines they could read as well as the frequency at which they are published and the location where they can access these magazines.

Search Firms. There are thousands of search firms and employment agencies throughout North America. Some, like Manpower and Adecco, have a broad scope, while others are much more targeted in scope—either geographically or by type of positions. While it is rare that recent immigrants have the profile that search firms are looking for on behalf of their clients, this job-search avenue should not be discounted. Immigrants should select the search firms that specialize in their fields or industry and send their résumés. Search firms can be a source of information on the status of the job market as well as a source of networking. When dealing with search firms, keep these two points in mind:

- Search firms do not ask candidates to pay any fee. Organizations that ask for a fee are usually not search firms. In this case, buyer beware! In North America, it is virtually impossible to find someone else a position (other than a low level, labor position), so many organizations that claim to find people a job for a fee are often not legitimate.
- Search firms are paid by their clients, namely, the organizations that have positions to be filled. Once a search firm has your résumé on file, there is no point in contacting them frequently to find out what is happening on their end. If you do not hear from a search firm, it means that none of their clients is looking for someone like you. When one of their clients needs someone like you, they will find you very quickly, so there is no major need to follow up frequently. Once every three months is probably sufficient.

Search firms can be found on the Internet or through specialized directories that can be purchased online or in bookstores.

This analysis is complete when job seekers have created a table or spread-sheet containing a comprehensive list of search firms that may be interested in receiving their résumés.

Job Postings. There are many sites where organizations can post their openings: Monster, Workopolis, Hotjobs, etc. One of the key pieces of information that job seekers need to gather is: What skills are organizations looking for? This can be done by collecting a large number of job postings (somewhere between 50 and 100 in order to get a good picture of organizations' requirements) and analyzing them to determine what specific technical and soft skills they require. Questions that can be answered in this manner include the following.

- Which software is commonly required?
- Which designation/certification is commonly required?
- Are there trends in these job postings? For example, do they come mostly from the same geographic location? Do they come mostly from large organizations or from their subcontractors?

Job seekers can easily get overwhelmed by the amount of information, so counselors can assist by helping them recognize trends and patterns that job seekers cannot see. One important piece of information that may come out of such an analysis is the need for job seekers to upgrade their qualifications by:

- **Obtaining certification.** For example, a Romanian IT specialist determined that he needed a Microsoft Certified Software Engineer (MCSE) certification to be competitive in his field; he found an IT position three months after obtaining his certification, whereas he had been unemployed for two years before that.
- **Obtaining a designation.** For example, Canadian auditors need a CA (Chartered Accountant) designation in order to obtain a position of manager with one of the big four accounting firms.
- **Learning a new piece of software.** For example, many mechanical design positions require the ability to use software like Catia or SolidWorks.

Counselors often have to remind job seekers that the job postings they see represent only a small fraction of all the positions that are out there. As discussed earlier, the vast majority of positions are never posted, not even on the companies' own websites, so it is important to keep some perspective. For example, the fact that most posted openings require at least two years of experience does not mean that people who have no North American experience cannot find jobs. It just means that they will need to find positions that have not been posted. Recent immigrants rarely obtain the positions that are posted, for two reasons:

- If a corporation has gone through the trouble of posting an opening, it has defined in detail what it wants and needs. It has a clear picture of what the ideal candidate looks like, and recent immigrants do not fit that picture because their careers and responsibilities do not fit the North American patterns.
- If a corporation has posted a position, it usually receives many applications, so competition is stiffer, and it is difficult for recent immigrants to edge out North American competitors because of their different approach to interviewing and different soft skills.

Nonprofit Organizations. Volunteering with a nonprofit organization can be an effective way for job seekers to demonstrate the skills they have. The advantage there is that it is usually much easier to get volunteer positions. Most nonprofit organizations are continually looking for more volunteers. Successful volunteer activities offer several benefits.

- They fill a résumé gap.
- They provide local references and the beginning of a network.
- They give job seekers a chance to demonstrate how good they are at applying their skills.

When recent immigrants decide to volunteer, many use the wrong criteria (by North American standards) to decide what volunteer activity to pursue. This may lead them to perform work that will not move their job search forward. For example, they may choose to volunteer within their ethnic group. While this may be beneficial on the social side, it rarely leads to the creation of a network that moves their job search along. They may also choose activities that are not in line with their skills. For example, a Pakistani mechanical designer who was volunteering for Meals on Wheels found that this did little for his job search. When he began designing and building new contraptions to help the people serviced by Tetra (a nonprofit association that recruits skilled volunteer engineers and technicians to create assistive devices for people with disabilities), he suddenly found that doors were opening for him. Counselors need to discuss with recent immigrants what volunteer activities they could pursue and ensure that these activities will be perceived by North American employers as adding to their experience.

Volunteer opportunities can be found through local government offices as well as specialized directories and websites. For example, in Toronto, www.211toronto.ca contains a comprehensive list of nonprofit organizations and provides links to their websites.

Salary Surveys. Knowing the going rate for your skills is an important piece of information for job seekers in North America. When prospective employers ask "What are your salary expectations?," quoting a figure that is too high means you have unrealistic expectations, and quoting too low a figure means you do not understand what the position requires. Immigrants need to be able to answer this question with data that demonstrates that they can do research and analyze the data they obtain through this research. The easiest way to obtain this information is to look at salary surveys published by professional associations and to analyze these surveys to understand your level and the range of remuneration that is associated with it.

Employment Targets. This category is listed last because most immigrants think of this one first. Many immigrants see that the fastest route to a job is to respond to online job postings by sending the same generic résumé to each posting, "just in case." As all counselors know, this is usually a very ineffective approach. Some immigrants have sent over 2,000 résumés and received not a single response. They get stuck, discouraged, as their skills become obsolete. It is therefore essential that counselors help immigrants understand that the fastest route to a good job consists in learning a lot about their labor market and the organizations in their sector before they even start creating their résumés.

Employment targets can be found through:

- Specialized directories, which are available online or through public libraries.
- Buyer's guides and ads published in trade magazines.

Digesting Information

The next step in the labor market analysis consists in digesting all the information gathered in the first phase. The objective is to find patterns and correlations and to create a picture of the industrial sectors where job seekers are likely to be of interest to corporations so that they can determine where they have their best chances. For example, immigrants who have obtained a Ph.D. and who have conducted research in the past are most likely to find employment in a research and development center, as opposed to any organization in their field.

Counselors need to help immigrants understand the limitations they face and the positions for which they will be considered as having "instant credibility." When potential North American employers meet a candidate, they assess, often within the first 30 seconds of their interactions with this candidate, whether or not this candidate has what it takes to do the job. They then make their decision, often within the first 10 minutes of the interview. This decision is based on the information on their résumés, which needs to convey an implicit message of "I can do this job because I have previously done all the elements it requires," and on their way of answering questions, which clearly shows that they think like the people who do this kind of job.

A good example of this "instant credibility" is the test that some Canadian professional engineer associations use to determine whether or not immigrants who have extensive engineering experience outside of Canada are engineers. The test they use is the "duck test," meaning that "if it quacks like a duck and walks like a duck, then it is probably a duck." Applied to engineering, this test becomes: If this person talks like an engineer and thinks like an engineer, then he or she is probably an engineer. These professional associations have immigrants come to meet a panel of engineers who will ask them questions to determine whether they think and speak like engineers. If the answer is yes, then these immigrants will be able to move to the next step of the licensing process.

Counselors sometimes need to be brutally honest and help immigrants stop looking for positions for which they will not be considered qualified. For example, a Serbian plant manager who immigrates to North America has very little chance of obtaining a plant manager position here—at least not initially. This message is often quite difficult to give, but it will benefit the recipients of these conversations tremendously, since it increases their probability of finding a job and getting started on their North American journey. They may come back to their dream at a later date, once they have established a network and learned to navigate the North American work culture.

One point to keep in mind is that immigrants have a much better chance of finding jobs in sectors that are experiencing rapid growth, as opposed to sectors that are not. While this is true for everyone, this point is far more important in the case of immigrants than in the case of mainstream North Americans, since immigrants have a much lower probability of being the preferred candidate when organizations have a choice among candidates. This was clearly the case in the recent past, with many immigrants finding employment easily as programmers when the IT sector was booming in the late 1990s. It is true again in the accounting profession because the Sarbanes–Oxley Act has created a tremendous need for auditing services, resulting in a global shortage of audit accountants. It is also true of the oil and gas industry, particularly in the Albertan oil sands.

Creating an Action Plan

The next phase consists in turning the information gathered up to this point into an action plan that immigrants will then implement. It requires setting priorities in each area.

- Which professional associations will job seekers join? In which association will they be active?
- Which conferences/events/presentations will they attend? Will they try to make a presentation at one of these conferences/events? With what kind of people are they trying to network?
- Which trade magazines will they read regularly?
- To which search firms will they send their résumés?
- To what kind of job postings will they respond? For which job postings will they be considered qualified?
- What kind of volunteer activity will they undertake?
- To which organizations will they send their résumés?

Other questions that need to be addressed by job seekers in collaboration with their counselors include the following.

- What kinds of positions will they apply for?
- What are their most significant accomplishments by North American standards?
- What kind of résumé will they create?
- How do they contact target employers, and in what order?

As mentioned earlier, the creation of a detailed action plan based on a thorough labor market analysis takes a lot of time—typically 5–8 weeks of solid work for someone who has 10–15 years of experience in a particular field.

The Job Search

Once job seekers have created a comprehensive action plan, the key becomes the implementation of this action plan. This implementation includes a number of steps:

- Creating a base résumé and customizing it to specific job postings.
- Preparing for and going through job interviews.
- Networking.
- Negotiating a job offer.

Since numerous books have been written on each of these topics, the remainder of this chapter focuses on the support that social workers can provide to immigrants to help them go through this process.

Résumés

There are many courses and books on how to write a good résumé. There is no magic formula—if there were, everyone would know what it is and the person who created it would be rich and/or famous! Therefore, everyone needs to find what works best for him or her. This section discusses specific points that counselors need to examine in more detail, since most immigrants are unaware of the issues related to these points.

Concise and Precise Self-Descriptions

Immigrants need to be able to define themselves in 15 words or less. Résumés that start with a short, concise, precise self-description are more likely to be read—provided, of course, this description corresponds to the kind of profile the organization is looking for. In contrast, lengthy and general statements that could describe thousands of people are likely to lead to rejection. For example, résumés that open with statements like

OBJECTIVE: A challenging position in research and development demanding creativity and innovation in chemical products and processes
OBJECTIVE: To obtain a mechanical designer position

do not have nearly as much impact on North American employers as résumés from the same people that start with statements like

Polymer synthetic chemist specialized in the development of new polymer molecules to achieve specific properties

Mechanical engineer specialized in the design of enclosures for electronic products and systems

Specific Profiles

The profiles that immigrants use to describe themselves need to support their specialization and need to be supported by their experience. Counselors must look at these with a critical eye to weed out statements that could apply to anyone (such as "Excellent team player who works well independently") or that are not supported by the experience of job seekers (such as "Excellent communication skills" when the person has difficulties speaking English).

Profiles need to highlight clearly the knowledge of job seekers by showing that they know what is important in the positions they are applying for. They must be able to demonstrate that they have what it takes by putting forward accomplishments that are specific to their field. For example, points such as the following clearly demonstrate the technical knowledge of this candidate, since people who have not worked in this field are usually unaware of the trade-offs involved in this line of work:

- Over 10 years of experience in the design and fabrication of plastic and metal enclosures for a wide range of electronic products and systems.
- Extensive experience in optimizing enclosure and product designs to minimize manufacturing costs while maximizing serviceability, weatherability, and product life.
- Strong experience in designing enclosures to manage electromagnetic interference (EMI), heat dissipation, and environmental issues.
- Experience in cost estimating, BOM preparation, GD&T, and DTC.

Profiles such as the following include specific accomplishments that give readers of this résumé a sense of the individual's capabilities:

- Over eight years' successful experience in helping manufacturing organizations improve processes and product quality.
- Saved a total of $80 M for customers by implementing process improvement programs in over 40 organizations.

Experience

When they describe their experience, immigrants often focus on points like the number of people who reported to them or their responsibilities. These points are considered less important or less relevant by North American organizations than the projects they worked on and the results they obtained. This latter information gives the company a much better idea of what this candidate can do. The comprehensive project descriptions created by job seekers in the initial stage of their job search for details (see the earlier section of this chapter on "Analyzing the Experience and Expertise of Immigrants") becomes handy at this point since they help job seekers and social workers create bullet points that describe the competencies of job seekers.

All project descriptions need to be quantified in order to make them concrete and real rather than abstract. For example:

Led a team of engineers and technicians in the development of three new materials for a new feminine hygiene product to be launched in several continents simultaneously. Reduced cost of raw materials in finished product by 10 percent.

Managed a complex chain of supply for test markets involving 15 suppliers (some working in parallel, others in series) located in seven countries in Europe and North America. Reduced the percentage of raw material orders delivered late from 50 percent to 0, which enabled the timely production and testing of developmental products.

They also need to be supporting the expertise claimed by the candidate in their one-line self-description and in their profile. North American interviewers often evaluate negatively descriptions of projects that are not relevant to the expertise required for the position. This indicates that job seekers have worked in areas unrelated to the job at hand and makes them look like a "jack of all trades, master of none."

Finally, it is essential that the résumés prepared by immigrants be reviewed by North American professionals who work in the same field as they do, to check whether they are using technical words that are common in North America. As well, they want to be sure that the figures they are using to quantify their accomplishments are in the right ball park. Figures that are too low or too high will be interpreted as unimpressive or exaggerated. In either case, they are viewed negatively by North American interviewers. Networking within one's profession becomes very helpful at this stage, since these are the people who can tell whether the résumé makes sense or not and what specific points need to be modified to make it attractive to people within the field.

Customization

Since North America is a land of specialists, immigrants need to customize their résumés for every job posting to which they respond. This does not mean creating an entirely new résumé each time: Eighty percent of the résumé should be the same for all job postings—this corresponds to the core part of their experience. The remaining 20 percent needs to be modified for each application. Sending the same résumés twice often means that at least one of these two will not hit its target, since it is not adapted to the specific requirements of the position.

Interviews

What follows are a few areas where immigrants often struggle. Suggestions for counselors to help them overcome these challenges are included.

Chitchat

Many immigrants have difficulties making chitchat in a way that fits the expectations of North Americans. The subjects of chitchat may be very different in their home countries (see Chapter 3 for more details). One suggestion counselors can make to immigrants who want to practice chitchat is to visit a shopping mall and go from store to store. Practice chitchatting with sales representatives. By observing the approach sales representatives take to initiate and carry the conversation (e.g., how much time does it take them to get down to business? What subjects do they bring up? How do they bring up these subjects?), immigrants can learn how to chitchat effectively.

Odor/Perfume

North Americans do not like odors—whether cigarette smoke, perfumes, cooking smells, or body odor, the goal of the North American workplace is to be odor free. People use a lot of deodorants to achieve this objective. In other parts of the world, odors are more common and often welcome; for example,

French people enjoy perfumes extensively. This creates major issues during job interviews, since North American interviewers will immediately cross off a candidate from their list if they can smell this candidate.

While this is a nonissue for most immigrants, social workers need to tell those for whom it is an issue, since it will decrease tremendously their chances of finding employment. Furthermore, interviewers will not tell candidates who have odor problems that they are turning them down because of an odor problem—most North Americans are very uncomfortable discussing this issue, even with people they know, let alone people they do not know. As a result, job seekers who have odor problems will not find out unless counselors tell them explicitly.

Counselors need to keep these two points in mind when they prepare for such a conversation:

As long as their intentions are clearly to help them, most immigrants will react positively to being told why they are not successful in their job search, since it gives them concrete suggestions to improve.

It is often easier for a man to discuss odor problems with another man than with a woman, and vice versa. Some counseling offices have set up a male/female team of "designated hitters," people who will deal with this issue when it arises.

Identifying Individual Contributions and Accomplishments

Counselors need to help immigrants differentiate between their contributions and the contributions of other team members as well as identify what are their personal accomplishments versus the accomplishments of others. This can be challenging at times; for example, Chinese professionals will often look at this exercise as making no sense at all, since they did everything together. The way to get to this information is to ask immigrants which tasks they performed most often as well as which tasks they tended to perform better or more quickly than other team members (chances are these would be the tasks for which North Americans would consider them responsible within this team).

Tell Nothing but the Truth

When immigrants prepare for job interviews, one point counselors need to emphasize is the very strong negative impact that telling something other than the truth has in North America. You do not have to tell the whole truth in North America, but you certainly do not want to say something you know is untrue, because, when people find out that you said something you knew was untrue, you lose all credibility and trust and you will never be able to regain them. Telling "white lies" or "stretching the truth" does not have consequences nearly as negative in many other parts of the world, so immigrants may sometimes "embellish" their experience. This approach is fraught with major perils in North America, because as soon as recruiters find out that one point has been embellished, they think to themselves: "What else has been embellished?" and eliminate this candidate from the running.

Interview Preparation

While there are many courses and books on how to prepare for interviews, these usually cover more of the soft skill part of the interview rather than the technical questions that candidates will have to field. Making lists of such questions would be an arduous task, and those lists would become obsolete as soon as they were published. Therefore, it is critical that immigrants prepare for interviews by asking people who work in their field to help them prepare by asking the kinds of technical questions that job seekers are likely to be asked. There is no substitute here for experience and being in the right field.

Networking

Networking with people within one's field provides incredible benefits to any professional in North America, particularly when they are looking for a job. People within your field can:

- Help you understand the trends that are taking shape within their industries and help you determine where your skills may be needed. They can add to and validate your labor market analysis.
- Help you refine your résumés by making sure you are using the technical words common in North America and that the numbers you are quoting to quantify your accomplishments are in the right ball park—impressive without being excessive.
- Help you prepare for interviews by giving you examples of the questions often asked and suggesting ways to improve the quality of your answers to these questions.

- Pass on your name to people who are looking for people with your skills, suggest opportunities for you to demonstrate your skills (through articles/presentations/volunteer activities), or suggest job opportunities.

Obviously, the last point (suggesting job opportunities) is the one that job seekers most want. Unfortunately, going straight to this one essentially shuts the door to all the others, because few approaches will terminate a conversation more quickly in North America than asking someone shortly after they have introduced themselves to you if there are positions open in their organizations.

Many immigrants tend to confuse information interviews with actual job interviews and give their résumés to the person who was giving them information. The two are quite different, and counselors can help job seekers understand the difference by insisting that they not give their résumés to anyone when networking unless that person asks for it explicitly. During information interviews, job seekers need to concentrate on gathering information and knowledge that cannot be obtained through other means. North Americans hate being asked questions that are answered on their organization's website. They must also avoid turning someone off by asking him or her for a position at this point.

Negotiating a Job Offer

For most immigrants, this is usually a moot point, in the sense that they usually have limited bargaining power. In most cases, they end up obtaining a position for which they are overqualified to some extent while being paid at the low end of the pay scale for that position. This usually reflects their lower-than-average soft skills by North American standards (see Chapter 9 for more details). As discussed in Chapter 9, one of the best routes for immigrants to move forward in their careers is to work on improving their soft skills—in particular, their negotiating skills so that they can negotiate job offers more effectively.

When they are asked for their salary expectations, immigrants need to give a range that is based on the research they have conducted (see the earlier section on "Salary Surveys") without putting themselves out of the race by giving figures that are either too low or too high. One good rule of thumb is to present a range where the high end is 50 percent higher than the low end (such as $40K to $60K or $80K to $120K). The range of remunerations in most professions is often of that magnitude when you consider the absolute lowest and highest figures, so these ranges are not an exaggeration, and they are wide enough to be able to fit the requirements of the organization that is interviewing you.

Keeping in Touch

Once job seekers have found jobs, most lose contact with their counselors. Since counselors have worked with job seekers for an extended period of time and have learned the strengths and limitations of the people they helped, this approach often limits the future career prospects of immigrants. Counselors can be an important element in their network, at least until they develop a network within their professions.

5

Helping International New Hires Adapt to the Organization

You have made the big decision and hired someone or many people who are culturally different. Now what? Kick back and watch them produce? Perhaps.

The new employee wants to make a positive early impression and perform meaningful work. The organization wants to help the new employee to feel welcome but also wants to get the person productive as quickly as possible. However, recent immigrants and existing employees will not always see eye to eye, due to the cultural differences discussed throughout this book. That being the case, who should adapt or change their ways—the new hires or the current people in the organization? We believe that the newcomer should be responsible for 80 percent of the adaptation and the existing employees 20 percent. The new hire should be relentlessly learning and adjusting to fit into the organization that he or she has joined. But the newcomer's integration is jeopardized without a helping hand from the receiving organization.

The amount of adaptation that new, culturally different employees need to go through depends significantly how much they have adapted to North America by the time they are hired. If they came to North America to join and work for an organization or if this is their first major job in North America, there is a good chance they will need a fair amount of support in order to integrate effectively into the organization.

This chapter provides the reader with a better understanding of relocation adjustment issues and offers strategies for the organization to help recent immigrants through the process. No organization wants to spoon-feed newcomers. But, on the other hand, it is a waste for an organization to lose people when small adjustments on their part could have made the difference. As with all important relationships, it is easier to get started right than it is to get back on track after a series of oversights or misunderstandings. The better prepared the new employee and employer, the smoother the transition will be.

The first section, on culture shock, describes the issues recent immigrants are facing and how unusual or inexplicable behavior may be put into context. The bulk of the chapter is then dedicated to initiatives the organization can undertake to help everyone get on track.

New employees benefit from an orientation to the company, to the office, to relevant people, and to the job itself. People will be very appreciative (and likely more productive) if the company takes an interest in the settling-in process of the entire family, not just of the employee. Employee retention and productivity is higher in companies with good orientation and support programs.

> Immigrants don't just bring their skills; they bring their whole culture with them.

Culture Shock and Adjustment

What Is Culture Shock?

Culture shock is a term used to describe the physical, emotional, and mental upset experienced when moving into a new environment. The combination of a new position, not knowing what is expected, not knowing how to make oneself understood, and not knowing how to meet one's needs can be debilitating.

Some researchers prefer the term *adjustment shock* or *role shock*. Much of the stress in a relocation is caused by so many of the anchors that make life normal changing in one moment. This radical upheaval requires adjusting to new patterns in every aspect of one's life.

What Are the Causes?

Anxiety and disorientation are often caused by so many combined changes coming together in one moment. Here are some examples of changes a newcomer has to deal with.

On the job, the new immigrant needs to adjust to the many cultural differences raised in this book, including:

- Nonverbal communication.
- Verbal communication.
- Punctuality.

- Manager–employee relations.
- Teamwork.
- Individualism.
- Risk aversion.

There is an incredible amount of information to process, decisions to make, and things to do on such topics as:

- Finding a permanent place to live.
- Home utilities.
- Schooling for the children.
- Childcare.
- Banking.
- Insurance.
- Licenses.
- Transportation.
- Shopping.
- Groceries the family likes.

Some of the sources of stress may include:

- Marital disagreements over all the changes and choices being made.
- When one spouse has stopped working.
- Financial issues.
- Changes in house, living, and cooking circumstances.
- Weather.
- Hours of daylight, hours of sunlight.
- Recreational habits.
- Religious activities.
- Social activities.
- Extended-family gatherings.
- Eating habits.
- Vacations.
- Laws, rules, and regulations.

The foregoing topics are most of the big ones. Culture shock or adjustment shock also comes as a result of all the little differences that individually would mean nothing but cumulatively can dramatically affect one's feeling of well-being. The effect of these variations remains largely unconscious for most people. Let's take a look at the first five minutes of one's day, which may appear very different in a new place:

- The alarm clock ringing or radio station playing has a different sound.
- The time to get up is earlier or later than it used to be, most likely earlier.
- The bed, pillows, and sheets are new and feel different.
- There is more or less natural light coming in the window, for sunrise is at a different hour.
- The temperature and humidity of the apartment or house is unusual.
- One's foot touches a new surface when getting out of bed.
- The layout of the bedroom, the wall colors, the decorations are unfamiliar.
- It doesn't feel like home, not yet.

We could continue through an entire day, listing the differences minute by minute. This list may remind the reader of when he or she left home for the first time to attend college or to take a new job in a different city. Indeed, the experience is similar; it is a matter of degree.

Interestingly, some of the lifestyle changes just mentioned actually invigorate or energize some people though debilitating and depressing others. Of the people who are negatively affected, each will have a slightly different source and symptom. Some individuals are more distraught by not having extended family nearby, while others find the multitude of decisions to be made most difficult. Each person is unique.

> Unlike some of my friends, I relocated to a smaller city in North America and into an office where everyone else was born in this country. I had heard that in a smaller center like this people are friendlier and more helpful. My experience in the first couple of months was the reverse. I wanted to quit and go home. At the office, I was given some brief instructions and set to work immediately. My assigned mentor took me to lunch, but I am a vegetarian and the restaurant he selected offered me very few menu choices. Coworkers didn't ask me about India, about my work there or anything else. I felt that to them it was like I had just dropped in from another planet. They didn't know what to do with me. There were a couple of misunderstandings where my colleagues got the impression I was lazy and trying to avoid work. It felt bad. Outside of work I spent a lot of time inside my apartment, alone. It was the first time I had ever lived alone. I was lonely and I missed my family in India so much.
>
> —Indian professional in North America

This poor fellow is suffering from a combination of culture shock and adapting to a new business culture. After three months, he was feeling much better about his work and his workmates. They had come to understand each other better, though he still felt that he would rather be in a larger city, where he would have had a chance to socialize with other Indians.

What Are the Symptoms?

The symptoms of culture shock may come to the awareness of the organization when coworkers complain of the new employee's rudeness, irritability, inexplicable behavior, and/or poor work habits. Of course, there could be other explanations for these behaviors. However, in most cases, culture shock or adjustment shock is a big factor when these types of concerns arise. Less dramatic symptoms might be that the new person is sticking with others from the same cultural group, not attending social functions, and remaining silent whenever possible.

The problem is better tackled prior to hearing from a manager or coworker that he or she refuses to work any longer with this new employee. Relationship damage is difficult to repair. While the culture shock experience is not likely to be averted completely, the problems associated with it can be minimized through proper preparation.

Symptoms and commonly associated comments:

Helplessness:	"This is too much for me."
Loneliness:	"Where are my family and friends?"
Frustration:	"Why is nothing simple here?"
Anger:	"That's the craziest thing I've ever heard."
Negative attitude:	"These people are so demanding. They don't care about me."

While in a negative state, newcomers may criticize the local people and their ways. They may blame the company for not taking care of them properly. Finally, they may blame themselves and feel they are not cut out for this new position or location. This loss of self-confidence can be particularly problematic to workplace performance.

How Long Will It Last?

The simplified U-curve in Figure 5.1 represents the adjustment process associated with an international move. Initial feelings of excitement and perhaps euphoria are replaced by an emotional downward slide. The newcomer realizes that things are very different but has not become accustomed to the new ways.

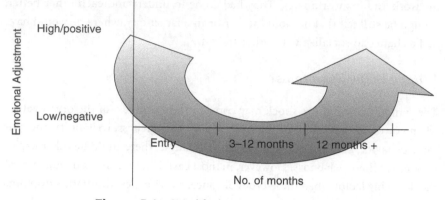

Figure 5.1 Simplified U-curve of adjustment.

Deep concerns over whether one made the right decision to relocate are common, as are the feelings listed earlier under "symptoms." People who consciously pursue positive adjustment strategies are more likely to make a smoother transition. The transition process, however, can take 12–18 months or longer. In reality, some will experience the most intense anxiety in the first few weeks or months; for others it doesn't begin until after a number of months in the new location. While culture shock anxiety affects people at different times and in different ways, most people experience it in some form.

Who Experiences It?

It should be noted that people can experience culture shock when relocating from one city to another in the same state or province. It is not exclusively international moves that bring it on.

There is nothing unusual or wrong with experiencing culture shock, even on repeated international assignments. Accepting that the process is normal, and understanding something of the stages helps in the positive adjustment. When the experience of culture shock is denied, people are more likely to blame someone or something for the challenges they face.

What Can Be Done to Help?

Assisting employees through the culture shock adjustment process includes the suggestions listed in the remainder of this chapter. Effective diversity programs combine "push and pull" strategies. The "push" strategies involve programs that are automatically provided for the new employee and receiving employees. The "pull" strategies include programs and support that the new employee and receiving employees may call on as they see fit.

Suggestions for assisting employees through the culture shock adjustment process include:

- Provide a thorough orientation to the organization, including information on its products and services, how to get around the building, access supplies, facilities, and safety and security.
- Provide an orientation to the job, including duties and responsibilities, standards for judging performance, reporting relationship, expected interactions with coworkers, suppliers and clients, wage structure, benefits, incentive pay, and anticipated training and development.
- Provide a business culture orientation, including factual background to the city and country, city logistics, cultural values and behaviors, business norms, and especially culture shock, describing symptoms and strategies for positive adjustment.
- Offer the assistance of an education consultant to help foreign-hired employees to find the optimal schooling fit for their children.
- Arrange for an external coach to provide over-the-phone information on the business culture, and answer questions, beginning while the candidate is still in his or her home country if applicable.
- Provide a settling-in mentor to help with basic questions about navigating around the office.
- Identify a business performance coach who provides regular and detailed feedback to the new employee on his or her job performance.
- Provide some form of support to the family of the employee, assisting in settling in, education, finding work, etc. In some cases, companies provide English-language lessons for family members.
- Prepare and support coworkers and managers of culturally diverse new hires so that they can better understand the needs of the newcomers and be in a better position to assist them.
- Schedule periodic meetings to discuss cultural integration within the organization.
- Be aware that some behaviors demonstrated by the new employee may not be typical for that person but rather the result of new levels of stress.
- Be flexible in allowing the employee time to take care of settling-in activities, such as house buying and selecting schools for children.

- Share best practices with other organizations and human resources professionals at local, national, and international human resources associations and conferences.
- Provide opportunities for social, team-building activities.

> If the company was the first choice of the employee and, conversely, the employee the first choice of the company, then there is a good deal of momentum to carry the early relationship over rocky times. However, if the matching was not a first choice for either party, then there tends to be greater wariness in the early part of the employee/company relationship.

New Employee Orientation, Coaching, and Support

Recruitment is a significant expense to an organization. Company personnel people and resources are tied up sifting through résumés, conducting interviews, and making hiring decisions. Then come orientation programs, coaching, and ramp-up time until the employee becomes fully productive.

Recruiting and orienting culturally different employees is typically more expensive to the organization than hiring local candidates. If the recruits are found internationally and brought into the country for the job, there is obviously an extra expense to that. However, the greater, often hidden, expense involves the recent immigrant's integration into the company and the society.

For companies without a plan, the pain is usually felt by the human resources department and/or by the new employee's colleagues. New hire workmates are typically bombarded with questions about work and nonwork issues. Coworkers feel bad for the new employee and try to help as best they can, but they also may begin to feel resentful.

Human resources personnel often bear the brunt of the poor preparation or underfunding of programs for the newcomers. Here are a few of the concerns voiced by human resources departments:

We are supposed to hire 100 new employees internationally and bring them here in the next six months. We have to assess their credentials, follow up with references on the other side of the planet, and arrange visas and temporary accommodations. We get questions on the climate, appropriate clothing, education for the children, daycare, whether the spouse can work, and dozens of other questions that we have never had to deal with before. The hours required are astronomical.

The manager of the apartment we are renting for our new employee has called to complain that the couple are allowing their toddler to defecate and urinate on the carpet, and he would like it to stop. [In some Southeast Asian cultures, toddlers are toilet trained without diapers. However, neither do they have carpets on their floors.]

I can't believe how difficult it is for our new immigrant employees to get basic things like credit cards or drivers licenses. They often need our help.

I know that one of the reasons our immigrant employees come to this country to work is to ensure a good education for their children. But their questions around the education system and options seem endless.

We need to set expectations with the work group manager and the executive that we in HR cannot handle all of these questions and issues on our own. They need to be shared within the organization.

The remainder of this chapter discusses programs an organization can offer that will assist the culturally different employees to integrate into the workplace. These programs can be arranged in-house or by outside service providers. The solutions presented are not meant to represent an exhaustive list. Organizations will always come up with creative and new ways to help newcomers.

Classroom-based programs described include an orientation to the organization, job, and business culture for the new employee and an orientation on cultural difference and support for the receiving work groups.

Coaching, mentoring, and other support programs are also outlined.

Organization Orientation

New employees want to learn quickly about the organization and the way things work in order to be productive. Details of the work group's or even the company's function need to be clearly stated verbally and on paper. Basics such as the location of the washrooms, expectations in the coffee room, how to get office supplies, the source of computer support, and safety and security procedures need to be covered.

Many North American offices rely heavily on the new employee's asking others for answers to questions. But with the intense pace of the average office, it is not easy to find someone who is available to answer the questions. Also, many North Americans are resentful of interruptions to their work.

A commonly voiced concern of new immigrants is that they are not given a complete orientation.

I was given a brief orientation to the company. But it was at a fairly high level and it was delivered quickly. Once I was back in my cubicle with my first small assignment in hand, I had a million questions. I didn't know where the washrooms were, how to use the photocopier, or who the people were in the work spaces next to me.

—Newly arrived professional in North America

We find it amazing how often we can mention this to companies around North America and have native-born employees nod, smile, and know exactly what we are talking about because they have experienced the same thing. They are typically able to give their own story of how they felt abandoned in their first few days or weeks on the job. This situation typically causes a higher level of stress for new immigrants.

There is no surer way to demoralize new employees than to leave them on their own without introduction to people or the organization. A North American may simply shrug his or her shoulders and accept "that this is the way it will be." It may be recognized as something uncomfortable but not entirely atypical. A recent immigrant may take it more personally. The abandonment may be interpreted as a snub and leave the person wondering either what is wrong with him or her or what is wrong with the company. Neither scenario is conducive to productivity gains.

Newcomers from more collective cultures (described in more detail in Chapter 8), such as India and Japan, are used to greater interaction with coworkers than is common in most North American offices. These interactions provide a source of valuable support and direction in the early stages. New to a more individualistic society, these people are unsure when it is appropriate to interrupt coworkers to ask questions.

When professional persons are hired in India, they are rarely left alone in the first few days or maybe even weeks. There is always someone at their side assisting them, answering questions, introducing them to others, and helping them become comfortable in the office. This applies to coffee breaks and lunch breaks as well. Coworkers will accompany the new employees every step of the way. You can imagine my shock when I moved to North America. I really believed that there was a serious problem either with me or with this organization. I was despondent.

—Indian professional in North America

A basic new employee orientation program might include the following topics:

- The company's core business.
- The location of relevant company facilities and equipment needed for day-to-day work.
- Meeting of the boss and coworkers.
- Security procedures.
- Safety requirements and procedures.
- Company policies.
- Company support services.
- Who to ask for different types of questions.

The most effective programs are more than one day in length. They begin within the first few days of employment. Don't assume, just because something was covered quickly in an orientation program or was included in the policy manual, that the recent immigrant will have absorbed it. There is much going on in those first few days.

> I sat down with the guy and went through our entire policy document, which included all the things he needed to be aware of and to do in the coming days. The next day I got a call from him asking which parking spot was his. A week later he asked about the process for medical attention, because one of his kids was sick. These were all things we discussed and were in his binder. Sometimes I feel like I'm wasting my time.
>
> —An HR specialist

First, patience is required, for much that is heard and read in the first few days will not be absorbed. A follow up session two or three weeks later to review the important points and deal with the new questions that have come up is highly recommended.

As well, there needs to be a designated person, who is easily accessible, to reinforce information and answer questions as they come up. This should not be "extra" work on top of this person's existing responsibilities—resentment can build if this is the case. Rather, their role should be seen as important and time should be allowed for it.

Job Orientation

While the new employee will have seen the job description and discussed the role during the interview process, now is the time to review roles, responsibilities, and expectations in greater detail. A performance review six or 12 months down the road is not the time for the employee to learn which job tasks were the most important or to learn the consequences of not achieving certain results.

A clear job description with duties and responsibilities will provide the employee with needed direction. This document then can be the basis for future performance evaluations.

An orientation to the job might include:

- The employee's duties and responsibilities in clear detail.
- The standards for judging performance.
- Reporting relationship.
- Expected interactions with coworkers, suppliers, and clients.
- Wage structure, benefits, incentive pay.
- Anticipated training and development.

In addition to the orientation, of course, there may be actual on-the-job training that takes place. This could last weeks or months. Once again, a clear sense of who is responsible for assisting in helping the new employees is recommended. Where should they go with their questions?

Business Culture Orientation

People new to North America may have very little idea of the business culture and office norms. They have been brought up and trained in a different system. Their expectations, developed perhaps from watching American television or Hollywood movies, can be wildly different from reality. The first step in helping employees learn corporate norms of behavior is to explain the expected behaviors. This is normally best accomplished through a formal business crosscultural orientation program in the first weeks on the job. An experienced cross-cultural trainer will have a good idea of typical areas of confusion and be able to help build new skills.

When employees are recent immigrants to the country, such a discussion might begin with the norms of the new national culture and follow through to regional culture and on to the specific corporate culture. All of these culture types will overlap and have a significant impact on the way things work.

Business culture orientations are typically one day long but can vary in length to suit company needs. Many companies find it beneficial to mix the participants to include those who have just arrived and those who have been with the organization for up to a couple of months. It is also recommended to include spouses in the orientation.

The benefit of inviting spouses of new employees to this orientation is three-fold. First, spouses will find the information on local business culture very helpful for their activities around town. Second, it will help the spouses understand what employees are dealing with at the workplace. For example, a spouse will hear what working hours might be normally and during busy season. A couple will be able to support one another more effectively through the issues discussed in the orientation. Finally, should a spouse end up in the workforce, then the orientation material will be completely relevant.

Some organizations precede this orientation program with a dinner the night before or some other social event. This might include people who have previously been through the same orientation program as a new employee. Another twist is to have longer-term existing employees participate in the program for their own learning, to assist in the learning of the culturally different employees and for team building.

Factual Background to the City and Country

Factual background information is a good starting point to understanding a new culture. Topics should, at a minimum, include:

- Historical highlights.
- Ethnic composition.
- Religion.
- Education system.
- Holidays.
- Government.
- Climate.
- Geography.
- Economics.
- Politics.
- Sports.
- Current news and events.

A country's culture has its origin in its history. Religion, ethnicity, the education system, government, and holidays are part of that history. This background gives the newcomer a sense of how local people look at the world, why they look at it that way, and subgroups within the country.

The climate and geography sections can include practical information on the seasons, average temperatures, and appropriate clothing for each. For people unaccustomed to winter, this information is particularly valuable. The concept of *wind chill*, or low temperature compounded by wind, is preferably understood before one's cheeks freeze from the experience.

Economics, politics, sports, and recent news topics help give North Americans context for what they see in the media and hear being discussed around the water cooler. The importance of knowing something about current events cannot be underestimated in the business environment. Though small talk is typically brief in North America, making an informed comment on a recent local sporting event can be a great opener to a business conversation.

City Logistics

For people who are completely new to the country, here is a list (suggestive but incomplete) of logistical topics that might be covered in an orientation program:

- **Health and safety:** emergency numbers, medical facilities, family doctors, dentists, locations, and times to be cautious.
- **Banking and currency:** bank accounts, credit cards, etc.
- **Transportation:** public transport, driver's license, renting or buying a vehicle, insurance.
- **Utilities:** electricity, gas, water, sewage, garbage, recycling.
- **Communication:** Internet, e-mail, telephone, fax, mail.
- **Shopping:** food, clothing, household goods, etc.
- **Recreation and leisure activities:** sports clubs, parks, museums, theaters, etc.

Cultural Values and Behaviors

Discussion of cultural values and behaviors is the core of an orientation program. Recent immigrants typically have already had exposure to other cultures prior to arriving at your workplace. They may come from a multicultural national environment, may have studied in a place other than their country of birth, and in most cases have learned to speak more than one language, possibly three or more.

Countries have dozens, if not hundreds or thousands, of behavior differences in the workplace. Examples of these differences include:

- The clothes to wear to work.
- The time to arrive at work.
- The greeting to use when you see a coworker for the first time that day, the second time, and so on.
- Social conversation prior to discussing work.
- Questions that can be asked and of whom.
- How and when to approach the boss.
- When and how to interrupt someone.
- When and how to correct someone.
- Meetings starting on time or not.
- In which situations to work alone and in which to collaborate with others.
- Whether to go for coffee or lunch alone or to invite coworkers.
- Whether to drink alcohol at lunch or not.

Here are a few comments we have heard from people new to the North American workplace.

I knew the work hours were going to be long and there would be little time or opportunity to make friends on weekends. So I had really hoped that I would be able to make a friend or two from the office. From my experience in the first few weeks, this is now looking unlikely.

I'm not surprised they don't know much about my home country, but I am disappointed that they are not even curious. They don't ask me about my country or my past experiences.

I was shown my cubicle and workstation, given my first assignment, and told to get to work and to ask if I had any questions. I was sitting there not knowing where the washrooms were, how to use the photocopier, or even the names of the people located near me.

I was used to an office environment where I could see the other people I was working with and felt comfortable asking them questions and enjoyed it when they asked me questions. We got a lot of work done, but we felt as though we were working together, kind of like a family. The long hours did not seem so bad. But here I cannot see into the other cubicles from my desk, I don't know who else is in the office, and it seems no one asks another person for information or advice, other than through an e-mail or telephone call. I feel lonely.

I understood that North Americans were private people and didn't expect colleagues to go out of their way to meet me. On the first day, from noon until one o'clock I noticed colleagues coming in and out of the office, some with food, some without, and I didn't understand the lunchtime ritual. At one o'clock, which is the normal lunchtime in India, I approached a colleague and asked if it was time for us to go to lunch. He paused and I could see the wheels in his head were working hard. He said that everyone had by then either gone out and had lunch or brought lunch back to their desks. He said that I should go to the nearby food court and get some food.

I offered some of my food to a colleague, to which he responded, "It is your food—why are you offering it to me?" I felt like I had done something wrong.

As well as representing people in culture shock, these quotes speak to cultural value differences around individualism, group orientation, friendship, privacy, independence, teamwork, and workplace relations. It takes months and possibly years to fully understand a national culture and its business culture. The recent immigrant knows that he or she is at a disadvantage. The goal is to get up to speed and fit in comfortably as quickly as possible.

Cultural Relativity

An orientation on cultural values and behaviors usually begins with a conversation on the topic of cultural relativity. By cultural relativity, we refer to the idea that people raised in one culture learn a set of beliefs and behaviors associated with what is right and what is wrong for thousands of situations, while people in another culture learn a somewhat different set of beliefs and behaviors connected with what is a better or worse thing to believe, say or do in the same situation.

This awareness that people in other cultures hold values different from ours is not something that comes naturally. The difference usually comes up with a statement like "What the heck is that person thinking or doing?" When people do become aware of the variance, the difference is often judged negatively, i.e., "their way is not as good as our way." Program participants are shown how to suspend judgment for a time in order to collect more information to better understand the context of the difference.

Communication styles, verbal and nonverbal, are described across cultures. When things go wrong, it usually begins with miscommunication. The orientation should include information on common differences in communication style and ways to bridge them. (Communication is described in more detail in Chapter 6.)

Value differences with the greatest impact on workplace interactions include individualism (more in Chapter 8), hierarchy (more in Chapter 7), teamwork (more in Chapter 8), and risk orientation (more in Chapter 8). These are presented from different cultural perspectives along with their connection to manager/employee relations, decision making, employee participation, teamwork, and workplace etiquette. Orientation participants learn and practice how to bridge the cultural divide.

Culture Shock and Adjustment

An orientation program for culturally different employees in the workplace should include a section on culture shock and adjustment. If your new employee has been in the country for only a short time, she or he will likely be going through some form of adjustment or culture shock. This is described in more detail in the first section of the chapter.

Education Consulting

When an organization hires employees internationally and brings them to North America, one of the key concerns for newcomers is their children's education. The combination of immigrants becoming more concerned with school selection and a proliferation of school choices make it important for human resources or an Education Consultant to assist the family. Within a public system there may be secular schools, Catholic schools, charter schools, science schools, fine arts schools, sports schools, and language schools—to name a few. Programming options may include Gifted and Talented Programming, English as a Second language Programming, and much more. Within the private system, the choice may be equally varied.

An emerging field in North America is education consulting. A company can either let the family work it out on their own, provide internal support through the human resources department, or use external resources. While leaving the family to their own devices may seem like the cost-saving answer, it is a false saving if your new employee is missing days of work in order to figure out the education system and get his or her children placed.

An education consultant can provide information on and assistance with the following:

- The structure of the local school system.
- The choices that exist in terms of school type, quality, size, special programs, registration process, etc.
- How one's choice of neighborhood affects school choices.
- Which schools have a strong ESL program.
- Setting up appointments for school tours and language assessment.

Receiving Work Group Orientation

With recent immigrants making a huge effort to adapt to and integrate into the workplace and the culture, a small corresponding effort on the part of company employees can complete the connection. A cultural orientation program for internal employees, such as HR professionals, coaches, coworkers, and managers, can provide invaluable knowledge on where the new employees are coming from and how to help them cross the bridge to full integration. The existing employees learn about common differences in communication, values, and behavior and how to overcome them.

This orientation program would use the components described earlier in the subsection "Business Culture Orientation," with particular focus on the discussions of cultural values and behaviors and culture shock and adjustment.

One concern sometimes raised by existing employees is, "Why should we be learning about this person's culture or adaptation issues, since he or she is joining *our* organization? This is *our* country." People often underestimate how far the newcomer is stretching and changing in order to fit in. One response to this question might include a description of the extent to which the newcomer has to adjust. Also, current employees can be encouraged to look upon it as an opportunity to learn new or different ways to solve business problems. It can make them more effective at their jobs.

External Coach

Orientation programs provide a great fast start for the recent immigrant. Naturally, there are also ongoing questions that need to be answered and support required for the person to fully integrate. However, many organizations find that an external coaching program can play a valuable role.

If the organization is bringing professionals directly from other countries, the first coaching telephone conversation should take place prior to the employee's actual arrival in the country, when possible. The incoming employee will learn what to bring and begin to consider how the new business environment may be different. Personal and specific questions can be answered. It is actually at this point, prior to relocation, that many people experience the greatest stress. Having their questions answered can relieve this stress.

"My son is in a gifted program here. Are there similar special programs there?"

A second coaching conversation takes place within the first month of a person's arrival.

"I am receiving very little feedback from my manager. I'm worried. What does this mean?"

A third conversation might be scheduled for two to three months after job placement.

"I don't seem to be able to complete the work in the time given. What should I do?"

On each occasion there is a discussion of the business culture norms of the country that the person is coming from, in contrast with the norms of the location where the employee now works. Where there are discrepancies, the new employee is asked how he or she will bridge the differences. The culturally different employee is able to ask about difficult situations or expected challenges at the workplace.

Settling-in Mentor or Buddy

Each newcomer should be assigned a buddy or mentor who would pick up where the orientation classes left off by showing the person around, making introductions, and answering questions. Ideally, but not necessarily, the mentor is from the same culture as the new employee. The mentor would share the differences and challenges he or she first experienced when entering the country and joining the company.

The mentor would have this role included in his or her job function for a period of time, perhaps three to six months. Time is allocated to this important function, with some current job tasks removed temporarily. There would be no hard feelings created on either side, by the new employees' feeling they are asking too many questions or being too needy or by the current employees' feeling resentful of the time taken. It would take pressure off coworkers and HR, who would otherwise informally fill this role.

Business Performance Coach

Culturally different employees are eager to receive feedback, positive and negative, but often receive neither, especially in the early stages. Complaints leveled against new employees in their early months often circulate throughout the whole department before finally making their way back to the person concerned. Perhaps the person complaining doesn't feel comfortable raising the topic, doesn't feel it is his or her role, doesn't feel it is fixable, or is just too busy. This, of course, is a disservice to the new employee and to the organization.

A vital role in assisting the integration of new employees is that of business performance coach. This is the person who monitors the newcomer's job performance and provides regular and detailed feedback to the individual. In most organizations, this will be the employee's direct manager. In organizations, such as consulting firms, where the employee works on short-term projects, each for a different manager, one senior person may need to be assigned to poll the respective managers and be the performance coach.

Family Support

> My company was very understanding of family issues when I moved to the city. Even though the project I was working on needed me right away, the company made sure I had help to find the right school for my daughter, a preschool for my son, and activities for my wife and youngest child. After three months, all is going well with me personally and with work. My children are adjusting well. My wife, however, is very unhappy. She misses her family, her job, her old life. By far, this move has required her to make the most adjustments.
>
> —A recent immigrant professional

Recent immigrants often request time off work to deal with family issues. The environment is new for the whole family, and they are typically cut off from the extended-family support they were used to in their home country. Many are used to the idea of "family comes first" being accepted by companies. If the family unit is severely stressed or is breaking down, then obviously the work of the employed spouse will suffer.

North American culture has been described as segmented, meaning that the different aspects of one's life (work, family, friends, recreation, religion, etc.) often form separate and distinct segments. During work time, that is the sole focus, and family, friends, religion, etc., are not to impinge on this time. Similarly, one's friends are often not one's workmates, who in turn are different from one's religious congregation. Each aspect of a North American life is often made up of different people. Neither people nor the times usually overlap.

Most culturally different employees come from countries where life is less segmented. One's family comes first, irrespective of whether one is at work or not. People's friends are often also their workmates. In these cultures, it is assumed that family situations will often take priority over workplace requirements.

The accompanying spouse was perhaps a working professional in the home country but now is, for one reason or another, not working. Often an accompanying spouse would like to work sooner or later. The company can create significant goodwill by assisting the spouse to prepare for or actually find employment.

Companies are encouraged to invite recent immigrant spouses to the cross-cultural orientation.

Affinity Networks

There are many types of innovative programs that companies are experimenting with to help culturally diverse people feel welcome and supported in the organization. GE's Affinity Networks (described below) is one example. Many organizations have similar networks; while they may go by different names, they usually have similar purpose: helping people who belong to the same cultural group share their experiences, their successes, their challenges, and their learnings when dealing with the dominant North American cultural group. One of the important benefits of such networks, when they include people in senior positions, is that junior people have a chance to see that people who belong to their cultural group can make it to the top (see Chapter 9 for more details on this point).

> One of the key mechanisms for facilitating dialogue and progress in our diversity efforts is GE's Affinity Networks: the African American Forum, the Asian Pacific American Forum, the Hispanic Forum, the Women's Network, and the Native American Forum. These Affinity Networks play a critical role in attracting, developing, engaging, and retaining employees at all levels across the company. These networks work in close partnership with our Chairman and CEO, business leaders, and the human resources team to continually uncover ways to improve in

this area and opportunities for growth. These range from mentoring employees for professional growth to engaging customers for business growth.

—GE website

Summary

In this chapter we have suggested a number of different steps and programs that an organization can implement to improve the integration and retention of its culturally diverse employees. This is not meant to be a definitive list or one that must be followed precisely as described. Organizations are encouraged to come up with creative new ways to assist in the integration of their new employees.

The organization itself is best suited to know what initiatives will best meet their specific needs. Some organizations very successfully combine their orientation programs into one large program. Others spread the programs out over more time rather than slot them all into the first two weeks. The company that hosts an orientation series every few months for new employees benefits from the mix of very new and slightly more experienced employees in the same class.

The key to successful orientation programs, whatever the topic, is that they be relevant, practical, timely, and interesting. Few things are more difficult than trying to get people to attend programs that are perceived to be boring and of little value.

The question is asked whether these programs should be optional for employees to attend. The difficulty in making orientation programs optional is that many of the people who don't attend are those who would benefit the most from being in the room. Either because they feel they don't need any outside help, because they can't spare the time, or because they feel it might reflect poorly on their ability, people may choose not to attend. Our advice is to make these programs compulsory and then ensure that they are relevant, practical, timely, and interesting. Request feedback from orientation program participants in order to continually improve future sessions.

The orientations and programs recommended in this chapter help to improve understanding and communication on all sides. It is only through understanding and communication that challenges can be overcome and rewards reaped by having a fully functioning, culturally diverse workforce.

Cross-Cultural Communication

Introduction to Communication

The foundation of all business interaction is communication. There is no recruitment, retention, or promotion of employees without it; there are no clients, nor is there a business, without it. People in organizations spend over 70 percent of their time in interpersonal situations, whether it is one-on-one, meetings, telephone, e-mail, or some other form of communication. It should come as no surprise, therefore, that poor communication is the source of much of any organization's problems. Conversely, improving communication likely represents the single greatest opportunity for organizations to reach higher levels of success, however they define it. With a culturally diverse workforce, the potential both for problems and for opportunities is greater.

"Getting it right" means building rapport, finding common interests, exchanging information, persuading, and getting the work done. "Getting it wrong," on the other hand, leads to confusion, anxiety, frustration, and misjudgments. Benignly, this can be visualized as two ships passing in the night. Or more negatively, it could mean offense, escalating insult, and conflict, like two ships colliding in the night.

Communication styles are so deeply ingrained that it is difficult for us to be consciously aware of them. Through hundreds and thousands of hours of relatively successful exchanges within our home culture, our responses tend to be automatic. In this chapter, we attempt to make conscious what is normally unconscious in our communication.

Unfortunately, there is no silver bullet leading to extraordinary communication. Rather, there are hundreds of small things we can do that cumulatively will make a big difference. Hearing or reading about the differences may have you nodding your head in recognition. To communicate successfully across cultures takes practice and more practice.

This chapter looks at dozens of ways miscommunication can occur across cultures, verbally and nonverbally, and provides corresponding strategies for improved communication. The list is not meant to be exhaustive, but rather to cover the more common themes of failed communication.

Who Is Responsible?

The responsibility for good communication lies with both the initiator and the receiver of the message. The initiator's responsibility is to send out his or her message in a way that is most likely to be received as intended. Good communicators will adjust their message based on the person they are talking to (i.e., to account for age, gender, relationship, familiarity, culture, language skill, etc.). Good listeners will similarly use what they know about the sender of the message to help them interpret the message accurately.

Basic Communication Process

Misunderstandings are seldom the result of harmful intent or trying to mislead another person. When a message makes its way out of the sender's cultural filter to be received through the listener's cultural filter, the meaning received is rarely the exact meaning intended. The idea has been distorted, sometimes a little and sometimes completely (Figure 6.1).

Readers have no doubt had the experience of communication going wrong with someone of their own culture, even with someone in their own family. Have you ever seen a married couple get into a dispute over a simple miscommunication? Imagine one-half of the marriage partnership pointing out an item in a store ("Oh honey! Isn't this great?"), assuming that the partner will pick up the real meaning ("I would really like this for my birthday next week"). When the birthday arrives and the item has not been purchased, there is disappointment, sometimes hurt feelings. Likely this occurred because the original message was never received as intended. As we move across cultures, the complexity of communication multiplies exponentially.

> I had been working with an American woman for a year or so and we got along great. We worked well together and shared jokes. One day I said, "You have put on weight. You look like a cow." I intended it as a casual, perhaps humorous comment. She got really mad. I had never seen her get mad before.
>
> —A Sudanese woman

A once popular game at children's birthday parties was "telephone." In the game, a phrase or sentence is passed from one player to another, whispered from ear to ear. The person at the end of the chain says out loud the phrase she thought she heard. Normally it has changed substantially and makes for a good laugh. This is a game people from different cultures unintentionally play all the time, often with less humorous results.

We can identify four steps of basic directional communication. The communication between Person A and Person B can be represented as follows (see also Figure 6.1):

Person A   1. Message initiator formulates an idea.
            2. The message is transmitted, in verbal, nonverbal, or written form, through A's cultural filter.
Person B   3. The message is received, through B's cultural filter.
            4. The message is interpreted.

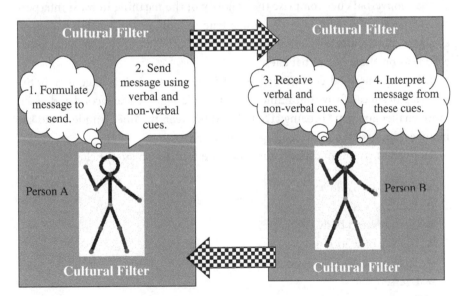

Figure 6.1 Basic one-directional communication through cultural filters.

Two points to note from our representation:

■ Messages are often distorted as they go through the cultural filter of each person. The filter refers to how a culture verbally and nonverbally packages a message. That packaging is typically significantly different from one culture to the next.

- Unintentional communication follows the same stages but without the first step of actually planning to send a message. We have all had the experience of a spouse or close friend saying "What's the matter? I can tell by the look on your face that something is wrong" or "I'm going as fast as I can," in response to your tapping foot, repeated glances at your watch, and clenched jaw. We were not intending to send a message, but our nonverbal actions are constantly sending some sort of message to other people. The chance is slim that people from other cultures will properly interpret this unintentional communication.

Nonverbal Communication Differences

Nonverbal communication refers to all information exchange except that involving the literal meaning of the words being used. Communication research tells us that nonverbal cues comprise the majority of the meaning in most interpersonal interactions. Although this holds true among North American English speakers, most cultures and languages of the world place, relatively, far more emphasis on these nonverbal cues.

Learning the word definitions and grammar of a new language is only the first step in successfully communicating in that language. The second and much more challenging part is being able to "read between the lines," understand the nuances, and use the nonverbal signals properly.

Nonverbal communication issues addressed in this chapter include:

- Space.
- Touch.
- Gestures and body language.
- Display of emotions.
- Tone of voice.
- Dress.
- Scent.

Space

While personal space may not be the "final frontier," it is an important factor in communication, from the first interview to the end of the probation period and beyond. *Proxemics*, the study of personal space, investigates the distance individuals maintain between one another and how this gap is significant. Personal space varies by one's emotional state, the type of activity, personality, and the relationship of the people. Only close personal friends or family members are typically allowed into our private space, while business associates are to remain at a culturally determined distance.

In multicultural situations, misunderstandings may arise during conversations because the size of this invisible private-space bubble varies from culture to culture. This can be especially tricky because normal distances between men and men, women and women, and men and women also vary by culture.

When a person with a smaller personal space moves in too close for the other person's comfort, what might be the outcome? The person with a larger personal-space need may feel, sometimes subconsciously:

- Panic, similar to the "flight or fight" reaction.
- Tense and defensive.
- Unable to follow the conversation.
- Annoyed because the former "does not have the right to come this close."
- That a sexual pass is being made.

The response may be to step back, cross arms over the chest, or laugh as a way either to reestablish the distance or to bring the person emotionally closer.

When a person with a larger personal space refuses to come close to someone expecting more physical intimacy, what might be the outcome? The person expecting to be physically closer may feel, sometimes subconsciously:

- "Snubbed"—perceiving the other as behaving in a standoffish manner and reading a put-down that is not intended.
- Too far apart to carry on a normal conversation.
- Distracted by other goings-on in the room or by trying to adjust the distance to his or her comfort zone.

José, my Venezuelan colleague, and I were working together on a project. We were in my office and referring to something on my computer. As I clicked away, José leaned over my shoulder, with both of us looking at the monitor. We chatted back and forth until I realized I could feel his breath on my neck. He was too close, much too close. I stood up and retreated some distance back so that I could carry on the conversation.

—North American office worker

Differences in the use of space can also be noticed in the following:

- How closely people stand to each other when waiting in a lineup at the coffee kiosk or the bank.
- How much distance people leave between their cars when lined up in traffic.
- How desks are arranged in an office, whether the space is open and the workstations close together or offices are more separate, with privacy and space.

The Japanese provide an interesting glimpse into the use of public and private space:

- Companies favor the open-office concept, where desks sit side by side and the manager's chair is slightly more elegant but very close by.
- The Tokyo subway system moves millions of people each day. Shinjuku Station, one of the busiest in the world, is a blur of fluid motion. Despite the multitudes making their way to their respective train platforms, rarely do strangers physically touch or bump. Physical contact only comes when the white-gloved attendants help the last few passengers get into a crowded car. The subway "pushers" make it socially okay for the riders to make physical contact in a situation where it is unavoidable.

North Americans maintain a physical space in conversation that is greater than in most parts of world, with the possible exception of northern Europeans. Most of the world's people, including those of Asia, Africa, Mediterranean Europe, eastern Europe, Latin America, and the Caribbean islands, tend to have a smaller personal-space comfort zone than North Americans. There are also differences in personal space among the ethnic groups of North America. Anglo North Americans tend to keep the larger space (Figure 6.2).

Here are some indications that you may be invading another person's personal space. The other person may:

- Take a step backwards.
- Raise his or her eyebrows.
- Lean backwards.
- Begin fidgeting.

- Speak to you while looking away rather than looking directly at you.
- Attempt to end the conversation.

Figure 6.2 Personal space.

Here are some indications that you may too distant from the other person. The other person may:

- Step toward you.
- Ask if there is a problem.
- Lose interest in or become distracted from the conversation.

Solution

How can you determine the size of someone's comfort zone? When people first shake hands, they stand at the distance that is most comfortable for them. The arm and hand is extended about halfway to where they expect the other person to be standing. Here is the guideline in North America: If one's arm were outstretched, one's thumb would reach the ear of the other person.

When working with someone who has a smaller personal-space zone and tends to move into yours:

- Try taking a step backwards to see if the person senses your discomfort.
- Try to accept the distance and carry on a normal conversation, in the name of stretching yourself and building rapport.
- Ask the person for the normal speaking distance between two people in their culture, as a lead-in to mentioning what is normal for you.
- If you are coaching this person as an employee, sit down privately with the person to explain the cultural norms in your organization and your region. Part of this conversation can include the local interpretation of sexual

harassment regarding the normal space between a man and woman in an office environment.

When working with someone who has a larger personal space and tends to stay distant from you:

- Try taking a step forward and see if the person is comfortable with this.
- Try to accept that this may be the normal distance for the other person and adjust your distance accordingly.
- Delicately mention the distractions you are experiencing over the large space between you.
- If you are coaching this person as an employee, sit down privately with the person to explain the distance norms in your culture.

Touch

It was the first time I ventured outside of North America. A group of coworkers and I traveled for miles on sand roads to reach a small village in central Senegal, West Africa. The village would be our home for the next six weeks. Huge baobab trees were about the only life forms to be seen en route. As we entered our village, which had no electricity or running water, a small crowd gathered around our bus. They stared at us as hard as we stared at them. I had never seen people with such black skin, beautiful smiles, or brightly colored clothes. As we disembarked, a huge fellow, he must have been 6 foot 4 with the physique of a wrestler, greeted me with a warm, gentle handshake. My hand disappeared inside of his. As I was about to retrieve my hand, I realized that he had no intention of letting it go. Still full of smiles, he began leading me away and showing me around the village. I felt so uncomfortable I could have passed out. But I realized that would be inappropriate. The fact that we did not have any language in common didn't stop him from enthusiastically explaining all about his small village. After five or 10 minutes of my sweating profusely into his hand, he wished me well, let me go, and went on his way.

—North American exchange program worker in Senegal

Physical touch is the most intimate form of communication. In most North American business settings, touch is disappearing, other than in handshake greetings. Women sometimes kiss on the cheek. Men sometimes slap backs or put a hand on the shoulder. To hold someone's hand for more than a few seconds is considered a very intimate gesture—especially man to man. Conversely, in rural Senegal it is a sign of friendship, acceptance, and welcome.

In North America, we say that the only part of a colleague's anatomy that one may safely touch is the upper arm, and that only briefly and lightly. Among colleagues who don't know each other well, not touching at all is the best advice, other than for the handshake. If a colleague shows the least discomfort with a light arm touch or actually remarks on it, then that too should be considered out of bounds. Again, a big concern around touching is the question of sexual harassment. The issue is a serious one in North America.

In Arab and North African countries, it is common to see men walking down the street hand in hand. Presidents George Bush Sr. and Jr. have been photographed hand in hand with Saudi King Saud. Latin American men will often walk or stand arm in arm. In North America, young women can often be seen walking arm in arm. These are not considered sexual gestures but, rather, signs of friendship.

You may find yourself in a situation where you extend your hand to shake with another person, but the other person does not engage your handshake. This may be most common between a North American man and a Muslim woman. The Muslim woman may feel it is inappropriate to shake a man's hand or to touch a man who is not a close relative.

I traveled to Iran to meet with some of our workers there. When I got out of the SUV at the work site, I saw a group of men I knew very well. We were pleased to see each other and gave brief hugs in greeting. There was one man in the group who was a local Iranian, and I didn't know him. I thought that, to be friendly and fair, I should give him a brief hug as well. It was a mistake. That man did not speak to me again during my entire visit.

—Female Canadian HR manager

Solution

When working with someone whose touch you feel is inappropriate in your workplace and/or for you personally:

- Explain that, in your culture, it is rare for people to touch.
- Explain that some people may misinterpret the intention.
- Explain clearly what is appropriate touch and what is inappropriate.
- Explain the meaning and seriousness of touch and sexual harassment in North America.

■ Ask the person to follow the guidelines you have laid out in his or her future behavior.

If you extend your hand to shake and the other person does not raise his or her hand:

■ Put down your hand and exchange a verbal greeting without making a big deal of it.
■ Later in the conversation, you may wish to ask if the person is offended by a handshake greeting and ask how best to greet in that person's culture.
■ Explain that in your culture, the handshake is the common greeting between men and women and that he or she will come across this repeatedly in interactions.

Gestures and Body Language

Gestures refer to the use of body movements to communicate.

> When Richard Nixon was Vice President of the United States, he made a state visit to Brazil. Relations between Brazil and the United States were somewhat strained, and Mr. Nixon, over the course of a few days' visit, tried to patch things up. Upon his departure, he climbed the steps of his aircraft, turned, and with a big smile gave the familiar "okay" sign (thumb and index finger curved together to form a circle). The next morning the photo of this gesture was splashed across the front pages of Brazilian newspapers. "This is what the United States thinks of us," was the message. While a positive gesture in United States, our "okay" sign has a highly offensive sexual connotation in Brazil!

Approaching a language barrier, we may feel that gestures are our best tool for getting our point across. Indeed, for early humans, before the evolution of language, all of our communication was through gestures and very basic sounds. Even today, it is estimated that over 70 percent of all communication is still of the nonverbal form. But gestures are not universal.

> I was new to driving in Mexico City and not at all sure about the local rules of the road. Traffic appeared to me to be in chaos, and a very fast-moving chaos at that. At one point, cars were merging into my lane. The driver in the car next to me lifted his arm, bent at the elbow, with the back of his hand facing upwards and toward me. There was a small back-and-forth movement in his hand. I could not tell from his expressionless face whether this was a good thing or a bad thing, but I

suspected the worst. I wondered what I had done wrong. Afterwards, I asked my Mexican friend the meaning of the gesture. To my surprise and relief, he explained that this was the Mexican gesture for "thank you." The next few times I received this gesture in traffic it still made me nervous. But, in time, I realized my friend's assessment was correct. It took longer for me to practice using it myself, for it felt very similar to an "up yours" gesture in Canada.

—Canadian consultant in Mexico City

Gestures that mean one thing in one place and something completely different in another place obviously will create challenges. It is not uncommon for Indians to wobble their heads side to side as they are listening. To them, this indicates that they are listening politely to what you are saying. We may misinterpret this gesture to mean that they are disagreeing with what we are saying. An Arab person might quickly move his head up and back, accompanied by a click of the tongue, to indicate "no." We may misinterpret this as a "yes" from the head movement but be confused by the tongue sound.

If you were to beckon someone into a room with a hand open, palm up, and fingers waggling, the newcomer to North America might not understand your meaning. The beckoning gesture in East Asia is palm down, with fingers waggling. If you use your index finger to point from the person to the seat you want him or her to take, it may cause offense. In East Asia, pointing is done with either the thumb or all fingers extended rather than just the index finger.

The handshake, while by no means universal, is the most common greeting gesture used in business today. But within the simple handshake, what is the correct amount of time to be holding hands and how much pressure should be applied? In North America, most are taught from a young age that a firm and brief handshake indicates a person of strong character. The converse belief is that a limp handshake shows no spine, "a dead fish," and a weak, untrustworthy character.

This attitude, however, does not extend to traditional Native American culture. A Native American friend once explained that among his people, they imagine holding the other person's heart in their hand while shaking. You can imagine how a crushing handshake would be received.

As well, some aboriginals prefer a one-pump handshake. A mainstream North American may be surprised when an aboriginal person withdraws his or her hand while the Anglo North American may feel they are still mid-handshake.

North Americans prefer a two- or three-pump handshake of moderate grip. There are also regional differences. And shakes between women and between a man and a woman are typically slightly less firm.

I was working with the Filipina technician and was fascinated by her culture. Sadly, her mother passed away and she returned to the Philippines for the funeral. When she came back I offered my condolences once again. Then I asked her about the funeral. "How was it?" "What kind of clothes do people wear to funerals in the Philippines?" etc. In response to my first question, she smiled. The more I asked, the more she smiled and eventually she started laughing. I realized I was probably being too forward, but I was bewildered by her response. Only afterwards did I find out that she was trying to tell me to drop the subject because she was intensely uncomfortable.

—North American office worker

Most people in the world recognize a smile to indicate amusement, pleasure, or approval. But depending on the circumstances and the culture, it can have other meanings as well. Some meanings of a smile, especially with strangers or new acquaintances, are described in Tables 6.1 and 6.2. Table 6.1 presents ges-

Table 6.1 Common Gestures in North America with Their Meanings in Other Countries

Gesture/body language	Meaning in North America	Meaning elsewhere
Thumbs up	Good job, good luck	"Up yours" (Australia, parts of Africa)
"Okay" sign (thumb and forefinger curled to make a circle)	Okay	Vulgar sexual connotation (South America) Zero (France) Money (Japan) Trouble (Egypt)
Index and middle finger pointing up, showing back of hand to other person	The number 2	"Up yours" (United Kingdom)
Smile to a stranger	Seen as friendly	Seldom seen; therefore, person may seem to be an idiot or a conartist (France) Embarrassment, discomfort (East Asia)

Table 6.2 Common Gestures in Other Countries and Their Meanings in North America

Gesture example	Meaning elsewhere	Meaning in North America
Head wobble side to side	Listening, paying attention (India)	No meaning
Move head up and back	No (Middle East, North Africa)	Yes or "so what" in a defensive or possibly aggressive way
Hand on hips	Overly aggressive (much of world)	No meaning, sometimes aggressive
Passing something to another person with the left hand	Offensive; the left hand is considered unclean (much of Asia and Africa)	No meaning
Gentle-grip handshake	Polite greeting (Gulf, Africa, SE Asia, Native American/First Nations)	Lacking character and integrity

tures we commonly use that may not be understood in the way we mean them. Table 6.2 presents gestures people from other cultures commonly use that carry a different meaning in North America (Figure 6.3).

Solution

Advice to the North American when interpreting the gestures of others:

- If you find a gesture offensive, you have likely misinterpreted it.
- When unclear, ask for the intended meaning.

Figure 6.3 Varying interpretations of hands-on-hips gesture.

Advice to the North American when making gestures:

- Don't assume that the meaning will be received the way you intended.
- If the person looks confused or offended by your gesture, then explain the intended meaning.

The diverse nature of gestures is well described by Robert Axtell in his book *Gestures: The Do's and Taboos of Gestures Around the World.*

Display of Emotions

People of all cultures have similar emotions, including happiness, sadness, anger, frustration, love, and fear. In the workplace, common emotions include contentment, enthusiasm, cheerfulness, optimism, and pride or, conversely, irritation, anxiety, frustration, and disappointment. How these emotions are expressed, especially in a business setting, varies significantly across cultures. In some cases, it takes an attentive observer to identify the emotion being expressed by another person. It may show in a subtle shift of body posture, a slight movement of the eyes, a shift in the eyebrows, or a change in the pitch of the voice. On the other hand, the behavior may be anything but subtle, with arms whirling like a cheerleader's, eyes bugging out, eyebrows lifting dramatically, or voice rising. While the physical behaviors are obvious, the meanings behind the expressions may not be.

Emotionally expressive communication may involve the following traits:

- Vocal variety—the voice rising and falling and changing in volume.
- Variety of facial expressions.
- Other body movements involving fingers, hands, arms, even legs.

I was walking down the hallway in an office in Sudan when I saw two acquaintances practically shouting at each other. Their arms were dancing and their faces alive with expression. They stood close enough that one's man spittle was practically reaching the other's face. I went up and asked, "What's the big argument?" hoping to diffuse the situation. The men paused and gave me a quizzical look that told me I had interpreted things all wrong. I meekly apologized for interrupting them and continued down the hallway.

—Canadian trainer in Sudan

In this case, the Canadian trainer didn't realize this was the men's normal way of talking. They weren't arguing, nor was there any ill feeling between them.

Figure 6.4 shows differing levels of expression by cultural region. People from the Far East tend to show minimal positive and negative emotions. At the other extreme, Italians tend to demonstrate greater emotion on both the negative and positive scales. A more emotional style produces open displays of feelings, such as laughing, crying, singing, shouting, fist-shaking, dancing, and cheering. Using the unemotional style, one tends to be passive, with little vocal variety.

One situation where these differences are readily visible are funerals: Compare the funerals of Yasser Arafat in Palestine with the funerals of Trudeau in Canada and of Reagan in the United States: The amount of emotion displayed by Palestinians during the funeral of Arafat (crying, wailing, shooting in the air) vastly exceeded the amount of emotion displayed by North Americans in similar circumstances.

The Italian movie *Life Is Beautiful* won two Academy Awards, one for best actor and one for best foreign movie. At the award ceremonies, when actor Roberto Benigni heard his name, he jumped up on his chair, then walked on the chairs of the people in front of him to get to the stage (he almost walked on the heads of the people in front of him) and then continued to jump up and down when he was onstage. He was clearly showing a large amount of positive emotion, far beyond the range of what is typically considered acceptable by North American standards.

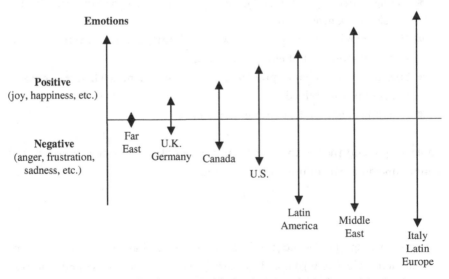

Figure 6.4 Strength of emotional behaviors in selected countries/regions.

People from cultures that value the free expression of emotions in business tend to view themselves as being transparent, open, honest, and trustworthy. They show respect for the other person by not holding back, not masking their true thoughts or feelings. Through a dramatic exchange, a stronger personal connection is made between the colleagues.

Less emotionally demonstrative cultures will try to limit their expression of emotion, especially in a business setting. By attempting to leave out the emotion, it is felt that communication can be less personal and more effective in working toward a common task.

Here are some workplace scenarios that represent a more emotional style:

- When a problem exists, employees clearly express dissatisfaction to help others know how strongly they feel.
- A major success at work might be followed up by "high fives" and hugs with colleagues.
- When showing a lot of emotion, happy or sad, at work, coworkers tend to become more trusted. Their candor is appreciated because it reflects sincerity.

Here are some workplace scenarios that represent a less emotional style:

- Saying something like "Good job everyone, now back to work" after having a major work group win.
- Having trouble trusting people "with such little control over themselves" that they show a lot of emotion at work.
- Speaking calmly about a problem and the consequences when an employee needs to be disciplined.
- Avoiding angry confrontations at all costs.

Table 6.3 presents the positive and negative views of an emotional approach and a more unemotional communication method.

Solution

Try not to judge people negatively based on their having a different communication style from yours. Be aware of your assumptions, and question them.

Table 6.3 Positive and Negative Views of Different Emotional Styles

	Positive view	Negative view
Emotional	■ Shows openness, honesty, sincerity, trust	■ Shows a lack of control ■ Immature, childish ■ Not leadership material
Unemotional	■ Clear, concise, and quick ■ Helps keep the focus on the task rather than on the people	■ Unreadable ■ Cold and distant ■ Noncommittal ■ Uncaring ■ "I'll surround myself with vending machines, computers, and robots if I can't deal with human emotion."

Here's how best to work with someone favoring a more expressive style:

■ Don't overreact or take an emotional outburst personally.
■ Be confident and comfortable with your own communication style.
■ Try to become a bit more expressive yourself.

Here's how best to work with someone favoring a less expressive style:

■ Don't assume the person has no emotions or feelings.
■ Look more closely for clues to the person's intended message.
■ Try to contain some of your expressiveness.

In coaching recent immigrant employees, you should describe the norms of expression in your company, your industry, and your region. Try to explain the normal range of expressiveness for various situations to help them understand what's going on and to express themselves appropriately.

Tone of Voice

The human voice is an instrument of incredible range. Some cultures take full advantage of that range in everyday communication. Other cultures seek to control the voice, limit its ups and downs, and instead rely on other verbal or nonverbal subtleties to get their meaning across. As you might guess, expressive peoples tend to use more vocal variety, while less expressive peoples tend to have more controlled speech.

Those from more expressive societies find it astounding that the two statements "You are doing a great job and you are promoted" and "You are doing a terrible job and you're fired" may be delivered with the same even speaking style. Yet this is considered the preferred "professional" style in North America. For people that favor the more monotone style, extensive variety in volume and pitch reminds them of an overdone farcical play or childish exuberance, something not to be taken seriously.

The Japanese minimize vocal variety in their business speech. Words in the Japanese language are pronounced without accents. Mandarin Chinese, on the other hand, is a tonal-based language and requires vocal variety in order to distinguish meanings between one word and another. The habits learned in one's first language are often transferred into the use of English.

In Japanese and Southeast Asian cultures, people are taught that to speak softly is to show respect. North Americans often interpret quiet speech as timid and lacking confidence. The differences are relative. Texans may appear loud and brash to Canadians, who may in turn appear loud and brash to Indonesians.

Solution

Here's some advice to employers:

- Explain to new employees how different tones of voice may be interpreted in your office setting.
- If your goal is to make the other person feel more comfortable, then you might mirror the other's tone of voice. For example, if the other person is speaking more softly than you, you might try to speak more softly as well. If the other person is trying to do the same, somewhere in the middle may be the comfort zone that works best for the two of you.

Dress

I was part of a Canadian delegation on an official visit to Peru. The delegation was led by an older woman who dressed quite conservatively—dark-colored suits, nothing feminine. Like many Québec women, I dressed more femininely, used brighter colors, makeup, and accessories (jewelry, scarf, etc.). When we met our

Peruvian counterparts, they thought I was the leader of the group and started paying me the corresponding respect. I had to redirect them to the actual delegation leader, who was not pleased.

—Female French Canadian engineer

Types and styles of clothing, material, and color vary by culture and climate. Employees in North American workplaces tend to dress in subdued colors. People from Africa, the Caribbean, and Latin America tend to prefer brighter colors.

Many countries have a traditional dress that is acceptable business attire, such as the sari for women in India and the gelaba, a long white shirt/dress worn by Arab men, cowboy boots worn with a business suit in Texas, and Bermuda shorts with knee-high socks and dress shoes in Bermuda (Table 6.4).

When George W. Bush entered the White House in 2001, he brought back the suit and tie as the standard dress code. This lead was followed by segments of corporate America. Despite this, it appears most workplaces in North America have been moving toward more informal business attire. Men have removed their ties for all but the most important business meetings in many parts of the continent and in many industries.

Table 6.4 Dress Considerations

Dress issue	Considerations
Formality	■ Suit, tie, collared shirt, dress shoes ■ Skirt, dress, pantsuit, jacket ■ Dress pants, open collar, casual shoes ■ Blue jeans, T-shirt, running shoes
Color	■ Bright, multicolored suits ■ Subdued tones
Design	■ Finely tailored ■ Revealing clothing ■ Ripped or shredded
Other	■ Body piercing ■ Visible tattoos
National dress	■ Indian sari ■ Arab gelaba gown

To say that an office is "business casual," is not enough information for the recent immigrant. The definition of business casual can vary considerably. In Silicon Valley in the summertime, business casual can mean shorts and T-shirt. It could mean blue jeans and a collar shirt. Or it may mean dress pants, a dress shirt, and a jacket.

People coming to North America from more formal cultures typically take very little time to adjust to the local attire. Many men are happy to abandon the tie and go casual, but not all. Some professional men coming from India, for example, are reluctant to show up at work in anything but a suit and tie. When given the option, they would just as soon keep wearing formal clothes.

In Latin America, a man is not taken seriously in a business meeting unless he's wearing a suit and tie. Clients and coworkers will feel that he is not showing them or their office suitable respect. Employees in a casual Californian IT company may wonder who you are trying to impress were you to arrive in a formal suit.

In 2005, Prime Minister Koizumi of Japan asked his country's office workers to dress more casually in the summertime. Tokyo summers are very hot, and the price of oil was high. If men didn't have to wear their neckties, it was reasoned, their air conditioners could be turned down a degree or two. The prime minister knew that the only way he could get office workers to change their dress habits was to lead by example from the top. He dressed more casually and instructed other government people and civil servants to do the same. An indication of how difficult that was for the Japanese surfaced when civil servants began sporting buttons saying "Excuse me for dressing casually." It is unlikely that workers in Silicon Valley would feel they have to, or want to, wear a button like that.

A Canadian national controversy erupted in 1989 about whether RCMP (Royal Canadian Mounted Police) officers should be allowed to wear turbans for religious reasons. The outcome was that the turban was made part of the official uniform of the RCMP. The blue turban corresponds to the forage cap for routine duties, and the brown turban is worn, like the Stetson hat, for ceremonial events.

Solution

What might a North American do when his or her employee is wearing clothes that he or she finds inappropriate for the situation?

- Typically, there is a range of appropriate clothing in any North American office. The human resources professional or coach of new employees should be able to articulate the accepted standards even if they are not written in policy. The meaning or purpose of the dress standards should be explained.

- Be aware that some of the factors influencing a change of dress are national customs, family pressure, and finances.

How could the immigrant approach the dress question?

- "When in Rome, do as the Romans do."
- If particular clothing is worn for religious or strong cultural reasons, take the issue up with the company.
- Recognize that clients and coworkers may make judgments based on a person's dress.
- Learn the acceptable range of personal choice in office clothing.
- Know that the clothing expectation may vary depending on the business circumstance—for example, whether one will be meeting with clients or not.

Scent

Our sense of smell is powerfully influential in how we evaluate a situation (Table 6.5). We know that certain food smells, such as blue cheese, make some people salivate and make others nauseous. The smell of a brewery elicits similar mixed responses.

Table 6.5 Odors from Body and Clothes

Situation	Issue
Natural odor from a clean body	People have different natural odors due to the food they eat and their unique physical makeup
Halitosis, or bad breath	Certain foods, such as garlic and onions, can leave a strong smell on the breath Dental hygene or health may also be an issue
The odor of an unwashed body	Bathing irregularly or not wearing an underarm deodorant
The odor of clothes	Wearing soiled clothes Wearing the same clothes that one has worn while preparing food
Perfumes or colognes	Some people have allergic reactions

Smells that come from the body can be seen as wonderful to some and disgusting to others. The use of perfumes and colognes can be similarly judged. In North America, scented products have been blamed for adversely affecting some people's health (because they cause headaches, dizziness, nausea, fatigue, and more). Many conferences and workplaces are now declared perfume free. By contrast, scented products and perfumes are regarded very positively in France and many Arab countries.

Odors considered offensive that come from a person will likely cause coworkers and clients to avoid the person. It is not good for teamwork, productivity, or social rapport within the office.

Solution

What the manager might do:

- First, determine in your own mind if this is an issue that needs to be addressed or not—if clients and/or coworkers are complaining, then it likely needs to be addressed.
- Bring the issue up with the employee to see if the individual is aware of the issue and if there is a known medical cause.
- With great sensitivity, explain hygiene expectations with the offending employee.
- If this is a candidate you would like to hire, you might mention the issue and ask whether the candidate would be able to come to work unscented.
- Set company guidelines for the use of perfumes and colognes.

I arrived at the California Institute of Technology at the beginning of September but learned that classes didn't begin until the end of the month. This was my first experience in California and I thought I would take advantage of these few weeks to discover and explore. A French friend of mine, who arrived at Caltech one year before I did, took me under his wing, and the two of us went out, partied, and generally tried to meet some girls. After three unsuccessful weeks of attempts to date, my friend sat me down for a serious little conversation. He started by asking me if I wanted to date women; since we had spent the last three few weeks trying to do this continually, I looked at him as if he was from Mars and told him, "Of course I want to date women." At this point, he went on and told me, "Then you need to have a shower every day. A shower once every other day just does not cut it here." I realized my friend was right—California is much warmer than Paris in September. I have had a shower every day since this little conversation and I am still thankful to this friend for telling me about this problem.

—French student at Caltech

Verbal Communication Differences

Now we come to the more familiar communications issues that surround verbal communication. There are many reasons why words that are spoken are not received as intended. We might think the other person didn't hear us, so we repeat ourselves, speaking more clearly and perhaps louder. If that doesn't work, we might think we are dealing with someone who is stupid or does not speak English very well. While either of these may be the correct assessment, it is more often something else. More commonly, the cause can be found in our use of the language. The following topics will be covered in this section:

- English as a second language.
- Different versions of English.
- Silence.
- Underlying language assumptions.
- Background noise.
- Speaking face to face versus side by side.
- Accents.
- Acronyms/abbreviations.
- Direct and indirect communication.
- Humor.
- Sports English.
- Connotations.
- Greetings.

English as a Second Language

Anyone who has attempted to learn a second language knows how tiring and frustrating the process can be. Until one becomes fluent, understanding and making oneself understood can be an exhausting process.

For the past few weeks, I have been using a voice recognition program on my computer. The program is sophisticated enough to learn from the mistakes that it makes. But I must first point out those mistakes. The software interprets some of my words wrong. I must go back and correct them. It's frustrating. Sometimes I think it would be easier to just type in the words myself rather than using the program. It reminds me of speaking with someone who does not speak English very well. Many of the issues are the same.

—Human resources consultant

As people learn a second language, they begin by translating word for word from their mother tongue into the new language. Words and phrases often precede actual sentences. There are pauses and lots of "ums," and they get stuck halfway through a sentence. For simplicity, they try to compress the translation, and sometimes important details are left out. Steps in the story being related are skipped, making the message less meaningful.

Canadians will often ask once or twice to try to get the meaning. If they have not understood by then, they will simply move on. U.S. Americans will typically keep asking until they get the meaning.

An all-too-common scenario is when a recent immigrant presents his or her idea at a meeting. Others in the room don't quite understand what is being said or what is meant. After at few polite questions, the conversation moves on to the next topic. Later in the meeting a native English speaker in the group presents the same idea that was presented earlier by the immigrant. His or hers is seen as a new and good idea. The latter speaker receives total credit for this fine idea. The former feels frustrated.

When speaking with nonnative English speakers, native English speakers may find that:

- The conversation is going slowly or there is such emphasis on each word that their concentration wanders from the topic.
- The use of incorrect words causes a loss of meaning and understanding.
- Technical words are misused, stumbled on, or not understood.
- When their counterpart pauses, they feel the urge to jump in with what they think is the word that the nonnative English speaker is looking for.
- They tend to avoid nonnative English speakers because more effort is required in communicating with them.

I was trying to make conversation with the daughter of our new employee from Venezuela. She was very proud of her beginning English skills and was trying very hard to communicate with me. I asked, "Do you miss any food from home? What is your favorite food?" She answered, "I like kitchen and rice best." When I didn't understand, she repeated, "Yes, I like kitchen and rice best." Still not understanding, I changed the topic and we moved on. However, on reflection later, I realized that she had just mixed up a few letters and was trying to say *chicken*.

—Canadian HR consultant

A common problem surrounds the correct use of technical words. North Americans tend to equate the ability to use technical words specific to their professions with the ability to understand the concepts these words represent. North Americans are often watching very closely for any indication that new immigrant employees do not "know their stuff." The first indication of this, thinks the local person, is when the newcomer either doesn't understand a common industry term or stumbles over the technical word when forming a sentence. Despite the judgment of the local person, this is usually a language issue. A new person may also be very reluctant to interrupt a conversation to ask about the meaning of a word, for fear of being labeled incompetent or stupid.

I had been working in North America for about two months as an accountant. I was working on an audit team for a large pharmaceutical company. In the documentation, there was reference to gift certificates. I am fluent in English, but I'd never heard of a "gift certificate" before, because they did not exist in Romania when I left. I asked the project manager what it meant. He looked at me as though it was the stupidest question he had ever heard. It took him a few moments to actually reply to my request.

—Romanian accountant in North America

A nonnative English speaker might notice that:

- Constantly using a language other than one's own native language is a very tiring process.
- Native English speakers have little concept of what you are going through or how to make it easier for you.
- Native English speakers prefer communicating with another native English speaker rather than the nonnative English speaker.

Solution

Tips for native English speakers:

- Simplify your message by using less complex sentence structure and vocabulary.
- Try to slow down your delivery, and articulate each word more clearly. Avoid contractions (*gonna, wanna,* etc.) that are quite difficult for non-native English speakers to catch. In writing, avoid nonstandard abbreviations, such "U R" for "you are" and "I C" for "I see."
- Don't shout to be understood.
- When speaking, watch for verbal and nonverbal clues (like facial expressions and body language) that the message was not received as you intended. If concerned about how it was received, rephrase it or check the person's understanding.
- Try to differentiate between an employee's ability to do something and his or her ability to communicate that he or she can do something.
- If the person does not know our acronyms or our technical words, do not assume the person is uneducated or inexperienced. He or she may completely understand the technical issues of a job but be unable to select the correct technical word in the English language.
- Avoid "isn't it?" or "aren't you?" type of questions, for example, "You are coming, aren't you?" Because this way of formulating questions does not exist in many other languages, it can be confusing for nonnative English speakers. To the question "You are coming, aren't you?" they may answer "Yes (I am coming)" or "No (I am coming)," depending on how they interpret the question.
- Ask whether or not they want help finding words that might convey their meaning.
- Provide written agendas and documentation of content prior to meetings whenever possible. The culturally different employee can then preview material and vocabulary.
- Review agenda items and documents prior to a meeting.
- Use visual aids in meetings whenever possible—charts, PowerPoint, etc.
- If you do not understand a particular word, you can ask the person to spell it, write it down, use a synonym, or say this word in his or her native language and have someone else translate. When this option is unavailable, have a bilingual dictionary at hand.

- Communicate important messages through several different media to ensure that they are fully received. Make sure you send consistent messages.
- Try to involve the nonnative speaker in the conversation by asking explicitly for the individual's input, particularly during brainstorming sessions and when the person has had time to preview and prepare for the meeting.
- If you get a voicemail message from a nonnative English speaker that you do not understand, if possible ask another nonnative English speaker from the same linguistic background to listen to it and "translate" for you. This person has a better chance of figuring out what the message means because he or she is familiar with the typical mistakes that people from that linguistic background make when speaking English.
- In continuous meetings, provide some rest time so that nonnative English speakers can take a break from the concentration required to follow the conversation.
- Avoid scheduling the presentations of nonnative English speakers at the end of the day, when fatigue has decreased their English-speaking and -comprehension skills.
- Consider providing ESL courses for the nonnative English speakers who are members of your staff or team. Courses designed to help participants modify their accents can be particularly beneficial, as can those that focus on specific industry terminology or technical English.
- Offer to proofread documents or presentations.
- When you feel strong emotion about something said or done by someone who comes from a culturally different background than you do, clarify the person's meanings and intentions before you express your emotions.
- If you cannot think of any positive interpretation of someone else's actions or words, chances are you are missing something. Clarify with the person or with someone who has experience in dealing with similar cultural groups.
- Be patient and try to follow newcomer's ideas and logic. They may be different from your own.

Tips for nonnative English speakers:

- If you do not mind people suggesting words or phrases as you are talking so that you can communicate more quickly, say so.

- Try to participate, even if you feel uncomfortable, particularly during brainstorming sessions.
- If your organization offers ESL courses, take them, even if your English is already functional. Courses designed to help you modify your accent to make it more understandable by native English speakers can be particularly beneficial. English speakers will see this as showing initiative in trying to participate fully in the work world.
- Keep a dictionary handy, and ensure that the words you use mean what you think they mean. Pay particular attention to the connotations (positive or negative) that words may have.
- Ask for, and get, help with your documents and presentations from a native English speaker. This approach may also be used in the case of sensitive e-mail messages or phone calls—running your approach or message by a native English speaker is likely to help remove some sources of potential misunderstandings.
- Before calling someone, think of what you want to say and look up the words you are likely to need. If you are leaving a voicemail message, compose this message on paper, and then read it aloud to the answering machine. This considerably decreases the chance of misunderstandings.
- Make sure you know, and use appropriately, the technical words that people use in your field. Find a native English speaker who will take the time to discuss this with you; use sketches, diagrams, and pictures to ensure that you understand all these technical terms. Use them repeatedly until they become second nature. Consider taking a technical English course or seeing if the company will assist in paying for a language coach for an initial period.
- Try to remain cool and composed, even when you have made a mistake that results in embarrassment for you or when you feel embarrassed by others (in most cases, they do not mean to embarrass you).

Different Versions of English

George Bernard Shaw once said that the United States and the United Kingdom are "two countries divided by a common language." Whether this is so or not, different versions of English can create some humorous and not-so-humorous encounters (Table 6.6).

Having everyone in the room speaking English is no indication that all the words have the same meaning. American English and British English have different meanings for at least several hundred words. Canadian English tends to be a confusing mixture of British English and American English. India and Australia have many words that are unique to their countries. Even within the United States and Canada, there are words and terms unique to specific regions of these countries.

Tables 6.7 and 6.8 present some examples from, respectively, Australian English and Indian English.

I had been working in the North American office for a few weeks and was feeling pretty good about my adaptation. I was getting along well with my colleagues and there were very few misunderstandings. One day a colleague had volunteered to share with me some data from his computer. In the afternoon, I approached him and asked, "Do you have a stiffy for me?" He asked me to repeat myself, which I did. He just gaped at me. Then he began to laugh. Then he began to relate what I

Table 6.6   Same Word, Different Meanings

Word or term	Britain	United States
mean	Not generous, tight fisted	Angry, bad humored
first floor	One floor above entrance level	Entrance floor
rubber	Pencil eraser	Condom
boot	Car trunk	Footwear
bonnet	Car hood	Headwear
biro	Ballpoint pen	No meaning
flyover	Overpass	No meaning
cash point	Automated teller machine	No meaning
table an issue	Delaying the discussion	Put the issue up for discussion
to strike out	To go after an opportunity	To fail
to luck out	To have no success	To succeed by amazingly good luck
to knock you up	To call on someone	To make pregnant
a joint	A leg of meat, usually lamb	Marijuana rolled into a cigarette

Table 6.7 Australian English Examples

Term	Meaning
bonzer	great
digger	soldier
feel crook	to feel unwell
Sheila	woman
tall poppies	successful people
root	have sex

Table 6.8 Indian English Examples

Term	Meaning in North America
open ("open the lights")	turn on/switch on
close ("close the lights")	turn off/switch off
softer (make fan softer)	slower (reduce fan speed)
pain (a noun; "Does it pain?")	hurt ("Does it hurt?")
rascal (dangerous offender, convict)	mischievous

said to other colleagues in the office. It was only later that they shared with me that the term *stiffy* was an informal reference to an aroused male penis, not the 3½-inch rigid computer diskette I meant.

—South African female accountant working in North America

Different uses of English words across cultures can be humorous, confusing, offensive, or all three.

Examples of differences in English language usage between Canada and the United States include the following.

- References to high school or college years as freshman, sophomore, junior, and senior are usually not used or understood outside of the United States, particularly not in Canada.
- A *toque* refers to a knit winter hat that covers the head and ears in Canada, whereas it might be called a *ski hat* in the United States.

- A bathroom, or public lavatory, in the United States is called a *washroom* in Canada.
- A *pop* in Canada is a *soda* in the United States.

Solution

How can a North American best deal with the issue of differing English versions?

- Recognize that immigrants may use different versions of English that are the norm in other parts of the world.
- Be patient when helping them use the local terms.
- Be aware that people from England especially, but also other English-speaking countries, may take offense if you suggest that their version of English is weird or wrong.

How can a recent immigrant best deal with the issue of differing English versions?

- Recognize that North Americans may use a different version of English than what you are used to.
- Begin learning the new terms and asking for meaning when hearing something different that you don't understand.

Silence

In the early 1980s, our company was in negotiations with a Japanese automobile parts supplier over a small, but critical, engine part. I put forward a price that our company would be willing to pay, $20 per unit. The Japanese team sat silently with serious faces. It didn't feel right. I felt we had to increase our offer in order to get the deal. I suggested a price of $21. Again the only Japanese response was a stony silence. I pictured myself returning to headquarters in the United States and trying to explain that I failed to secure this vital piece of equipment. I took a deep breath and gave my final price, $22 per unit. After a few more minutes of excruciating silence, the Japanese nodded and said that price would be fine.

I learned afterwards that the Japanese negotiators were pleasantly surprised but very confused by the one-way negotiation. Apparently, they were showing their respect to me by taking several moments to consider my words and proposal before giving their response. I had totally misinterpreted this and thought the Japanese were disapproving of my price proposals.

—American negotiator in Japan

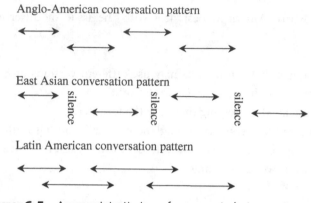

Figure 6.5 Appropriate timing of comments between two people in conversation.

The use of silence or pauses in conversation can mean very different things in different cultures, as Figure 6.5 and Table 6.9 show. When you are having a conversation with another person and the other person is speaking, which of the following is the appropriate time for you to begin speaking?

a. Before the other person is finished speaking.
b. At the moment the other person finishes.
c. Several moments after the other person finishes.

Many people say it depends on who you are talking with and on the nature of the conversation. Cultural background also plays a significant role.

Figure 6.5 presents graphically these differences across cultures. Typically Anglo-Americans will not overlap or leave breaks between speakers but neatly pick up where the other left off. This may be called the "jazz band" style of communication. One player does his or her solo and is immediately followed by another musician. People demonstrate respect for the speaker by waiting for him or her to finish. At that point another speaker can take the floor.

Table 6.9 Interpretation of Different Timing Patterns in Communication

Cultural group	Speech pattern	Positive view	Negative view
Anglo-American	One speaker begins the moment another speaker stops	Each person is able to speak uninterrupted, and no time is wasted	■ No time is given to ponder words of speaker (Far Eastern) ■ Shows a lack of interest and passion in the conversation (Latin American)
Far Eastern	After each speaker there is a momentary pause	Each person takes time to consider the words of the speaker	■ People are stuck for words to say or are disapproving (Anglo-American) ■ Shows a lack of interest and passion in the conversation (Latin American)
Latin American	Speakers overlap each other in conversation	Speakers are showing interest and passion in the conversation	■ Speakers are showing a lack of control and a lack of respect for the speaker (Far Eastern and Anglo-American)

People from the Far East are more likely to pause briefly between speakers. As well as showing respect, the silence may be used to process information and to think about what they will say next. Another possibility is that silence may indicate disapproval.

Latin American and Mediterranean cultures will often overlap each other. Latin conversations may be compared to symphonies, where multiple people play at the same time. One begins before another is finished. One may finish the sentence of another to indicate that that person is intently following the conversation. In some cases, Latin Americans will speak to one person with their hands while they are responding verbally to someone else's question.

The highest form of listening in Latin cultures is reflexive speaking. Partway through a sentence, the other person will speak with the same words at the same tone and at the same pace, thereby demonstrating he or she was listening carefully. This requires successfully anticipating what the speaker is going to say. However, this type of interaction is normally considered rude by North Americans.

As with all cultural generalizations, these patterns do not apply in all situations. For example, when interacting with Latin Americans you don't know very well in a business situation, you will rarely be interrupted. The interruptions are more likely to come after you have developed a closer personal relationship.

Periods of silence in a business conversation are probably least likely to occur in North America. Perhaps this can be attributed to North Americans' seemingly constant need for action and stimulation as well as a time consciousness. The experience of sitting quietly and comfortably with another person or even with oneself is a rarity. Time that is not actively filled by work, play, or some other clear purpose is considered wasted time. Conversely, most traditional cultures of the world continue to appreciate quiet time. Regions where the overlapping speech pattern is common among friends, such as Arab countries, there is also comfort with periods of silence.

Solution

The solutions or advice given in Table 6.10 are generalizations based on the majority of the population. There are people in the Far East who will speak over the top of another person's sentence. Also, there are people in Latin America who will pause before making comment. Individuals exist in every culture. Once again, more successful communication often comes by imitating the style of the other person (to a degree).

Underlying Language Assumptions

The key purpose of language communication in North America is to get one's point across. Communication tends to be utilitarian, concise, and to the point. People who can get a complex point across using simple language are highly valued. Conversely, people who use long or obscure words, complex grammar, and extended sentences are accused of being too academic or "full of themselves." Speakers using literary techniques and flowery language are said to be "out of touch with business." Those who use more indirect communication patterns are accused of beating around the bush, wasting time, and risking clarity. Most business people in North America subscribe to the "K.I.S.S." (keep it simple stupid) philosophy of communication. Using correct grammar is not as important as clarity and brevity.

Table 6.10 Advice to Help People Work with People Who Have a Different Sense of Conversational Timing

Cultural group	Talking with	Advice
Anglo-American	Far Eastern	■ Give others time to complete sentences ■ Don't rush to fill silences ■ Ask for ideas if they have not been offered and wait patiently for the answer ■ Communicate in a more controlled and even manner
	Latin American	■ Don't be put off by interruptions ■ Show a bit more emotion in your conversational style
Far Eastern	Latin American	■ Don't be put off by interruptions ■ Show a bit more emotion in your conversational style and excitement about the topic
	Anglo-American	■ Don't be put off by how quickly they jump into the silences in the conversation ■ Show a bit more emotion in your conversational style
Latin American	Anglo-American	■ Give others time to complete sentences ■ Communicate in a more controlled and even manner
	Far Eastern	■ Give others time to complete sentences ■ Don't rush to fill silences ■ Ask for ideas if they have not been offered and wait for the answer ■ Communicate in a more controlled and even manner

In most of the rest of the world, including Europe, the Middle East, and Latin America, how you speak the language tells a great deal about your education, your class, and where you came from. The French will keep track of the number of words you use with three syllables or more, to help gauge your intelligence and education. Being referred to as a complicated person can be a compliment in France and yet be derogatory in North America.

> I was teaching five-year-olds at an international school in Malta. The kids were from a dozen different countries. I hadn't realized how much I missed real English until a new boy from England joined our class. Instead of hearing the usual "Please pass the water," I heard from this boy's mouth "Would you be so kind as to pass the water, please?" I nearly fell off my chair. It sounded so civilized and right.
>
> —English school teacher in Malta

In the Arabic language, businesspeople who speak like poets are respected. Clever and subtle phrases are seen as the products of a cultured person. The Muslim holy book, the Koran, is written in a poetic structure. It is often quoted in business.

Recent immigrants will often assume that success in the new land will come in the same way it did at home. They will try to demonstrate their fine upbringing in education by using, or trying to use, more complex words and linguistic structures. Because English is probably their second language, this may not be well received in North America. They're putting emphasis on something that does not matter in North America or, worse, is judged negatively.

Solution

In working with recent immigrants:

- Beware that they may be trying to impress you with their linguistic abilities, and don't judge too quickly.
- Be prepared to explain the norms around English usage, and the K.I.S.S. concept and how it is highly valued.

Background Noise

Business conversations increasingly take place in airplanes, restaurants, and other public places. Office environments can be loud, with open office floor plans becoming standard. Carrying on a conversation with background noise is challenging at the best of times. When conversation partners don't share a common first language or common accent, the risk of miscommunication increases. People speaking English as a second language will be at a distinct disadvantage. The more noise, the greater the disadvantage.

Sources of background noise might include:

- Being in an airplane, car, train, bus.
- Being in a coffee shop or restaurant.
- Being in a louder work site, such as a construction zone or manufacturing facility.
- Being in an open office with people talking, phones ringing, and printers functioning.
- Background music or a radio playing.
- Cleaners vacuuming.
- Nasty weather outside.

Figure 6.6 graphically shows how comprehension decreases dramatically with increased background noise.

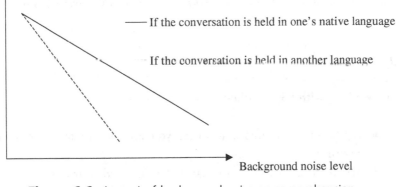

Figure 6.6 Impact of background noise on comprehension.

Solution

What might you do when you want to have a conversation with someone whose first language is not English and there is a lot of background noise?

- See if there is another place you can go where it is quieter, e.g., a meeting room with a closed door.
- Turn off your radio.
- Reschedule the meeting until the area is quieter.
- Ask other people in the area to keep their voices down.
- Get closer together and ensure you are face to face so that following the lips and facial gestures can aid in communication.
- Use visual aids to help reinforce meaning, e.g., charts, documents you look at together, maps.

Speaking Face to Face Versus Side by Side

Communication is typically at its best when two people are face to face and close to each other. Reading the other person's lips is a complement to the words being heard. Seeing facial expressions provides more clues to the speaker's meaning. Having a direct line from the speaker's mouth to both of the listeners' ears gives the best audio reception. These conditions do not apply when conversation partners are side by side. Comprehension will typically suffer.

Some professionals are more likely to find themselves working side by side rather than face to face. For example, if professionals are working at a counter, as pharmacists often do, they may find communication inhibited by their physical positions.

Communication is potentially further degraded as the participants use remote devices such as telephone, fax, and e-mail.

Solution

When working with ESL candidates and employees:

- Try to meet in situations where you are face to face and in close proximity.
- Articulate so that they can hear better and read your lips.

Accents

On more than one occasion when I was introduced to a U.S. American, I heard the American refer to me with what I thought was the name *Dan*. I corrected Americans, saying my name is *Don*, only to have them, perplexed, say that is what they said, *Dan*. When I ask them to spell it, D-O-N, I realized that we were talking about the same word.

—Canadian commenting on American pronunciation

My first language is English, so when I came to North America I did not imagine that there would be a problem with communication. In the first few days especially, I had trouble understanding what others were trying to say. Others seemed to have even more difficulty understanding what I was trying to say. After a few weeks, there was no problem. I grew accustomed to how people were speaking, and I learned how to mimic more closely the accents of the people around me.

—Irish accountant in North America

After university, in 1982, my girlfriend and I bought one-way tickets for Tokyo to look for work. The only jobs we were offered were English-teaching positions. We were told that our accents were just what they were looking for, a typical U.S. midwestern, TV announcer accent.

—Traveler from Canada

My family and I stopped at the McDonald's drive-through menu board and ordering station in Calgary. I began speaking into the microphone to place my order. After each item, the voice came back through the speaker but I couldn't understand what she was saying. Fortunately, the items also showed up visually on the screen in front of me. I assumed the problem was with the low-quality microphone/speaker equipment. When I drove up to the window to receive the order and pay for it, it was obvious that the woman spoke with a French accent. In person, I could understand her fine. But over the speaker system, it was very difficult indeed.

—Fast-food customer in Calgary

We must be cautious about our assumptions when we hear people using English in a way that is foreign to us. It doesn't mean they don't speak English well or necessarily that English is not the mother tongue. Indians from the subcontinent can be offended by asking them how they learned to speak English, when English may be their first language and likely their command of its grammar far exceeds that of most North Americans.

The George Bernard Shaw play *Pygmalion*, which was later made into the stage musical and movie *My Fair Lady*, featured the numerous types of English accents in 19th century England. One's accent supposedly reflected one's social status and could be traced to specific locations. Within the English-speaking parts of North America alone, there are many different accents, varying from north to south and east to west.

Accents tend to be more of a problem when people are encountering each other for the first time. For our purposes, this would represent the interview period and as a new employee. After people have worked together for time, accents have a less detrimental effect on communication.

Solution

When you have trouble understanding someone's accent, you might:

- Try to maximize face-to-face conversations, at least initially.
- Try to figure out the meaning from the rest of the sentence or the context.
- Ask the other person to repeat him- or herself.
- Ask the meaning of the particular word or phrase you do not understand.
- Ask the person to restate the message in a different way.
- Get the person to write it down.
- Ask someone else with the same accent who you know better to explain things to you.
- Use written references and visuals whenever possible, as in a good reference.
- As an employer, consider providing an accent-reduction class.

When another person has trouble understanding your accent, you might:

- Try to maximize face-to-face conversations, at least initially.
- Restate in a different way the message or the particular words not understood.
- Write it down.
- Ask someone else with the same accent who you know better to explain things.
- In face-to-face meetings, face the person to whom you speak so that he or she can read your lips at the same time as he or she hears your words.
- Consider taking an accent-reduction class—it can be very helpful.

Acronyms/Abbreviations

AASLCAPNNA stands for "Acronyms are a source of a lot of confusion among people new to North America." Even terms ubiquitous in this region, such as IRS (Internal Revenue Service), ASAP (as soon as possible), and RSVP (répondez s'il vous plaît, or please reply), may not be understood by many people new to the country. Unique lists of acronyms can be specific to a company, industry, business in general, government, education, health care, and so on.

Sometimes acronyms leave people bewildered. But worse are the situations where the acronym does mean something to the listener, but something completely different from what the speaker intended. STD is a common acronym in North America for "sexually transmitted disease." In India, STD more commonly stands for "short trunk dialing," which refers to long-distance calling.

The Canadian International Development Agency, CIDA, is pronounced the same way as the word for AIDS (acquired immune deficiency syndrome) in Spanish. The Canadians found they were not very well received in small Latin American communities when they introduced themselves as being with CIDA.

> I was facilitating a cultural orientation program for a Venezuelan family that had recently relocated to North America. I was describing some of the economic issues of the continent. I explained that the NAFTA treaty was signed by the United States, Canada, and Mexico in 1994 and that there continues to be some debate in each country about the merits of the agreement. During the next coffee break, the Venezuelan fellow politely asked me what NAFTA stood for. In my description of NAFTA, I had failed to give the exact words that are represented in the acronym NAFTA.
>
> —Cross-cultural trainer

Multinational organizations and the military are often the worst offenders when it comes to using acronyms and abbreviations. In the accounting world, the U.S. Sarbanes–Oxley Act of 2002 meant to bring greater financial accountability and transparency to companies, is often referred to as SOX, but in the UK as Sarbox. Unless you are on the inside, both terms are likely to confuse.

Solution

How can a North American best deal with the acronym issue?

- Try to avoid using acronyms with new people, at least initially.
- Explain the meaning of the acronyms as you use them to the newcomer acquiring new terms.
- Create a list of commonly used acronyms in your organization. Post these lists on the walls in strategic places or on the intranet of your organization.
- Remind newcomers that they should ask if they hear or see an acronym that they do not understand.

How can a recent immigrant best deal with the acronym issue?

- Ask for clarification if an acronym is used that is not understood.
- Ask for a list of commonly used acronyms in the organization, and keep it handy for reference.

Direct Versus Indirect Communication (Table 6.11)

Direct communication refers to when a message is put across as clearly and concisely as possible. If additional information is required to put a point across, the background information usually follows the central point. The message

Table 6.11 Differences Between Direct and Indirect Communication

Direct communication	Indirect communication
First focuses on task accomplishment	First focuses on relationship
Message is in a few clear words	Message is in the context of the word usage, vocal variety, nonverbal clues, relationships, and more words
Explicit (clear, obvious) meaning	Implicit (implied, hidden) meaning
Communication tends to be impersonal	Communication tends to be personal
"To the point," open	"Read between the lines," subtle language
Deal with conflict directly, head on	Deal with conflict indirectly, "save face"
Go face to face with person to resolve conflict	Use trusted third party to assist

sender is more concerned with getting the precise meaning across than with the possibility of hurting the other person's feelings. Communication is viewed primarily as an exchange of information, facts, and opinions. It is thought to be impersonal and is focused on accomplishing the task at hand. Direct communicators don't usually need to have a previous relationship or a warm relationship in order to function effectively with another person.

In a conflict situation, people who favor direct communication tend to be to the point, open, and face to face with their issues. The communication is often impersonal, with the focus being on the issue rather than on the personalities. People on the outside of the conflict are expected to stay outside, except in exceptional circumstances. Requiring the help of a third party means the two in the conflict have failed and now they are wasting the time of another person.

People with an indirect communication style will typically provide general background information first and then work their way toward the heart of the matter. This is especially true if the subject is a sensitive one. Extra words are used to help soften the message. The true point of the conversation may not explicitly be mentioned. This allows the receiver of the message to save face. For the meaning to be properly interpreted, the communicating parties need to have a common context or culture. Otherwise, the message may be misunderstood.

Direct communication is sometimes graphically represented by placing a dot in the middle of the page and drawing a line that spirals away from the center in a circular fashion. This shows that the conversation point is made initially and then additional background information is added as necessary.

Indirect communication may be graphically represented by starting at a point near the edge of the page and drawing a circular spiral that winds inward toward the center. This represents beginning the conversation with general background information and making one's way toward the center, or to the main point.

An indirect technique might be to invite a trusted third party to act as a neutral go-between. This person helps the two people in this agreement or conflict to see each other's point of view and find common ground.

An example of indirect communication would be the way the word *yes* in many Asian countries can mean "yes," "maybe," "I understand," or "not likely." The true meaning can only be known through the context of the communication. This "reading between the lines" might involve the speaker's stance, arm position, facial movements, vocal variety, the use of metaphor, and so on.

I like living in Canada. My wife and I raised our kids here. It's home now. But one thing that has always bothered me is that Canadians will not tell you what they think. I don't know if they are trying to be nice, trying to be politically correct, or trying to avoid conflict, but they have a hard time dealing with open and honest comments. Each year during annual performance review at my company, managers tell me that I'm too blunt and that I need to be more diplomatic in the way I speak. Well, I am not a diplomat. I am an engineer and this is who I am. I'm not going to start diluting my message just because of some oversensitive Canadians. I have come to accept that I may not get the promotions I deserve because of my communication style.

—Dutch engineer at a Canadian company

Clearly, this Dutch engineer has a more direct approach to communication than the average Canadian, and his feedback style does not sit well with Canadians (see Chapter 7 for more on cross-cultural feedback).

Here are some situations that would represent a more direct approach:

- When there is a conflict, speaking with the person first to try to resolve the issue.
- When it appears that the work group is going to miss an important deadline, speaking to one's boss as soon as possible with a clear message.
- When having to deliver a message about poor performance to an employee, trying to avoid confusion by stating concerns clearly and concisely.

Here are some situations that would represent a more indirect approach:

- Going to the boss or another colleague first when having a problem with a colleague.
- In speaking with the boss, trying to put into context the challenges one's hardworking group is facing when experiencing some sort of delay. And then mentioning the delay only if absolutely necessary.
- Delivering messages about poor performance delicately so as not to embarrass or demoralize the employee.
- Using a third party to deliver a negative message.

I had a friend in Indonesia who explained the indirect nature of communication in that country with the following story. A young man met a girl with whom he fell hopelessly in love. The girl came to love him as well. He realized that the chances of getting permission to marry the girl were slim because he was from a poor family and she was from a wealthy one. He pestered his mother until she conceded that she would go to meet with his girlfriend's mother to see if a marriage could be considered. The mother of the love-struck boy made an appointment to go and meet the other mother. She was welcomed graciously to the home and offered tea. The tea came accompanied with a banana. After a nice social visit, the woman returned to her son. Nothing about the marriage request was discussed, but the boy's mother knew that they had been rejected. She told her son that the answer was no.

Seeing my bewilderment, my Indonesian friend explained that in this region of the country, serving a banana with tea was not normal and represented two things that did not belong together. The girl's mother knew why the other mother had come to see her and provided the answer in this indirect way, to save face.

—North American businessperson in Indonesia

Most North Americans reading this story are simply amazed. In our cultures it is difficult to fathom this type of indirect communication. The benefit to understanding this style in recruitment is that we may encounter people who are far more indirect in their communication than we are. They may not get the point the way we would like them to. Conversely, people from cultures such as Germany and the Netherlands may make comments that we simply find too blunt, bordering on rude.

Here are the impressions direct communicators have of indirect communicators (Table 6.12):

- They beat around the bush and don't get the point.
- "I sometimes don't even know the point they are trying to make."
- "I don't know when "yes" means "yes" or "no" means "no.""
- There seems to be more going on than I can figure.
- They can't keep focused on the business at hand.

Here is the impression indirect communicators may have of direct communicators:

- They are blunt, rude, and unsophisticated.
- They think everything can be simplified to the point of absurdity.
- They don't seem to care about people's feelings, just the business.
- They make strong comments and judgments on topics that are not necessary.

Table 6.12 Positive and Negative Judgments of Direct and Indirect Communication

	Positive view	Negative view
Direct communication	The message is perfectly clear	The message is unnecessarily blunt and offensive: "They don't care about anyone or anything but their own ideas."
Indirect communication	People's feelings are protected; it is a more sophisticated way of communicating	People are too easily confused or deluded by the lack of clarity: "What are you trying to say?"

The national tendencies of selected countries/regions along the continuum from direct to indirect are presented in Figure 6.7.

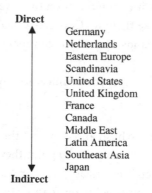

Direct

Germany
Netherlands
Eastern Europe
Scandinavia
United States
United Kingdom
France
Canada
Middle East
Latin America
Southeast Asia
Japan

Indirect

Figure 6.7 Direct and indirect communication preferences, by country.

Solution

Here is how best to manage people who favor a direct communication style:

- If they are offending clients or coworkers by their bluntness, you can help them see how they are being perceived and suggest a more subtle style for certain situations.
- Encourage them to pick up on the subtleties of communication.

Here's how best to manage people who favor an indirect communication style:

- Mirror back the more indirect style if time permits. If meaning is unclear, then be more direct.
- Try to have them give more context or background to their communication, if this is required in your office environment.
- Explain that in the North American business environment, a direct style is preferred and describe the behaviors associated with it.
- Practice and role-play typical direct communication.

Humor

Sharing a laugh is probably the best way to build rapport with another person. But the key element is "sharing" the laugh versus laughing over what might be funny to one and offensive to the other. A good joke brings people together, but a bad one pulls them apart. It is very difficult to undo the damage of one bad joke. Telling five good jokes won't make up for one bad one. In some cases, one cannot recover from a bad joke.

For example, much French and Italian humor includes sexual innuendo, which could very well result in a sexual harassment case in North America. Similarly, the cartoons published by a Danish newspaper in late 2005, which depicted the prophet Muhammad with a turban in the form of a time bomb, may have been meant as a joke, but the reactions they generated within the Muslim world were very negative (Danish products were boycotted throughout the Muslim world, riots ensued, and many people were killed). There was nothing this newspaper could have said or done after the fact that could have undone the damage done by the publication of those cartoons.

The challenge in using humor across cultures is that humor typically represents the most complex combination of verbal nuance and nonverbal action of any language or cultural group. Topics are often selected from the culture's taboo list—sex, politics, religion. This makes for dangerous ground.

Sarcasm, which mocks others, can be seen as insensitive and hurtful. Irony, which plays on opposite meanings, may leave the newcomer wondering if you literally meant what you just said. Puns, which are based on the fact that one word has several different meanings, do not translate into other languages since each meaning is translated by a different word.

Here we differentiate between telling a joke to try to make the other person laugh and sharing a smile or laugh over something unexpected. When the other person makes a faux pas, it may be best to ignore it. But if the other person laughs at him- or herself, that is our introduction to smile as well and perhaps to support the other person by retelling a similar faux pas we have made. By revealing our mutual humanness, we become closer.

An English teacher in Japan reports his experience of failed humor through his attempt to tell jokes.

> I was working with a group of engineers in a Japanese automobile factory. We had been working together long enough that we felt comfortable with each other and occasionally joked around. One engineer complained that the company sales in North America were slow. I joked that perhaps they should use a clown to help market their products, like the popular hamburger franchise does. They appeared confused by my comments. I made a couple of other silly suggestions trying to lighten it up. The group neither laughed nor cracked smiles. In my growing discomfort, I didn't know whether I had offended them with my comments or confused them with my words. I quickly moved on to another topic. Humor seems to be the last thing I figure out when I live in a new culture.

An Irishman who had immigrated to Canada many years earlier still recalls the most difficult part of his transition.

> I would make a joke and no one would laugh. I soon realized that it wasn't just my accent that was causing the problem. I learned from watching Canadians tell jokes that the person telling the joke must smile or laugh to indicate to others that this was a joke and it is safe to laugh. It seems that in this politically correct environment people are afraid to laugh unless they are sure you meant to be funny. That wrecks the joke for me. The best kind of joke is given with a straight face.

It's also been said that the British like to laugh at others and that Canadians like to laugh at themselves; when a Canadian and a Brit work together, they are both making fun of the Canadian. Though this may be true, it is also true that sooner or later, this wears thin on the Canadian.

Using humor to break the ice can backfire in a major way, as the following situation illustrates.

> We hosted a few Russian consulting engineers who were in Canada as part of a trade mission organized jointly by the Russian government. The owner of our engineering consulting firm, who is Jewish, invited them and a few of his employees for dinner at his place. The Russians arrived after I did, so I had a chance to see

what happened when they came in: They brought several nice Russian gifts and they tried to break the ice by cracking some jokes. One of them made a Jewish joke—that one went over like a lead balloon. I remember that the mood of the whole place really lightened up a lot when the guy who had made the jokes left.

—Canadian consulting engineer

When we come face to face with a conflicting or nonmatching gesture (for example, when a North American attempts to bow to a Japanese who extends his or her hand), do we stay formal, try to hide our anxieties, and apologize profusely or move on as though it didn't happen? Or do we boldly engage the other person with a smile or a laugh at our own missteps? In most situations, we recommend finding the humor in the situation. Laughing at ourselves is probably the safest of all humor forms. It breaks down barriers and introduces a personal touch. Such responses represent seminal moments in our relationships with others.

Solution

When you are considering injecting humor into a situation that involves an immigrant:

- When in doubt about how it will be received, avoid humor.
- Learn what that person and that person's culture find funny before you attempt to make them laugh.
- Make any jokes self-deprecating; definitely don't be laughing at others.
- Watch for signs that the humor was misinterpreted.
- Avoid the topics of sex, politics, religion, nationality, and ethnicity.
- Don't use humor to break the ice.

When people make jokes you consider inappropriate, you are doing them a favor by pointing that out. It helps them understand how their words could be interpreted poorly.

Sports English

Canadians and U.S. Americans use many sports expressions, particularly from baseball, basketball, football, track and field, and ice hockey. Many immigrants are completely confused by the use of these terms when they come from countries where these sports are not played.

It is common in our offices to hear people say, "You are way out in left field," "Go hit a home run," or "Let's go for the touchdown." These baseball/football terms have no literal meaning in the office setting.

Here are some cricket expressions.

- He lost his wicket: He failed (the batsman let the ball by him).
- It's like winning the Ashes: The biggest win (the Ashes is the perpetual prize in England vs. Australia Test match series).

These cricket expressions help North Americans put in perspective the challenge of the sports terms, if you are unfamiliar with the sport. In countries where cricket is king, like England, India, and Australia, these expressions are commonplace. How would we react to hearing phrases like these that are completely meaningless to us?

As soccer becomes more popular in North America, terms such as *receiving a yellow card* (for unsportsmanlike behavior) are more likely to be understood. But don't assume so.

Generally, the sports whose terms are being borrowed to be used in business settings are played and watched in greater numbers by men than women. Women are often, but not always, put at disadvantage when sports terms are blended into the business vocabulary.

Solution

Here are some suggestions to reduce misunderstanding:

- Immigrants should go to watch at least one live game of each popular sport with someone who can describe what is happening.
- Avoid using sports English whenever possible.
- When you have used a sports English expression, ask your culturally different colleagues whether they understand the expression. If you do not get a firm yes, then explain the term. Remember that others may be reluctant to admit they don't know English words.
- Provide new employees a list of common, local sports terms.

Connotations

A recently arrived Indian colleague and I were discussing the attributes of Indians in our workforce. I was taken aback when my colleague made the claim that

"Indian people are too good." I thought, "Too good for what or too good for whom?" It was only later that I learned he was using *too* in a way that I would use the word *very*. I completely agree with the statement that "Indian people are very good," but not that "they are too good."

—North American accountant

The issue with connotation is that the word fits normally within the sentence and in the context of the conversation. There may be no red flag to denote a problem. But the intended meaning and the other person's understanding are quite different.

Connotation refers to the implied additional meaning of a word, phrase, sentence, or paragraph. Here are some examples:

- The French word *demander* translates in English into "to ask for." Because it is closer to "to demand," many French people end up "demanding an explanation" when they are just trying to ask for an explanation. A French accountant working for one of the Big Four accounting firms in Montreal had to be removed from an assignment when he "demanded data" from the client.
- The Japanese word *hai* translates as "yes," but its connotation may be "yes, I'm listening" rather than "yes, I agree." This is the source of considerable confusion among English-speaking businesspeople. North Americans think they have reached agreements with Japanese, only to find out some time later that their Japanese counterparts have not agreed to anything yet, and are still at the stage of information gathering.
- When Japanese say, "It is going to be a little difficult," the cultural translation in English may be anywhere from the literal translation to "Forget it, that is not going to happen in a million years." Americans may see this statement as a challenge to be overcome and get into problem-solving mode immediately, to the confusion of their Japanese counterparts, who may be thinking "What are you trying to do? I just told you it is not possible!" The broader context and body language, such as sucking air in the teeth (bad news), will give more clues to the intended meaning.
- In Russia, customer service representatives who answer calls from clients experiencing difficulties with a given product or service will typically ask the equivalent of, "What is your problem?" or "What's wrong with you?" in their own language. When they translate this sentence literally into English, their question is interpreted very differently because this question

has, in North America, a very negative connotation toward the client. A Russian IT specialist was almost fired at one of the major Canadian department stores when he asked the executive assistant of the CEO, "What is wrong with you?" after she had called for help with her computer.

■ A North American sent an e-mail message to an Iranian who did not speak English well. The message stated that his spouse had been hospitalized and that he had therefore to cancel the meeting they had previously scheduled. His Iranian counterpart responded: "Of course, I understand your excuse" when he meant "Of course, I understand your reasons." Such differences can result in significantly damaged relationships, because the people involved may not realize that they are dealing with a misunderstanding.

Related to connotation is the trendy "word of the month."

I recall some time in the 1980s when our company's annual meeting was held in Toronto. All the managers from across the country were eagerly waiting to hear our company president's speech. He told us that our industry, the computer industry, needed a new paradigm. He explained that our company was moving into a new paradigm. I had heard the word before but had no clue as to its meaning. In a whispered voice, I asked a colleague on my left. He was not sure. I asked the colleague on my right, who happened to be an immigrant. He admitted to not having even heard of the word *paradigm* before. Over the months and years that followed, everything was a new paradigm. It had become a golden word.

—Canadian computer store manager

Some people suggest that the best way to tell which employees are on the inside track is by the language they use and how closely it mirrors the language of the movers and shakers in the company.

Solution

Recent immigrants may consider the following action items:

■ Do not attempt to use slang and idiomatic expressions until you are quite comfortable with the language. You may use them in the wrong situation, which may significantly backfire on you.

■ Avoid swear words, because they come across much more powerfully than may be meant. It may be okay for 25-year-olds to say certain swear words among friends away from work, but not at the workplace or with others.

- Learn the connotations of the words you use. In particular, buy and use a thesaurus or the online version of your favorite word processing software.

Greetings and Chitchat Topics

Before we open our mouths to speak to a new person, we are, largely unconsciously, sizing them up from what we see, and adjusting accordingly. Is the person male or female? Bigger or smaller? Younger or older? Light-skinned or dark-skinned? Anything in the person's clothing that might indicate where the person is from or his or her religion? Pleasant disposition or unpleasant? Clear eye or an unfocused gaze? Light step or a heavy one? An open look or a closed one? These evaluations take place in the blink of an eye and mostly unconsciously on our part.

Our senses may be heightened if we know the person we are meeting is from another country or another culture within our country. We have a sense in our minds that the communication may be different from what we were used to. We pay more attention to such things as clothes, stature, use of English, even smell, and how comfortable the person looks in this setting.

One of the most ubiquitous activities in our lives is the greeting we give other people. Unless we are complete hermits, we greet numerous, maybe dozens of people every day. In North America, these greetings tend to be predictable and very brief. Table 6.13 gives a few examples.

North American greeting times are among the briefest on the planet. For most of us, the greeting is a necessary evil that is kept as brief as possible so that we can get on with the purpose of our communication or interaction.

For people in many cultures, the greeting is one of the most important elements of communication and business relationships. It is through the greeting that we establish or reestablish our connection and rapport with the other person. It is on this necessary foundation that all other interaction is built. Getting it wrong can seriously jeopardize the work that is to follow.

Bob and I had been working together for six months. He worked on rotation, which meant he was in Sudan for 30 days and then would return home to Canada for 30 days. I was constantly astounded when he would return from Canada and the only greeting he would give me was his "Hi Mohamed. How are you?" And then he would proceed to ask about some business report. I wanted to know about his trip and his family and what he'd been doing for the last 30 days and also to relate to him some of the things that were going on in my life. Over the next few days, we might get to these topics, but it always seemed like after a five-word greeting it was business first.

—Sudanese oil worker in Sudan

Table 6.13 Sample Greetings, Moving Through the Day in North America

Spouse	"Morning," kiss on the lips, hug
Child	"Good morning. How did you sleep?," kiss on the cheek, hug
Neighbor from driveway	Arm wave and perhaps "Morning"
Office security guard, parking attendant	"Good morning"
Receptionist	"Good morning. How are you?"
Boss	"Good morning. How are you?"
Coworker	"Good morning. How's it going?"
Coworker/friend	"How's it going? Did you see the game last night?"
Second time past the same person	"Hi," nod of head, hand up in abbreviated wave, smile, or nothing

A traditional Sudanese greeting may last 10 or 15 minutes, covering topics such as praising God, one's state of mind, health, family health, recent activities, and more. They complain that the brief North American greeting makes them wonder if they have done something wrong or are in disfavor with the boss. Many Sudanese will claim that a proper greeting will foster better relationships and result in significantly improved productivity in the workplace. By contrast, North America is among the few places where people routinely do business with people they may not like or even respect.

The topics considered appropriate for casual conversation in the workplace are not constant from country to country. In France, for example, politics is a safe topic. Some of the most popular Sunday evening programs on French TV are political talk shows. It is then common for people on Monday morning at work to discuss the topics raised in these programs.

In North America, politics is typically avoided in casual conversation. The favored topics in North America include the weather, sports, traffic, recent news stories, and weekend activities. In countries where there is a wet season and a dry season, the weather is not often discussed. It is far too predictable.

Solution

A North American might consider the following regarding greetings:

- Be aware that the person you are meeting with from another culture is likely trying very hard to adjust his or her greeting to what is thought to be your preference; i.e., the Latin American is trying not to kiss you on the cheek, the Arab is trying to give a firmer handshake, the Native American is trying to make eye contact, etc.
- Be flexible with the person who gives you a greeting that is not normal for you.
- Be prepared to explain to new employees the standard greetings in various scenarios in your company and your industry.
- Ask if the person has any questions regarding standard greetings or if the person would like to practice the standard greeting a couple of times with you.

A recent immigrant might consider the following regarding greetings:

- Remind yourself not to take offense at greetings that are different from what you are used to.
- Observe the greetings being used among coworkers and try to mirror their behavior.
- When in doubt, ask someone what the appropriate greeting is for a particular situation.

Here are some suggestions for the recent immigrant regarding conversation topics:

- Be prepared to talk about the topics that other people talk about.
- Read, watch, or listen to local news, sports, and weather to be ready for casual conversation.
- Practice greetings by going to a mall and meeting sales representatives.

Written Communication

Chances are that the written English of an immigrant will appear different from what is standard in a North American office. Some of the factors that will affect one's writing style include:

- Whether English is one's first language.
- The form of English learned.
- The degree of formality considered appropriate.
- The expectation of what is wanted.

Table 6.14 presents some examples of differences between written British English and written American English. Canadians use a mixture of British and

Table 6.14 Differences Between British and American English

	British	American
Formality	"Dear sir" or "Dear Mr. Bob Harding" "Yours respectfully" or "Yours truly" "I write to inquire upon the status of our accounts"	"Dear Bob" or "Hello Bob" or "Bob" "Best regards" or "Warm wishes" "Where is our check?"
Plural form	"The team are worried"	"The team is worried"
Verb tense	"Have you finished the project?"	"Did you finish the project?"
Preposition	"She resigned on Thursday." "Our manager is in hospital."	"She resigned Thursday." "Our manager is in the hospital."
Christmas day 2007	25/12/07	12/25/07
Education	"She read history at Oxford."	"She majored in history at Oxford."
Spelling	"Organise," "legalise" "Colour," "humour," "flavour" "Co-operate," "co-ordinate"	"Organize," "legalize" "Color," "humor," "flavor" "Cooperate," "coordinate"[a]
[a] http://en.wikipedia.org/wiki/American_and_British_English_differences		

American language styles. When we first encounter an immigrant's written English looking different than we expect, we may leap to the erroneous judgment that the person is uneducated or poorly educated.

Solution

In evaluating written communication from immigrants, keep the following points in mind:

- Differences may be due to different styles or usages of the English language.
- Help your employees to be aware of technical terms in English and in your industry.
- Distinguish between a person's ability to write English and a knowledge of the field and the person's ability to do the job.
- Monitor the correspondence of new employees to see that it meets corporate standards.
- Consider providing new employees training in written English.

"The Medium Is the Message"

Marshall McLuhan said, "The medium is the message." Nowhere is this truer than in cross-cultural communication. Cultures have unique preferences and bias toward oral versus written communication and face-to-face versus remote communication.

> I came from an office in Dublin, Ireland, to work in an office in a large North American city. My expectation was that office processes would be fairly familiar. The big surprise was when someone in the same office had a question or comment for me; it would come by e-mail, even if the person was just two desks away. It seemed like such a waste of time and so impersonal. When I would step over to the desk of a colleague and ask a quick question, I sensed that I was breaking some unwritten rule.
>
> —Mutual funds professional from Dublin

Professionals in many other countries tend to prefer face-to-face communication, for the following reasons:

- Personal communication is preferred.
- It is quicker in many situations; one conversation can eliminate numerous e-mails.
- One is able to pick up nuances in body language and tone of voice that enhance understanding.
- It builds social cohesion in the office.

Professionals in North America tend to prefer e-mail, for the following reasons:

- Impersonal communication is often preferred.
- It reduces the number of interruptions (working without interruptions is thought to increase productivity).
- It allows the recipient to handle the question or message at the time and in the manner that best suits the person.
- It allows the recipient time to do some research prior to responding.
- It provides a written record of progress on a project.
- It allows the participation of numerous people without getting everyone together in one physical location.

I once worked with a fellow from India named Gupta who practically never left voice messages. Instead, if I didn't answer my phone, he would call again in 10 minutes and again 10 minutes later. This pattern would continue until I finally picked up the phone. Sometimes I would be meeting with someone and would have to put up with the incessant ringing. I resented the interruptions. On the rare occasions he did leave a message, it would simply say, "This is Gupta. Please call me." There was never an explanation of what he wanted from me. I thought this was such a waste of the capability of voicemail.

—American steel company manager

In this example, the American steel company manager is quite happy to leave the communication impersonal and to take advantage of voicemail. Gupta wants the personal communication that a telephone conversation can provide over a voice message.

It's not uncommon for a Mexican to leave a voice message for a colleague that simply says, "Hi, it's me. Call me back." The idea is that the colleague will know who the person is from the voice and will have a sense of the importance of the call from the tone of voice. This subtlety is lost on most North Americans.

Solution

A North American might consider the following regarding communication method (face to face, telephone, e-mail, etc.):

- Recognize that using a particular communication medium will likely be interpreted in different ways by different employees in your organization.
- Select the medium that might work best for the person with whom you are communicating.
- Perhaps develop some informal company guidelines on when to use the different methods of communication.
- Coach employees on standard methods of communication within your corporate and national cultures.

A recent immigrant might consider the following regarding communication method:

- Understand that communication is relatively impersonal in North America.
- Get used to putting clear, concise, and complete messages into e-mails.
- A single e-mail message should contain only one major idea.
- E-mail messages should typically be no longer than one page. Either figure out how to make the message concise or consider using another form of communication, such as a telephone call or a face-to-face meeting.
- Leave some detail in your voicemail.
- Don't leave voice messages for the same person on the same topic more often than once every two or three days.
- If you are concerned about how coherent your voicemail will sound, you might write out the message in advance and then read it into the machine.

More Communication Ideas

Motivation or Mental Preparedness to Communicate

Underlying the skills or mechanics of successful communication, within a culture or across cultures, is motivation. The best communicators typically have a greater desire to understand the other person and to have their message understood by the other (Table 6.15).

Table 6.15 Impact of Motivation or Mental State on Communication

Motivation or mental state more likely to succeed	Motivation or mental state more likely to fail
Interested in meeting new people	Not interested in meeting new people
Interested in hearing about and learning different ways of doing things	Not interested in hearing about and learning different ways of doing things
Patient with people who are different	Impatient with people who are different
Curious to learn about other cultures	Not curious to learn about other cultures
Interested in building better relationships with people by working together	Interested in getting the work done, with little interest in the people
See the best in people and situations	See the worst in people and situations

Solution

Here's how to build interest in communicating with and working with others:

- Provide employees with some background on the newcomer.
- Share organizational success stories on teamwork, where fresh ideas and perspectives made a positive difference.
- Provide an opportunity to learn about new cultures through speakers from your international operations, movie viewings, books, articles, etc.
- Provide opportunity for social mixing, for example, ethnic lunches, international holidays, birthday parties, and team building exercises.
- Reward collaboration, and reward collaboration across cultures.

LLIIAA Formula for Cross-Cultural Communication

Look
Listen
Interpret
Interpret again!
Act
Assess

North American society values one's ability to see a situation, interpret it quickly, and act swiftly. This usually works well for us. In a cross-cultural situation, taking a moment to try a second interpretation can protect against causing offense or creating a misunderstanding.

Be Confident

> I traveled with a group of North American businesspeople on a trade mission to South Korea. We carefully arranged to have the appropriate Korean businesspeople at the opening reception in Seoul. When I walked into the reception room, I was shocked to see my group of North American businesspeople chatting among themselves, with the Koreans doing the same on the other side of the room. When I asked one of the North Americans what the heck was going on, he replied, "We weren't sure how to properly greet the Koreans and what we should talk about." Needless to say, not many business deals were signed on this trip.
>
> —North American trade representative

Some people avoid communicating across cultures for fear of offending another person. The sentiment of not wanting to insult another person is a good one. But if it paralyzes us and stops us from engaging with others, then it is a problem. Most recent immigrants are appreciative when others take the initiative to speak with them, even if some of their cultural norms are broken. When we are respectful of others, have good intentions, and do some preparation, we rarely go far wrong.

The story in the upcoming section on "When You Do Something Culturally Offensive" illustrates how to overcome a cultural faux pas and how to even improve relationships through them.

Being Present with All Your Senses

Beyond the mechanics of verbal and nonverbal communication is the idea of "being present" with the person with whom you are in communication. All the cross-cultural skill in the world will not be of great value if the two people can't "connect." For example, a person can learn traditional actions associated with greetings in Japan. But going through the motions alone is no guarantee of a successful greeting or introduction. It helps, but behind the motions is a constant assessment and reassessment of one's connection with the other person. The anxiety and intense mental processing ("And now I bend at the waist. My gosh, is this right?") can stand in the way of making a personal connection with the other person.

Ideally, one is in a relaxed and comfortable state when entering an interaction with another person. If we can pay attention using all of our senses, we are in a better position to understand how the other person feels and what he or she is trying to say. Good communication is really a fluid and somewhat unpredictable process. Successful communication is like a dance. Each participant adjusts according to the responses of the other person.

Mirroring the Behavior of Others

The single most effective technique for improving cross-cultural communication with new acquaintances is called *mirroring*. It involves adjusting our behavior to more closely match the behavior we see in the person opposite us. For example, if the person is sitting ramrod straight in a chair, we might check our posture to see that we are not slouching. If the person is speaking slowly, we might monitor our own speech to make sure we are not speaking too quickly.

Mirroring is something most people do naturally. Have you ever noticed that when you speak with someone with an accent different from yours, you end up adopting a bit of that accent, or that when you speak with someone who doesn't make a lot of eye contact, you don't attempt as much eye contact either? If the other person is speaking softly, then you can try to match that. When you observe two people talking, you might notice how one seems to imitate the other's mannerisms. If one person has his or her hands in pockets, often the other one does too. If one person is touching his or her face while speaking, often the other person does too—as one person laughs, the conversation partner tends to laugh as well. These are all examples of mirroring.

Typically, it is the person with less power that tries to emulate behaviors and speech patterns of the more powerful person. In an interview situation it would typically be the interviewee that would be trying to match the style of the interviewer. The subordinate follows the lead of the manager. The manager in turn follows the lead of the executive.

Checking for Understanding

We are constantly looking for clues indicating that the other person understands our meaning the way we intend it. This can't be taken for granted. Clues that we are not coming across clearly to the other person might include a question, a blank look, or a change of topic.

When in doubt, you might try to:

- Ask people to repeat once, maybe twice, if you do not understand.
- Ask them to say it in a different manner.
- Summarize the parts you do understand, and be specific on the part you missed.
- Ask them to write it down.
- Ask for a diagram if it might be helpful on a technical topic.
- Apologize for not understanding, and ask people to repeat or rephrase.

When You Do Something Culturally Offensive

An environmental consultant working in Indonesia reported how a misused gesture actually improved his relations.

> I was with five Indonesians in their Jakarta office boardroom. We had worked together for some time and our relationships were good. In concluding the business of that meeting, I gave the fingers-crossed (middle and index fingers crossed) good luck gesture and said, "Good luck." The Indonesians looked surprised. One of them advised me that that gesture was offensive in Indonesia and that I certainly shouldn't use it in public. I apologized and assured them I wouldn't use it again.
>
> When I was later asked what impact using that gesture had on my relationships with the Indonesians, I had to admit that it probably improved our relations. Because the Indonesians knew I was not trying to be offensive, they were pleased to be able to help me to be more successful in their country.
>
> —North American environmental engineer in Indonesia

If we hope to succeed when we travel internationally to do business or are receiving foreign clients as guests, particular care needs to be taken not to do or say things that are culturally offensive. In the case of a recent immigrant employee, we expect the newcomer to do most of the adjusting. Avoiding cultural offense is still helpful, but more importantly the new employee needs to be given guidance as to the norms of the current environment. If the employee finds it rude, for example, to have things handed to him or her from the other person's left hand or to receive no morning greeting, the new employee may need to adjust.

If you are working with a recent immigrant employee, you might:

- Point out behaviors and comments that may serve to confuse or offend, with a description of the intended meaning.
- Help the employee's work group understand some of the cultural differences so that they can help ease the new employee into the new environment.
- As in the preceding example of the engineer in Indonesia, look for the positive side of any cultural misstep.

When in Doubt, Ask

When working with people from another culture, we are often unsure of the intended meaning of their words or behavior. Rather than assuming the worst, we should, in our own minds, step through different possible explanations. When we are still unsure about what is going on, then it is time to ask. Keeping the information flow going in both directions is the key to smoother cross-cultural relations.

Summary

Humans are remarkably adaptable and resourceful. When people are motivated to accomplish something together, they can be very ingenious in understanding and making themselves understood. If there is little motivation to make it work or there is some suspicion about others, then interpretations tend to be more negative.

In this chapter, we have covered dozens of areas for miscommunication across cultures. The list is by no means complete. However, following the solutions listed throughout this chapter will get you started on the right path.

Our existing communication skills are not to be underestimated. Every adult has fine-tuned his or her skills through thousands of interactions. Many of these contacts were with people very different from ourselves. Building on your existing communication skills, continually asking yourself for another interpretation, and listening with all of your senses will help keep you on the right path.

As mentioned earlier in the chapter, there is no "silver bullet" leading to great communication. It takes the practice of doing many small things differently and enjoying "the dance!"

7

Retention—Part 1: Manager– Employee Relations

The great Chinese social philosopher Confucius taught about the Five Proper Relationships, one of which was ruler and subject. This can be extended to the bond between employer and employee. While Confucius did say that a junior person should point out if the senior person errs, most of the advice given involves deep respect and loyalty to the superior. Western philosophy, on the other hand, is more grounded in Socrates, who suggests that while these employer/employee relationships are important, there are societal rules and/or laws that supersede them. Both cultural differences go deep and historically far into the past.

In order for culturally different employees to stay in the organizations that have hired them, they need to work effectively with their managers. If their managers consider them poor employees, they are unlikely to get past the probation period; if they do, they are likely to feel that they are going nowhere in the organization and will probably leave after a few years because they believe they have no future there. When employees do not come from the same cultural backgrounds as their direct managers, two major issues commonly arise.

- Employees and managers may have very different ideas of what "being a good employee" means because they have different perceptions of hierarchy. As a result, employees may feel they are doing an excellent job when their managers are ready to terminate their probation period or to put them on a performance-improvement plan.
- Employees and managers may have very different ways of giving and receiving feedback. As a result, the feedback provided by managers to their employees may not be received the way it was meant, resulting in unexpected reactions on both sides.

This chapter examines in detail how cultural differences often lead to poor cross-cultural employee–manager relations even though employees and managers are trying their best to work together. It concludes with advice on how to help those of different cultural beliefs and experiences to understand and work with the norms found in North America.

Perhaps the single biggest cultural difference in manager/employee expectations and behaviors across cultures has to do with the concepts of power, authority, and hierarchy. For the purposes of this chapter, these words will be used interchangeably and the term *hierarchy* used primarily. Hierarchy here refers to the psychological distance between employees and their direct managers. It is the degree to which less powerful and more powerful members of organizations accept the fact that power is unequally distributed between them. Interculturalist Geert Hofstede uses the term *power distance* to describe this phenomenon.

Hierarchy in Manager–Employee Relations

In hierarchical societies, dependence of subordinates on superiors is accepted as the norm by both sides. Roles are clearly defined and distinct. There is a clear delineation of expectations and behaviors separating the subordinate and the superior. Individuals are unlikely to question the boss's decisions. A primary, if not the primary, task of an employee is to follow orders and to please the boss. The subordinate keeps the boss "in the loop" on all activities, never going over the boss's head, and taking great care not to embarrass the boss. This may be recognized as a more traditional authoritarian, or a military, model.

> We were working in partnership with the Chinese National Petroleum Company in Africa. It seemed every time there was a decision to be made it had to go back to Beijing. These were decisions that didn't seem very important to us. Going back to Beijing meant delays in the project. I'm sure there were multiple people involved in coming up with the final answer in Beijing before it came back to us in Africa. The answers that came back often seemed completely irrational to us, and we were rarely given an explanation.
>
> —North American oil executive

In less hierarchical or more egalitarian societies, a consultative style, equality of status, and interdependence between different layers of power are considered desirable. Subordinates will, and are expected to question, and even disagree with, those in more senior positions. People from less hierarchical societies tend to focus on the business objectives first. They consider what the organization and work group are trying to accomplish, and they put their energies first toward that end. The manager encourages this approach and does not expect a great deal of attention. Employees initiate new projects, make independent decisions, and consult with people inside and outside the organization at various levels without necessarily informing their boss.

Hierarchical organizations, such as the military, have more levels than egalitarian ones. There may be over two dozen levels or layers between the lowest-ranking private and the most senior-ranking general. A flatter pyramid represents less hierarchy and fewer levels from bottom to top. These are probably best represented in the high-tech industry in North American society.

When someone has grown up in a particular society favoring one model or the other, the associated values and behaviors are deeply ingrained. Simply arriving in a new country or organization with the instruction that "things are done differently here" does not overcome one's habitual behavior. A common tendency is for an employee or a manager to assume that everyone else in the organization sees things the same way as him- or herself—the "normal," "logical," "right" way. The person remains blissfully ignorant until a conflict in approach to hierarchy arises.

Should senior people be treated differently from others? Consider the following situation. On December 23, 1988, the following news item appeared in the press:

> The Swedish king, Carl Gustav, experienced considerable delay while shopping for Christmas presents for his children when he wanted to pay by check but did not have a "check card" (like an ID card). The salesperson refused to accept the check without the check card ID. Only when helpful bystanders dug into their pockets for 1-crown coins showing the face of the king did the salesperson decide to accept this for ID—not, however, without testing the check thoroughly for authenticity and noting the name and address of the holder.

By contrast, many heads of state do not go shopping themselves, and they abide by a different set of unwritten rules than the majority. This is accepted as natural and normal by their countrymen. Here are some examples.

- Harrods department store in London used to close for the Queen of England to do her Christmas shopping. This type of special status and exceptional rule was accepted by most of the population.

- The prime minister in India does not do his own shopping. Wherever he goes, the street is typically cleared of people in advance. In the unlikely event he went into a store, only the most senior person, preferably the CEO, would serve the prime minister and would give the prime minister whatever he or she wanted, without payment.
- In Russia or Romania prior to the collapse of the Soviet Union, the clerk's life may have been at risk for being so unhelpful and disrespectful to the national leader (from previous Swedish example).
- In France, Mexico, or Peru, the clerk would likely have been fired on the spot for being so disrespectful (from previous Swedish example).

You may ask what possible relevance do shopping customs have to do with manager–employee relations. The interesting thing about values and culture is that the patterns found in one area, such as manager–employee relations, will also appear in other power or status situations, such as serving an important person in a shop. There is a consistency.

When the more hierarchical immigrant is managing North Americans, the complexity increases. Managers senior to the newcomer may be pleased with the extreme politeness and deference with which they are treated. But it may come as a real surprise to them and be difficult for them to believe when subordinates of the new manager report that he or she is a tyrant.

My manager was from Iran. While he was pretty good to work for, there were some things he did that took some getting used to. His style of management was very much command and control. When he made decisions, he expected us to act without asking questions. I think loyalty is important too, but this guy took it to extremes. He was furious when a guy in our department quit his job a few months ago.

—North American professional

Hierarchical cultures tend to see hierarchy everywhere, because it is considered, not only important, but essential. People in these cultures are constantly trying to figure out in any situation who is of higher status and how people should behave accordingly. Egalitarian people tend not to see hierarchy, because it is a lower priority for them. They are generally not conscious of people's status and whether one's behavior should vary based on it. As you can imagine, when hierarchical and egalitarian people mix there are many surprises and few of them are pleasant.

Though there seems to be a slow global trend away from hierarchical systems and toward egalitarian ones, societal changes such as these are typically very slow-moving. In a global economy, expect to be interacting with people from both systems. Keep in mind, too, that in reality, societies and individuals can be seen at varying stages along the continuum between egalitarian and hierarchical, with every society and every individual manifesting some tendencies of each to differing degrees.

In this chapter, we step through the following topics as they relate to hierarchy and to the relations between culturally different managers and employees:

- Respect of position.
- Ranking.
- Communication.
- Decision making and delegation.
- Compensation.
- Performance evaluation.

We explore where countries tentatively fit on the hierarchical/egalitarian continuum and how to interact more effectively with someone from another culture who has a different sense of hierarchy in the employee/manager relationship.

For our purposes, the reference to an individual or society being "hierarchical" is equivalent to "high hierarchy," and "egalitarian" refers to a person or society with a "low hierarchy" rating.

Hierarchy National Comparison Chart

The hierarchy chart shown in Figure 7.1 is adapted from Lionel Laroche's book *Managing Cultural Diversity in Technical Professions*, which in turn is adapted from the work of Dutch interculturalist Geert Hofstede. Hofstede's global study, first done in 1980 and since extended, lays important groundwork for studying *power distance* or *hierarchy* and how it affects manager/employee relations. The purpose of including the country ranking here is to give the reader a sense of the significant differences among countries on this dimension. People are often curious where their country ranks and where the country of their employee or manager ranks.

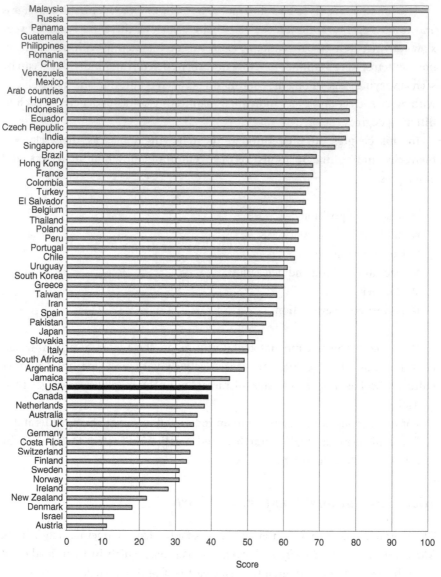

Figure 7.1 Hierarchy national comparison chart.

The danger in interpreting this data too exactly is twofold:

- Each country's rank may not be exact, due to imperfect research methods or changes in a national culture.
- One cannot assume when meeting someone that the person will follow the norm of his or her culture. For example, because the Philippines show up as being more hierarchical than the United States doesn't mean that each person from the Philippines will be more hierarchical than each person in the United States. Cultural traits tend to follow the normal bell curve of distribution, so there will, in fact, be some Filipinos who are more egalitarian than some Americans.

Understanding these dangers is very important. We do not want to make sweeping assumptions about people from a culture. This leads to stereotyping, inflexible negative assumptions about a group of people, and can result in moving backward rather than forward in our working relationships.

When looking at Figure 7.1, keep these points in mind:

- High scores correspond to countries that are more hierarchical. Conversely, low scores correspond to countries that are less hierarchical.
- There is no absolute right or wrong on this scale (a score of 80 is not better than a score of 20), but there is a relative right and wrong (people who have scores of 80 will experience difficulties in a country where the average score is 20). A difference of 10 is considered meaningful.
- The implications of score differences on this scale are discussed in the following pages.

Respect of Position

In keeping with minimizing the differences between people of more and less power, egalitarian cultures avoid the use of titles, protocol, and special privileges. These are felt to create artificial barriers between people. They are seen to create the wrong environment for creative, successful organizations.

More hierarchical cultures, on the other hand, place great value on titles, protocol, and special privileges, as means for maintaining order, control, and predictability in an organization (Table 7.1). The fear is that, without these formalities, the organization will descend into chaos. These titles also show the progression of people as they gather more and more experience. For example, while North American accounting firms might lump all Seniors (auditors who have typically between 2 and 5 years of experience) into one category with a single title and a fairly wide range of salaries, their hierarchical counterparts in France and India have Senior 1, Senior 2, and Senior 3, depending on how many years of seniority they have as Seniors.

The perks that are offered at more senior levels are considered deserved and fair. It is easy to see how what is considered fair will vary by culture, depending on how egalitarian or hierarchical the viewpoint.

> When we bought the bank in Mexico, we knew we had to make some radical changes. It was being sold because it was losing a lot of money. We felt that the camaraderie within levels was great but that across levels it was terrible, and there were a lot of levels. The first thing we did was to close the executive dining room. Employees at the senior levels were shocked and appalled. There was great resistance. A fine executive dining room was considered essential to encourage aspiring employees to move up the ranks and, more importantly, to give the right impression to potential clients. Among the junior levels, there was amazement. We felt it would save some money, get different levels mixing over lunch, and send the right message.
>
> —Canadian banking vice president in Mexico

A general acceptance of greater privileges reflects a more hierarchical orientation. The use of titles, or a lack of them, may be the first indicator of a person's sense of hierarchy. In North America, there has been a general decline in the use of formal titles, though for every trend there seems to be a countertrend.

> In 1999, the legislature of the State of Louisiana passed a bill requiring students to show respect to teachers and school personnel by addressing them courteously using the terms *ma'am* and *sir*. It was introduced out of a concern over the decline in respect or the practice of respect. The emphasis of the bill was to develop good habits of civility and courtesy.[1]

Generally, more hierarchical societies also tend to be more formal, which is reflected in the way hierarchical candidates address recruiters in their cover letters or during interviews (see Chapters 2 and 3 for more details on these points). The two concepts are closely related.

[1]http://house.legis.state.la.us/pubinfo/Press_Releases/PDF/DeathofRepHudson.pdf

During an oil embargo in 1974, most countries were struggling to reduce their energy consumption. At the time, Norway was not an energy-producing country. The king of Norway began riding the bus like everyone else. In an egalitarian country like Norway, this was perceived as an appropriate gesture and a sign of good leadership. More hierarchical societies might respond with disapproval and embarrassment. They might feel that, no matter how difficult things were for the people, their king should ride in style in order to give the right impression both inside and outside the country.

Also connected to respect and hierarchy, is the concept of *face*. Face can be viewed as the status or prestige a person has in the eyes of others. A loss of face occurs when one's image in the eyes of others is threatened. Causing one's boss to lose face is not appreciated anywhere, but it can have very serious repercussions in more hierarchical cultures. In these cultures, an employee's primary function may be to help his or her superior to gain face, to look good in the eyes of others. The value of saving face may show up in specific behaviors many times each and every day, such as agreeing with the boss in a meeting or privately correcting an error the boss made. A related but less pervasive concept in North America is reputation.

> My new Venezuelan employee just wasn't quite fitting in. I received complaints from secretaries, the mail delivery person, and the cleaning staff about her rudeness. I asked some of my peers and they said she was always extremely pleasant and polite. I eventually figured out that my Venezuelan employee showed senior people more respect than they expected and junior people less respect. After a few coaching sessions, she eventually got the hang of the way things work in our office, and now she fits in just fine.
>
> —North American manager

The use of titles and protocol is considered a way of showing respect to the other person in hierarchical societies. Recognize that when you ask someone to stop using titles or formal salutations, it will likely be very uncomfortable for the person. For him or her, it is asking the individual to be rude and disrespectful to seniors. Similarly, a superior who is more hierarchical may consider your informal and casual manner equivalent to insubordination. Ingrained practices and associated feelings can take a long time to overcome.

> I transferred from the Mumbai office of one of the Big Four accounting firms to another one in the United States. Back in India, I was expected to stand, almost at

Table 7.1 Comparison of Egalitarian and Hierarchical People with Respect to Titles, Protocol, Face, and Privileges

	Compared with egalitarian people, hierarchical people tend to:	Compared with hierarchical people, egalitarian people tend to:
Titles	■ Prefer using formal forms of address ("Sir," "Your Excellency," or "Mr./Mrs./Ms.") ■ Use position title to address people ("Director Jones," "Professor Swanson," "Manager," etc.) ■ Place significant importance on job titles ■ Expect the use of titles and protocol from subordinates	■ Prefer using first name and informal forms of address ■ Place little importance on job titles
Protocol	■ View introductions and greetings as important customs ■ Pay more attention to protocol, such as: ☐ Where people sit in a meeting ☐ In which order they enter a room ☐ In which order they speak ☐ How a meeting is run ☐ The exchange of business cards ☐ Standing when the boss enters the room ■ React strongly and negatively to lack of respect of hierarchy and to breach of protocol	■ Minimize or bypass introductions and greetings ■ Pay little attention to protocol ■ Speak to and interact with the boss as one would with a coworker ■ Be unaware of protocol ■ Be dismissive of the importance of protocol ■ Believe that people should act naturally and that showing respect is found elsewhere than protocol
Loss of face	■ Pay more attention to how self, subordinate, peer, or superior is viewed in the eyes of others	■ Pay little attention to how they're viewed by others, though there is still some concern for one's reputation
Special privileges	■ Assume senior people deserve special parking, special dining facilities, bigger and better offices, a golf club membership, tickets to premiere sporting events, etc.	■ Assume everyone should receive the same perks and benefits; special parking or tickets to a game may be awarded by lottery or given to the employee of the month

attention, when a partner walked by and to call him or her "Sir" or "Madam." As a senior auditor, I only dealt with managers, sometimes senior managers, but virtually never with partners. I was so surprised when my American partner came to meet me during the week in the office, told me to use her first name, and said, "Let me know if you have any problem."

—Indian auditor in the United States

Solution

Once you have identified whether your recruit or employee is more or less hierarchical than you, you have the choice of adapting your style to meet his or her expectations or not. Once again, the purpose of cross-cultural understanding is not so that we can necessarily do things in the style of the other person. Rather, the purpose is that from a position of understanding we can choose our preferred approach for the particular situation and communicate this clearly.

If your new hire is more hierarchical around titles, protocol, face, and privileges than is the norm in your organization, you could:

- Explain the norms of the office and industry environment around titles and protocol and set expectations.
- Ask the individual to observe and follow the lead of coworkers.
- Introduce the new person to colleagues and clients to get the relationships started more comfortably.
- Accept that it may take some time for the employee to become comfortable using first names.
- Be cautious not to embarrass the person in front of others.

If your employee is less hierarchical around titles and protocol than you are, you could:

- Explain the norms of the office and industry environment around titles and protocol and set expectations.
- Explain the reasons that these norms are in place and the problems that arise when they are not followed.
- Ask the person to observe and follow the lead of coworkers.
- Accept that it may take some time for the employee to show respect in ways that are considered normal in North America.

North Americans demonstrate respect in the workplace by:

- Saying good morning.
- Learning and using the person's name.
- Shaking hands on occasion but not often (typically when one has not seem the other person for a couple of weeks).
- Arriving on time for work and meetings (in North America, "on time" means less than five minutes late in most cases and just before the appointed time when meeting someone to whom you want to make a good first impression, such as senior manager, a prospective client, or a recruiter for a job interview).
- Respecting the privacy of coworkers by asking their permission before sharing information about them to others or before looking at their work, books, or documents.
- Fulfilling commitments or giving early warning if a piece of work is going to be delayed.
- Not speaking negatively about other people without them being present (i.e., "behind their back").
- Giving others the freedom and space to be individuals.

Ranking People

People from hierarchical cultures are used to being ranked and are taught to rank others. At high schools in France, for example, students are individually ranked on each exam, and the standings are made public. Assignments and exams are handed out in order, from top marks to bottom, for everyone to see. At one of the top universities in France, the École Polytechnique, students are given a number based on their ranking with others being admitted in the first year. That number is public and is used as the students' identifier rather than their name. No two students can have the same rank. People coming out of this type of system find themselves naturally ranking themselves and others inside and outside of work.

I was working with two people from Sweden and trying to figure out which one was the senior person. Each time I thought I had figured which was the leader, they would do something that would suggest the contrary. On occasion, I would send an e-mail to one Swede and would receive a response back from the other one.

Eventually it dawned on me that they were acting as an egalitarian partnership. This was new to me and was very confusing at first.

—French professional in the United States

The relevance to the workplace of this type of ranking comes when an immigrant is keenly aware of his or her place in the work group. Through a complex measure of colleagues' educational backgrounds, job performance, years of experience, and time at the company, a person from a more hierarchical culture, like India, Japan, or France, may well create a mental ranking of each person in the work group. Carrying this ranking around in his or her head, the employee has certain expectations of those imagined of higher rank and other expectations of those imagined to be of lower rank.

As an example, the typical North American manager might feel he or she is managing two levels of engineers, junior and senior. Within each level there may be five sublevels for the purposes of pay and official seniority. But in the practicality of day-to-day work there is little or no difference in the treatment toward all those designated junior engineers. The need for recognition of the immigrant's place in the hierarchy is not likely to be met.

If the manager is more hierarchical, he or she will have a sense of ranking among peers and subordinates that may be oblivious to others. The manager may be seen to be hung up on details and too focused on his or her own power rather than on the function of the business unit.

Hierarchical people place far more importance on the university from which they graduated, because that has a lot more weight in their home countries than it has in North America. In North America, some universities are considered better than others—Harvard is considered better than many state universities in the United States, while MacLean's publishes a ranking of Canadian universities every year. However, the difference between top-ranking universities is not major, because there is considerable overlap in the skills of their respective student populations. The situation can be represented graphically as in Figure 7.2, which indicates that, while the average student of university 1 may be slightly better than the average student of university 2, an employer needs to look at the accomplishments of each individual student to determine whether a particular student from university 1 is better than a particular student from university 2.

The situation in hierarchical cultures is quite different. In these cultures, a ranking of universities is almost universally accepted. This ranking is not published, since it does not change from one year to the next, and everyone knows it. The situation there is represented schematically in Figure 7.3. As this figure suggests, in hierarchical cultures most students from university 1 are considered better than most students of university 2. Entering students in universities often follow a very rigorous process, and being accepted in the best university ensures a great professional future to students.

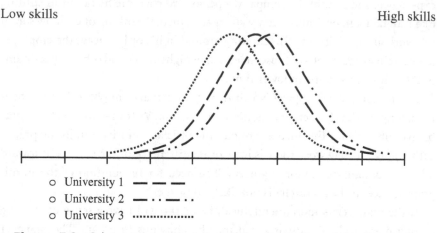

Figure 7.2 Schematic representation of the distribution of the skills of the students enrolled at the top three universities in the United States or in Canada.

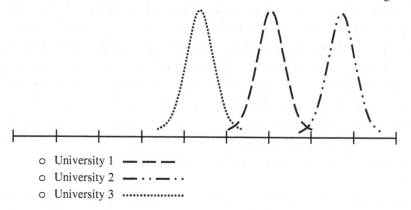

Figure 7.3 Schematic representation of the distribution of the skills of the students enrolled in the top three universities in hierarchical cultures.

Solution

If your recent immigrant counterpart is more rank conscious than is the norm in your organization, you can:

- Explain the smaller role that rank plays in your organization.
- Review what matters more in your organization and how the person can get ahead.
- Reassure the person on the value of the person's work to the organization.
- Explain to the person that degrees have a limited shelf life in North America and that what matters to the organization is what problems the individual solves.

If your employee is less hierarchical around ranking than is the norm in your organization, you could:

- Explain the logic and the function of the levels.
- Explain the expectations of employees regarding interactions with other levels.

Decision Making and Delegating

Toward the end of World War II, American bombers were targeting locations in Japan. Though Russia was an ally, the pilots were given strict instructions that never, no matter how severe their damage, were they to make an emergency landing anywhere in Russia. This was at the start of the Cold War. Three American crews, their planes hit and damaged by enemy fire, knew they wouldn't make it back to their home base. Rather than go down in Japanese territory, they landed in Russia. The country's leader, Joseph Stalin, returned the American pilots unharmed but kept their planes. Russia wanted the American technology. Stalin demanded that his people study the planes and copy them. His engineers did as they were told, exactly, and created replicas right down to the bullet holes in the sides of the aircraft.

At the time, Russia was a country where one obeyed the orders of the top person unquestioningly and exactly. The consequences of failure were dire. Whether the request made any sense to the worker was superfluous. While there are few places today where a failure to follow the orders of one's superior will cost one their life, the unquestioned following of a boss's orders is not uncommon.

I had a Russian intern last summer who was studying at one of the universities in town. At one point, one of our clients faxed a table of financial results; this table included both numbers and comments. I needed a soft copy of this table, so I asked my intern to copy the numbers into an Excel spreadsheet. He did exactly that: He copied the numbers but not the comments. When I looked at his spreadsheet, I shook my head in disbelief. Why did he copy only the numbers? What point is a financial table without the comments? I realized then that I had to think far more about the instructions I gave him, because he followed my instructions as I gave them to him and did not deviate from those instructions.

—American manager in one of the Big Four accounting firms

One of the areas of greatest challenge for new employees to North America is the issue of decision making. Who makes what decisions, and do they make those decisions in isolation or together with others? In hierarchical cultures, employees are carefully taught to get the boss's opinion and follow it for practically every decision that is made. This is what defines a good employee. Add to this the immigrant's uncertainty about many business processes in the North American environment, a possible lack of confidence in understanding what is meant when using English as a second or third language, and an intense desire to avoid failure. The resulting behavior may be interpreted as a lack of initiative that frustrates the North American manager.

Here is how the direction given by a manager might differ between cultures of low, medium, and high hierarchy.

- In low-hierarchy countries, the most common form of organization is the self-empowered individual and team. Managers act like coaches: They have influence only through their ability to convince team members. Directions are given in a general sense ("Acquire some technology that will help us get this work done"). Many projects are actually initiated by staff members.
- In medium-hierarchy countries (middle of the scale), the most common form of organization is the matrix. Managers are expected to make the final decision after consultation with their employees. Directions are given with more details ("Buy computers for the office that use the speediest Pentium chip available"). Staff members are expected to balance taking initiative on their own and implementing decisions made by superiors.
- In high-hierarchy countries, the boss has the first word and the last word. Here the most common form of organization can be represented as a steep pyramid. Managers (often referred to by a title such as boss, chief, or direc-

tor) make decisions based on their experience and position. Explicit and detailed directives are given to employees ("Buy six computers for the office with the latest Pentium chip, 6 gigabytes of RAM, 4-terabyte hard drives, 21" flat screen monitors"). Staff members are expected to implement the decisions made by managers.

When an employee makes a presentation in a hierarchical society, the manager will want to know or perhaps even provide the details, such as date, location, attendees, points to be made, structure of the presentation, data to be used as supporting evidence, sometimes even the type of font to be used. He (and it more typically is "he" in hierarchical cultures) will want to preview the presentation prior to its being viewed by clients. By contrast, many North American managers will say something like: "Prepare a presentation on this topic by next Tuesday. You will have 20 minutes; you will be presenting to senior managers. Go for it."

Hierarchical managers give a lot more instructions when they delegate a task to their employees than do egalitarian managers. They may also use a tone of voice that is more "top-down," "do-exactly-as-I-say" compared with the tone of voice of egalitarian managers, which tends to invite more employee questions and suggestions. When hierarchical people immigrate to North America and use this tone of voice with people who are in lower positions than they in the organizations, this often creates major problems, as the following illustrates.

One of the employees was really difficult to deal with. He was of Polish origin; he immigrated to Canada in the early 1980s. Technically, he was one of our best engineers, if not the best. He had obtained all the awards the company could give him. At the same time, he was impossible to deal with. One of his colleagues joked once that she wished they could install a toilet and make two slots in the door of his office, one for incoming work and one for outgoing work, then lock him in there. His top-down approach resulted in grievance upon grievance; keeping him out of trouble probably took 25 percent of his manager's time and 10 percent of mine.

—American HR manager

The same decisions are usually made at higher levels in hierarchical societies than in egalitarian societies, as the following example illustrates.

I sell transportation services in Monterrey, Mexico. I have been doing this job for over 10 years, so I have seen a lot of unusual client reactions. This still did not prepare me for what happened when I made a presentation to the CEO of the Mexican subsidiary of a Canadian automotive parts company. Through the Canadian Chamber of Commerce in Monterrey, I got to meet him and set up an appointment to make a presentation on the services my company offers. At the end of the presentation, he said: "Ricardo, that was an excellent presentation. Now you have to go and convince my purchasing manager to give you a trial order." I was floored! Any Mexican CEO would have said something like "Ricardo, that was an excellent presentation. I will ask my purchasing manager to give you a trial order." I never got the trial order!

—Mexican sales representative

Differences in the levels at which the same decision is made create major issues when employees are either less hierarchical than their managers, in which case employees are perceived as loose cannons, or more hierarchical than their managers, in which case they are often perceived as lacking initiative.

I had an accountant from one of our India offices working for me. He worked hard and really knew his stuff. The part that bugged me was that every time there was a decision to be made he came back to me to make it. This included things that he could easily have decided for himself, such as whether to send a thank you note to the client or to expense a business book he purchased. We reviewed the kinds of decisions I expected him to make by himself and which ones I expected him to consult with me on. It took a long time for him to feel comfortable making those decisions without running it by me. But eventually he got the hang of it.

—Senior accountant in North America

Lack of Initiative

Lack of initiative is one of the most common complaints from North American managers regarding new hires from a different culture. It is often applied to people from East Asia, southern Asia, Eastern Europe, Latin America, and Africa. The behaviors associated with this label include the following.

- These employees are thought to be competent, but they rarely step forward to offer their ideas. They don't volunteer to assist in projects where their expertise is unchallenged.
- They rarely speak out or challenge someone else. They may have concerns with the direction a conversation or project is going, but they don't

say anything. Or if they do, it is only to someone in their cultural group.

- In meetings, they sit silently while observing the conversation. "It's like pulling teeth" to get them to share their own ideas, the manager might say.
- They keep running back to the manager's office to ask for clarification, request a decision, or report back on a decision just made.
- Another fact of this problem is when employees sit in their cubicles being ineffective because they're unclear about the priorities of a project but also are not comfortable going back to the manager for clarification.

I have had some difficulties with one of my Pakistani pharmacists. He is technically really good, but I sure wish he could take more initiative. When the batteries of the emergency exit sign ran out, he kept telling every employee in the pharmacy that the batteries ran out. He even called me at home to tell me about it. My reaction was: "Just take new batteries from the ones we sell at the cash register and change them!"

—American pharmacy manager

Loose Cannon

In contrast to the issue of lack of initiative the "loose cannon" refers to the employee that is making decisions that others find unpredictable or beyond the scope of the person's responsibilities. This may be found when Scandinavians, from lowest-hierarchy cultures, are working for a North American manager. Perhaps more commonly, it is a term used by recent immigrant managers to describe their independent-minded local employees.

Here the issue is that the "loose cannon" is perceived as making too many independent decisions. He or she is seen to be making decisions on topics the manager feels the employee lacks either the expertise or the authority or both. The employee may be going over the manager's head to collect information or to get opinions or to promote his or her ideas. The manager may feel threatened and not in control of the employee. The employee can get the reputation of being a "loose cannon." The manager may grudgingly feel sometimes that he or she is working for the employee, rather than the other way around.

I was working at a high-tech company when I wrote an article on work relations across cultures. The article was about to be published when I learned that my company had a policy that prior to an employee's publishing an article it had to be reviewed by several layers of management. My direct manager was originally from the Middle East. He suggested that I rewrite the article to promote the great cross-cultural work environment of our company. That being in contradiction to my opinion of our workplace, I declined his advice. My manager pressed again, suggesting that the article could be much improved. Again, I stood my ground. From the perplexed and agitated look on his face, I knew that this was not the last I would hear about this. The next day I was transferred into a different department, based on a request from my manager.

—North American engineer at a high-tech company

The manager's sense of hierarchy had been offended. He could not fathom or tolerate that his subordinate would ignore his direction. It is interesting in this story that the issue at hand does not relate directly to the work group tasks or objectives. As is common in more hierarchical cultures, the span of a manager's authority over a subordinate is often broader than the mere work functions. Table 7.2 will help you determine if your new hire is more or less hierarchical than is the norm in your organization.

Solution

An important exercise for any employee and manager working together for the first time is to discuss the types of decisions they will be making, followed by clarification about who will be making which decisions. You might list all the decisions the employee and manager need to make on a regular basis and classify them in five categories:

- Decisions the manager makes on his or her own.
- Decisions the manager makes based on input from the employee.
- Decisions made jointly.
- Decisions the employee makes but first running the idea past the manager.
- Decisions the employee makes on his or her own.

If your new employee is more hierarchical in decision making and delegating than is the norm for you or in your organization, you could:

- Understand that simply telling the employee that you would like him or her to make more independent decisions will likely not yield good results.

Table 7.2 Comparison of Hierarchical and Egalitarian People on Decision Making and Delegation

Compared with egalitarian people, hierarchical people tend to:	Compared with hierarchical people, egalitarian people tend to:
■ Be obedient ■ Provide frequent updates to their managers ■ Ask more questions ■ Keep asking questions after egalitarian people consider that they have given sufficiently clear directions ■ Ask their managers to make decisions ■ Ask permission for small decisions, such as leaving early for lunch or taking office supplies from the supply room ■ Prefer closed-ended assignments ■ Prefer detailed instructions and will follow those instructions completely ■ Prioritize tasks and responsibilities based on the position and title of the delegating person ■ Report frequently to their managers and verify that their managers concur with their suggested direction ■ Rarely, if ever, disagree with their boss	■ Be empowered ■ Provide infrequent updates to their managers ■ Make decisions without consulting their managers ■ Stop asking questions and are ready to leave before hierarchical people consider that they have given sufficient direction ■ Prefer open-ended assignments ■ Prefer general instructions and the freedom to use one's own approach ■ Prioritize tasks and responsibilities based on urgency and importance ■ Take extensive initiative; make decisions and implement them without checking with their managers first ■ Feel relatively comfortable disagreeing with their boss

It is necessary to provide clear parameters within which you expect the employee to make decisions. Give examples.

■ Closely monitor and provide feedback as the employee adjusts to new decision-making rules.

■ Be quick with positive feedback when the employee has successfully taken on more responsibility or initiative.

■ Be patient with the employee if the early steps at taking on more initiative don't bring the results that you anticipated. There will be mistakes made along the way.

- Be quick with corrective feedback. Don't save it for the annual performance review.

I encourage my Mexican staff to take more initiative in making decisions rather than coming to me every time. On one occasion, we were hosting a large presentation. The fellow setting up the auditorium decided to use our small speakers, while I felt the size of the room and the audience was going to require large speakers. It turned out the small speakers were inadequate for the job. I tried to contain my frustration. Afterwards, the employee came to my office and apologized, admitting that he had made the wrong call. He said he learned something and would do it differently next time. I really appreciated that. He was learning to make decisions on his own.

—American administrator in Mexico

If your new employee is more egalitarian in decision making and delegating than is the norm for you and your organization, you could request that the employee report back to you with his or her progress and question more frequently than the individual may be accustomed to. Make sure that the employee is aware of why you are doing this and how this is the norm in your culture.

If your manager is more hierarchical than you are, you could:

- Get back to your manager more often to ensure alignment. Your manager expects more frequent reports than you may consider necessary.
- Check with your manager before taking new initiatives. In particular, check with him or her before starting a new endeavor.
- When your manager has made a decision, implement it.
- Quote experts in the field. Hierarchical people tend to respect the opinion of experts and follow their recommendations. A quote from an expert that your manager respects that supports your point is likely to have significant weight for a hierarchical manager.
- Request projects that are "off the beaten path" and not on your manager's critical path. Your manager is more likely to "cut you some slack" on such projects than on projects that are critical to his or her success.

If your manager is less hierarchical than you are, you could:

- Avoid asking open-ended questions of your manager. Your manager expects you to take the initiative and make suggestions. Asking your manager

"What do you think?," "How would you like me to do it?," or "What approach should I take?" is likely to irritate him or her, since he or she expects you to answer these questions for yourself.

- Do your homework before asking questions of your manager. Think of all the ways of achieving the objective you have been assigned, and rate the various options according to their pros and cons. Then ask your manager whether you are on the right track.
- Take initiative. Get involved in new task forces, new projects, and new initiatives—do not wait for your manager to suggest this to you.
- Find data. A nonhierarchical manager is less influenced by expert opinion; data has more weight with such a manager.
- Request projects that are really important to your manager. He or she is likely to provide you with more direction on such projects than on others.

Responsibilities

In hierarchical cultures, there is a much stronger sense of one's rank in society and people at certain levels do not perform tasks that are considered beneath them. In North America, CEOs of large organizations rarely sweep the floor, but they are expected to do whatever it takes to get the job done. We have found this difference in the distribution of responsibilities among the various levels of an organization and the more or less strict adherence to these job descriptions to cut across professions. Here are some examples that our clients have mentioned on various occasions.

An Egyptian pharmacy intern mentioned to his teacher at the end of his internship that, when he thought back on his internship, the event that stood in his mind was the fact that, on his second day on the job, he saw his teacher empty the paper-recycling box. The box was full, so every time the preceptor added paper to it, it fell on the floor. So he got up and emptied it in the larger recycling bin outside the store. The intern told his teacher that, in Egypt, the teacher would have asked someone (likely one of the lower-level staff members) to empty the recycling box for him.

—Canadian pharmacy teacher

We had a German engineering student work in our plant as part of his studies. At one point, we needed to do an inventory of the warehouse. It had to be done quickly, so everybody, from plant manager down, was asked to come in over the weekend to help. When we asked this German student when he would be coming in, he answered that he did not do inventory. We sent him back to his university shortly after that.

—American engineer

We experienced a bit of a challenge with one of our Filipino seniors. Every time he needed copies, he brought the documents to the receptionist and asked her to make copies for him. Initially, she did it without any problem because she was not really busy at that time. He kept asking her to make copies, even at times when she was clearly busy with clients on the phone and in the reception area. I sat him down and discussed the situation with him. When I told him that making copies was not part of Maggie's job, he asked who was responsible for that. I told him that we all make our own copies. He was silent for a while then answered that, in the Manila office, they have a whole department of people who make copies for everyone. He never made copies before and had no idea how to use the photocopier.

—American accountant

I studied finance in the United States and decided to stay there at the end of my studies. I got a job in one of the banks and worked my way up there. I went back to India for a vacation and visited my father in his office. We talked about some legal documents I needed and I realized I needed copies. I got up and started to walk toward the nearest photocopy machine when my Dad said, "Usha, give this document to me. You and I don't make copies—I will have one of the staff members copy this document for us." I sat down, surprised at how much I had forgotten about the way things work in India.

—Indian finance specialist working in the United States

In North America, tasks generally correspond to specific levels in organizations; for example, a pharmacist is expected to counsel patients, whereas a pharmacy technician is expected to count the pills needed by the patient. However, this split of responsibilities is usually not a hard-and-fast split; it will change based on circumstances. For example, when the pharmacy is really busy, it is expected that pharmacists count pills rather than wait until technicians have completed that task. Understanding when employees are expected to go beyond the tasks that they typically take care of is essential for the success of every recent immigrant.

Here in Mexico, people outside of the professional class are expected to be clearly told what to do, and they will do it with conviction. If a person has six primary tasks, it would take quite a calamity to get that person to make an exception to do something beyond those assigned tasks, whatever the emergency.

—North American businessperson in Mexico

By contrast, employees who have a lower sense of hierarchy than their colleagues will often be perceived as intruding into the work of the people below and above them in the organization. In unionized environments, this often results in grievances, since they may be perceived as threatening the employment of the people below them. They may also be perceived as insubordinate when they start taking on some of the responsibilities of their managers (see Chapter 9 for more details on this point).

Solution

If your employee is more hierarchical than you are in this respect, you could:

- Explain what is expected of him or her in normal circumstances and what is expected of him or her in unusual circumstances.
- Lead by example. As the Egyptian intern case indicates, this usually registers deeply in the minds of new immigrants.
- When you do something that is not part of your usual responsibilities, explain why you are doing it, so your employee does not perceive you as "dropping a level."

If your employee is less hierarchical than you are in this respect, you could:

- Explain to him or her the impact on others of his or her approach.
- Lead by example. Show how to delegate tasks that the employee would take on him- or herself when other people are expected to take care of these tasks.

Compensation

In most countries and organizations, managers earn more than their subordinates. In hierarchical cultures, this statement goes without saying. However, in more egalitarian cultures, there are exceptions. For example, a senior technical person in a technical industry may choose to pursue technical excellence and have no interest in managing people. If the company values that technical expertise, they may be happy to pay this individual more than a manager. (See Table 7.3.)

One measure of a nation's inequality is the comparison of the difference in income between the poorest 20 percent and the richest 20 percent of the population. Consistent with our hierarchy chart, Denmark, Sweden, Norway, and Finland have among the most equally distributed incomes.[2]

Canada and the United States appear as having a slightly lower hierarchy level than the average of other countries in the world. The initial reaction of a professional new to North America from a more hierarchical culture may be one of shock to learn that a person more junior is earning as much or more money than he or she. This may be viewed as disrespectful and completely inappropriate.

Solution

The solution here is simply to explain the situation and set expectations. Give the reasons and the scenarios when a subordinate may earn more than a manager. It does not mean that the manager is respected or valued any less.

Performance Evaluation

Who is in the best position to judge an employee's performance? The employee's manager may be the most obvious answer. In more hierarchical cultures, it is

Table 7.3 Comparison of Hierarchical and Egalitarian People on Compensation

Compared with egalitarian people, hierarchical people tend to:	Compared with hierarchical people, egalitarian people tend to:
■ Consider inconceivable the idea that people might earn more money than their managers ■ Expect that senior people will earn considerably more money than junior people	■ Experience situations where they earn more than their managers ■ Believe that the compensation of senior and junior people should not be too different and should be based on how these skills are valued

[2]http://en.wikipedia.org/wiki/List_of_countries_by_income_equality

assumed that the direct manager is the best person; and possibly the manager's manager will also be involved. One's place in the organizational universe is made or broken by the immediate boss. The importance of pleasing this person cannot be overstated.

In more egalitarian organizations, employees are encouraged to and primarily rewarded for helping to achieve the organization's objectives. These organizations are more likely to involve coworkers and even subordinates in an employee's evaluation. It is recognized that working well with all levels contributes to the organization's meeting its objectives. In this scenario, the manager, though still important, is not the sole focus of the employee. (See Table 7.4.)

Table 7.4 Comparison of Hierarchical and Egalitarian People on Performance Evaluation

Compared with egalitarian people, hierarchical people tend to:	Compared with hierarchical people, egalitarian people tend to:
■ Avoid evaluating the performance of their managers—360° feedback is difficult to use; managers do not accept the idea that employees can evaluate their performance; employees generally rate their managers as excellent in every area ■ Avoid writing the first draft of their own performance evaluations—only managers are considered qualified to evaluate their performance	■ Participate in the evaluation of the performance of people below, above, and on the side ■ Write the first draft of their own performance appraisal

A major accounting firm tried to implement 360° feedback in their Middle East office. On the first go-round no one evaluated their manager. When questioned about it, employees claimed that they considered themselves incompetent to evaluate their own managers. They also possibly didn't want their managers to know what they really thought of their superiors. Human resources mandated that everyone complete the feedback. On the second go-round all managers received excellent reviews on all criteria. Employees couldn't see how to rate their managers negatively without showing disrespect and causing loss of face. Also, they were concerned that if they gave a poor rating to their manager, it would come back to haunt them. The staff was not convinced of the confidentiality of the process.

A similar breakdown occurred when a group of Russian engineers was asked to create the first draft of their own performance appraisal. They also felt that they were incompetent to evaluate themselves.

Those from hierarchical cultures may find it tremendously uncomfortable to be asked to evaluate the manager or to have a subordinate evaluate them. For them, it flies in the face of everything that the manager/employee relationship represents. To give negative feedback to one's boss is contrary to everything they have been taught about showing respect.

Solution

To help a newcomer use your performance evaluation system:

- Provide clear instructions and training on performance evaluation practices. Model and practice with them.
- Explain the rationale and perceived benefits of the system.
- Closely monitor progress, and provide support in using evaluations properly.
- Consider ways of easing the staff into this process—perhaps by using a more simplified but specific set of questions.
- Provide sample evaluations to help culturally different employees new to your organization understand what is expected of them.

Other Hierarchy Issues

A number of other workplace differences may show up in manager/employee relations that relate to hierarchy. Some examples are presented in Table 7.5.

Another important difference between hierarchical and egalitarian managers is that hierarchical managers will rarely say things like "I don't know," "You figure it out," "It depends," or "It is up to you" in response to a question asked by their employees. In hierarchical cultures, managers are expected to know and will provide specific answers to most questions asked by employees. By contrast, North American managers will often give this kind of answer in response to queries from their employees.

Hierarchical managers and employees alike cringe when they hear egalitarian managers answer in this manner. In their minds, these managers are clearly not good managers, while egalitarian managers consider themselves good managers when they answer in this manner, since they offer their employees freedom and room for creativity.

Table 7.5 Comparison of Hierarchical and Egalitarian People on Distribution Lists, E-mail History, Problem Solving, and Influence

	Compared with egalitarian people, hierarchical people tend to:	Compared with hierarchical people, egalitarian people tend to:
Distribution lists	■ List people in decreasing hierarchical order	■ List people in alphabetical order or randomly
E-mail history	■ Keep old e-mail messages, primarily to protect their own interests or to allocate blame appropriately	■ Keep old e-mail primarily for reference to assist in future projects
Problems	■ Focus more on finding why the problem exists and who created it than on solving it and on preventing it from occurring again ■ Place significant importance on finding who created the problem (blame)	■ Focus more on solving the problem and preventing it from occurring again than on understanding who is responsible for creating the problem ■ Gloss over personal responsibilities in the creation of a problem
Influence others	■ Quote senior people in the organization ■ Quote famous people, articles, and books ■ Refer to the title and/or position of people in conversations (name-dropping) ■ Refer to company policies	■ Follow the example of successful project leaders ■ Refer to personal past experience ■ Not mention the title and/or position of people in conversations ■ Promote the idea that makes the most sense to them

Solution

- Be aware of possible differences, and help others to understand those differences.
- Point out to newcomers the norms in your company and industry.

If your employees are more hierarchi cal than you are, you may:

- Explain how you see the situation. If the answer is "it depends," describe the factors on which your answer depends. If the answer is "it does not make much difference," explain this point.
- Tell your employees that you plan to make them think, because you want them to learn to solve these problems on their own.
- Explain that you could work out the solution but that it is not your role to do so—your role is to coordinate their activities with the activities of other people in the organization.
- Use role-playing as a way to teach your employees some skills (particularly soft skills). When you do, warn them ahead of time that you will use role-playing as a teaching method; for many people coming from hierarchical people (particularly East Asia), role-playing is quite threatening since there is a good chance they will not act in the best possible manner and may therefore lose face.

If your employees are less hierarchical than you are, you may:

- Explain that you are giving them specific answers because you have a specific idea in mind and want them to do a task in this manner.
- Explain your reasons for doing it this way rather than giving them leeway to try and figure it out their own way. Expect some reluctance at times.

Client–Professional Service Provider Relations

When service professionals, such as accountants, lawyers, engineers, and information technology specialists, communicate with their client organization, at what level do they communicate? Do people communicate only with others of a similar level in the hierarchy of the client organization?

Communication Between Layers

In more egalitarian cultures, people are more likely to communicate across levels when it best serves the needs of the project at hand. Hierarchical cultures are more likely to communicate only up one level and down one level in their own organization and directly across in the client organization. This communication process is presented in Figure 7.4.

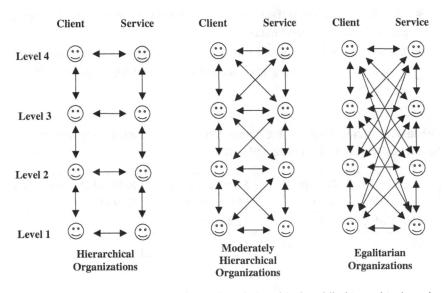

Figure 7.4 Communication channels in hierarchical, mildly hierarchical, and egalitarian organizations.

Providing Good Service

The relative position of professional service providers (such as accountants, medical doctors, pharmacists, and engineers), their managers, and their clients is not the same in hierarchical cultures and in North America.

- In North America, the client is on top, the manager is in the middle, and the professional service provider is at the bottom.
- In hierarchical cultures, the manager is on top, the professional service provider is in the middle, and the client is at the bottom.

In other words, the relationship between professional service providers and their clients is quite different. This difference comes from the difference in relative position these people have in hierarchical societies relative to North America. The best way to understand this point is through Table 7.6. The figures presented in the table are approximate. Exact figures are not needed to illustrate the general trend. Though India and the United State are used in this table to illustrate the point we want to make, similar points can be made by comparing virtually any developed country with any developing country.

- The GDP per capita is used here as an approximation of what the average person in that country makes.
- The starting salary is based on the average salary of recent graduates in large organizations; they are rounded to exact multiples of the GDP, for simplicity.

Table 7.6 Comparison of the Gross Domestic Product (GDP) and Starting Salaries of Professionals in India and in the United States

	GDP per capita	Starting salary of professionals	Ratio of starting salary to GDP
United States	$30K per year	$60K per year	2×
India	$700 per year	$14K per year	20×

These figures demonstrate the following:

- For the price of one professional in the United States, an organization can hire six professionals in India. These six professionals have learned virtually the same material, from the same books, from professors who graduated from the same universities. This is a strong motivator for offshoring.
- A professional can earn several times more in the United States than in India for the same kind of work. This is a clear incentive to immigrate to the United States or any developing country.
- The ratio between the starting salary of professionals and the average salary of people in the country is 10 times higher in India than in the United States. This means that the position of professionals in Indian society is much higher in India than it is in the United States. In India,

an accountant, pharmacist, engineer, medical doctor, etc. can afford to have many staff people taking care of his or her family. Most professional Indians have at least one full-time staff member, often two or three. Compare this situation to that of most North Americans, who rarely have house help. To understand the social position of Indian professionals in Indian society, imagine the situation where the average starting salary in your profession was $600K per year. Would people in your profession have a somewhat superior attitude toward the general population?

This explains the major difference that exists in the relationships between professional service providers in hierarchical cultures and in North America:

- In hierarchical cultures, clients are thankful that professional service providers help them. Professional service providers are expected to analyze the situation of their clients in detail and then to tell their clients what to do in their particular situations.
- In North America, professional service providers are thankful to their clients for buying the services they need from them. Professional service providers are expected to offer choices to their clients and to let them decide what is best in their situations.

When hierarchical service providers come to North America, their approach to client relationship management often creates major challenges, as the following anecdotes illustrate.

I was the teacher of a Korean pharmacy intern. One of the patients came to her to renew his prescriptions; he was late by a month. She and I went to talk to this patient. She started the conversation by saying, in a very negative tone of voice, "You are late!" I saw the client's face start to change and I immediately jumped in: "I am sorry; we do not mean to put you on the spot. We are concerned for your health. Taking this medication regularly is important, and what we are trying to say is that it is important for you to renew your prescription on time so that there is no lapse in your use of this medication." I had to do some serious damage control. After the client left, I had an extensive conversation with my Korean intern. She had difficulties understanding why she could not tell this patient that he was late in renewing his prescription, since he obviously was!

—American pharmacist

I own four pharmacies that are open 24/7, so I need a lot of staff, and I found it difficult to find people for the night shift. So I was glad when a Romanian pharmacist who recently obtained his license agreed to staff the night shift. Unfortunately, I am now caught between a rock and a hard place. I don't know if it is better to have him there or not to have anyone. Every morning or so, I find some complaint, either from one of the technicians or one of the customers, stating the pharmacist was quite disrespectful toward them. One client wrote that the pharmacist told him when he was supposed to take his medication, that the times really did not fit his schedule since he was working night shifts, and that the pharmacist told him: "It is really important that you take these medications at the times I told you to." Then he went on with the side effects. I had a chat with him and asked him to thank customers for coming to our store for service. He looked at me strangely and answered, "Why should I thank them? They should thank me! I am solving their problem."

—American pharmacist

Solution

To help culturally different employees learn how to serve North American clients as they want to be served, you may consider:

- Having them shadow people who have good client-relationship-management skills.
- Providing training in this area; the most effective training programs include simulations where service providers interact with people who behave like clients (these people might be coworkers or trained actors, depending on the situation).
- Coaching them extensively.

Once again, we cannot assume, simply because someone is a recent immigrant, that he or she will be more hierarchical in his or her beliefs and behaviors. As the country-ranking hierarchy chart of Figure 7.1 shows, the national tendencies of Australia, Israel, Denmark, and New Zealand, to name a few, are to be more egalitarian than Canada and the United States. Also, there are individual and regional differences within all countries.

Probation Period

Hierarchy differences between managers and employees often play havoc during the probation period of culturally different employees, because they usually work very closely with their managers during this period of time. If they do not show enough initiative, they often lose their positions at the end of their probation period. One of the most common challenges experienced by managers of recent immigrant employees during the probation period is the situation where managers delegate tasks or responsibilities to their employees without giving them enough instructions (by their employees' standards) to complete the task.

For example, imagine the situation where a manager needs a picture of a horse and simply says to the employee, "Draw me a horse." If the manager has a bit more of an idea of what he or she wants, the manager might say, "Here is a sketch of a horse; go complete it." Hierarchical employees are used to being delegated tasks through paint-by-number pictures: "Here is a paint-by-number picture of a horse; go fill it." When employees are used to paint-by-number pictures and they hear, "Draw me a horse," a zillion questions come to their minds. "What kind of horse? A plow horse or a racehorse? Male or female? Black or white? How big should the picture be? How big should the horse be in the picture? Should the whole horse be in the picture or just the head? Should it be front, side, or back? Should the horse be eating, drinking, walking, running? What kind of background? What kind of foreground?" And so on.

In this case, employees often react in one of three ways:

- They are overwhelmed by the task and completely paralyzed.
- They try to think of all the possible ways in which they could complete the task and then do them. For example, they will prepare every picture of a horse they can think of so that their manager can choose. When managers see that, they may react by thinking something like "What an incredible waste of time! These employees cannot make any decision on their own."
- The most common reaction consists of going back to their manager and asking all the questions on their mind. When they do, their manager usually answers something like "I don't know—you figure it out." Culturally different employees often interpret this statement as a test; since managers always know in hierarchical cultures, they assume this means their manager is testing them. In that case, they usually observe their manager to gather clues as to what the manager really wants. For example, they will try to see if their manager leans more toward a male horse or a female horse. If the manager makes an off-the-cuff remark like "Maybe a female horse," then they think that this is what their manager wants and they work on drawing a female horse.

In practice, managers have given it no thought, and they expect employees to come up with these answers. If it becomes clear during the time it takes them to draw the horse that a male horse is needed, they will still do the drawing of a female horse because, in their minds, this is what their manager wants. So when they present their female horse picture to their manager, the conversation goes along the following lines:

> Manager: *But we need a picture of a male horse here.*
> Employee: *You told me you wanted a female horse, so I drew a female horse.*
> Manager: *I never asked for a picture of a female horse.*
> Employee: *You certainly did.*

None of these reactions is likely to help employees get through the probation period. Over time, employees often ask questions of their managers but get no responses to these questions. In the mind of the manager, it is the employee's responsibility to find the answers to these questions. In the minds of the employee, it is the responsibility of the manager to provide the answers to these questions. As a result, both feel the other is incompetent. Culturally different employees who are on probation often are let go at the end. Many recent immigrants go from probation period to probation period or short-term contract to short-term contract specifically for this reason, i.e., their idea of what being a good employee means is very different from their manager's idea of what being a good employee means.

North Americans managers usually have little patience for questions that clearly demonstrate that the person asking the question has not researched the issue. For example, any question that can be answered by entering a keyword in a web search engine or by looking at the company's website will make the person asking this question look like he or she is unprofessional. They also do not like being asked an open-ended question like "What should I do?" or "What do you want me to do?" As many North American managers will say, "Don't come to me with problems, come to me with solutions." At the same time, they do not want their employees to waste time floundering by trying to answer questions that have already been answered ("reinventing the wheel"), by becoming paralyzed, or by going in the wrong direction.

Solution

Because being considered as lacking initiative is a major problem in North America, the responsibility of adaptation in this area falls primarily on the shoulders of culturally different employees—their careers will be impacted very negatively if they do not learn this. The approach that seems to yield the best results consists of coaching culturally different employees in the following manner.

- When managers delegate a task or a project to them, managers and employees discuss the amount of time this task or project is expected to take. During this initial meeting, hierarchical employees are tempted to ask many questions in order to get a good sense of what their managers want; this is usually not the best time for so many questions. The best approach is to ask a few questions and then leave.
- Employees set aside 5 percent of the total time allocated to this task or project to gather information and to create a plan. This plan may contain options—there may be slightly different ways to complete parts of this task or project. This preparation phase ends when 5 percent of the time has been used—for a one-week project, 5 percent represents a couple of hours.
- Employees then meet with their managers and review the plans they created. They will tell their managers: "Here is how I plan to proceed. I am not 100 percent sure of these points. I can think of three ways of doing this part—A, B, and C. I think A is best for XYZ reason. What do you think? Am I missing anything?" The key here is that employees are giving to their managers the implicit message that, in the absence of input from their managers, they have a plan that will get them to their goals. It may not be the most elegant, the quickest, or the easiest solution, but it is likely to work.

By using this approach, culturally different employees can be seen as "doing their homework," i.e., doing all the work they can possibly do on their own in a reasonable amount of time and presenting options and solutions to their managers, rather than problems.

Cross-Cultural Feedback

This section examines how cultural differences related to feedback can create major challenges for culturally different employees and their managers. We have found that giving feedback to and receiving feedback from culturally different colleagues the way it was meant to be given or received is one of the biggest challenges faced by recent immigrants, particularly when they have arrived recently in North America. In many cases, they are given feedback in ways that are very different from what they are used to and have virtually no idea of whether they are doing well, okay, or not well at all. Here is one example.

> I had been working in the Canadian company for two months and the only feedback I received was that I was doing fine. I wanted to hear which parts of my job could be improved, which parts I could do better, but I never received that kind of detail. It was as if the Canadians were trying to protect my feelings or something. I found it very unhelpful.
>
> —Australian professional in Canada

The way people provide feedback to one another is quite different in different countries, as another example demonstrates.

> During one of our meetings, there were four Italian plant engineers and technicians and three Canadian engineers in the office of the plant manager. The plant manager proceeded to give feedback to his people. He did it all in Italian, but you did not really need subtitles. He was taking them one by one, telling them how bad a job they were doing, using all kinds of names of rare birds and dragging them through the mud. This went on for about half an hour; then we all went for lunch together.
>
> —Canadian engineer working in Italy

Cross-cultural collaboration is complicated by the fact that feedback is not provided in the same manner in all countries. For example, North American listeners often interpret comments made by their Polish teammates as harsh criticism when, in fact, they were intended to be only slightly negative. Figure 7.5 presents a schematic description of the dynamics that lead to feedback misinterpretation.

Feedback Within a Single Cultural Context

As shown in Figure 7.5, the range of possible feedback can be represented along an axis in the following manner:

- The left side of the axis, marked "Unacceptable," corresponds to feedback of unacceptable performance. A manager commenting to a subordinate that his or her performance falls in this area would in essence be giving him or her notice that some very fast and significant corrective action is needed.

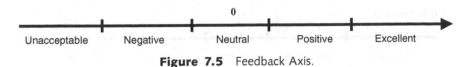

Figure 7.5 Feedback Axis.

- The area between the first and second marks, in the range marked "Negative," corresponds to negative feedback. A manager commenting to a subordinate that his or her performance falls in this area expects corrective action from his or her subordinate.
- The next range, marked "Neutral," corresponds to the neutral zone, where feedback falls when it is neither positive nor negative.
- The next range, marked "Positive," corresponds to positive feedback.
- The range on the far right, marked "Excellent," corresponds to feedback for outstanding performance.

When feedback is given and received by people of similar cultural backgrounds, the interpretation of feedback is relatively straightforward, since both giver and receiver interpret feedback using similar scales. As always, there are differences between people within each culture: Some people are more sensitive to feedback than others. On average, however, most people are able to evaluate how much of a reaction they should expect from their managers for a given type of mistake.

Feedback Within a Multicultural Context

Misunderstandings often arise when giver and receiver do not have the same cultural background. Different cultures have different scales for interpreting feedback. This situation is schematically represented in Figure 7.6 for the case of North America and Poland. On average, people from the Middle East, Eastern Europe, Israel, Germany, the Netherlands, Belgium, France, and Italy tend to be less sensitive to feedback than North Americans. As this figure implies, a comment intended to be neutral by a Pole may already be in the negative or positive range of a North American listener, prompting him or her to react in an unintended manner. Conversely, a Pole may not interpret feedback from a North American properly if this feedback is mildly negative or positive, since it may still be in the Polish neutral range.

   In the context of teams, this difference of interpretation of feedback can wreak havoc on a project. Most people make a comment that straddles the line

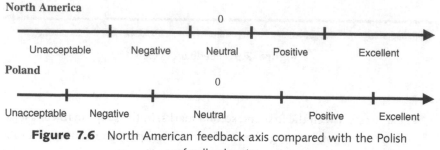

Figure 7.6   North American feedback axis compared with the Polish feedback axis.

between negative and neutral when they want to give negative feedback to their teammates. A mild negative criticism made by a Pole may be interpreted as very negative by the Americans. As a result, indirect comments often miss their mark, since they are not evaluated based on the proper context.

There are differences in this respect between Americans and Canadians. Americans often will give feedback more quickly and more directly than Canadians. Americans will clearly and precisely lay out problem areas. If Canadians are on the receiving end of this feedback, they may feel that Americans are overreacting or coming on too strong. Americans may be confused by the more subtle feedback given by Canadians. They may fail to see where the problem lies and then accuse the Canadians of being wishy-washy. Here is an example that illustrates this difference.

> I work in the career center of the School of Management of a Canadian university and I report to a Canadian woman. On several occasions, she came to my office, closed my door, and started to talk to me about things that seemed inconsequential to me—as if she was talking about the weather. I typically ignored her comments since they did not seem to amount to anything, but it often came back and haunted me later on. Eventually, I realized that, when she closed the door, this meant that she was giving me negative feedback and I had to make sure that I understood what the problem was before she left.
>
> —American working in Canada

Note that in other cases (China and Mexico in particular), the relative positions of the two axes are reversed, as shown in Figure 7.7: While North Americans have a narrower neutral zone than Poles, their neutral zone is wider than the Chinese/Mexican neutral zone. On average, people who come from Latin America or East Asia tend to be more sensitive to feedback than North Americans.

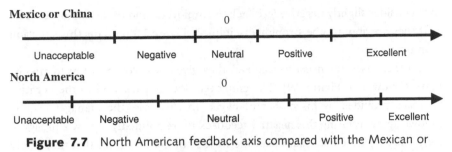

Figure 7.7 North American feedback axis compared with the Mexican or Chinese feedback axis.

In this case, mild criticisms or jokes made by North Americans may be taken very seriously by Mexicans or Chinese, more seriously than they were intended. Conversely, comments made by Mexicans or Chinese may not elicit any reaction from North Americans, contrary to their authors' expectations. Here are two situations that illustrate this point.

> I was really surprised when one of my Mexican employees gave me his resignation. I gave him slightly negative feedback during a meeting and moved on. To me, it was no big deal and I thought everything was fine. The way I said it made it almost like a joke. Clearly, it was a big deal to him. Our HR manager told me later that I had offended him gravely by giving this feedback in a meeting, and he felt he had no choice but to resign since he thought I would fire him next. That idea never crossed my mind.
>
> —American plant manager in Mexico

> I had a really difficult time with one of my Chinese employees. On one occasion, I gave her negative feedback, and she was in tears at the end of the discussion. So the next time I had to give her negative feedback, I was really careful and said it very, very softly. She still ended up crying at the end of the conversation. I had to ask one of my female supervisors to give her feedback on my behalf so that she would find words that would not make her break down while still giving her the message that I wanted her to change her behavior.
>
> —Canadian manager

Dealing with Performance Issues

When managers and employees come from different cultural backgrounds, dealing with performance issues can be quite tricky. In some cases, the negative feedback they give to employees appears to blow up in their face: They give what they consider slightly negative feedback to employees, and these employees react as if they are about to be strongly disciplined. Figure 7.8 presents this situation graphically.

In other cases, the negative feedback they give to employees seems to miss its mark (arrow 1 in Figure 7.9). The employee does not respond to the negative feedback provided by his or her manager. In this case, the manager usually follows up by restating this negative feedback more pointedly (arrow 2 in Figure 7.9). The employee may again hear the words but not recognize that they imply that his or her manager wants him or her to change his or her behavior. If there is still no change, the manager might say it again; this time, the feedback is quite negative (arrow 3 in Figure 7.9).

In this situation, the manager is starting to lose patience ("Three strikes and you're out"). To the employee, this negative feedback is like lightning in a blue sky ("Why is my manager so upset with me? This is news to me!"). The manager often interprets this situation to mean that the employee does not want to change his or her behavior. The reality is that the employee does not know that he or she needs to change behavior.

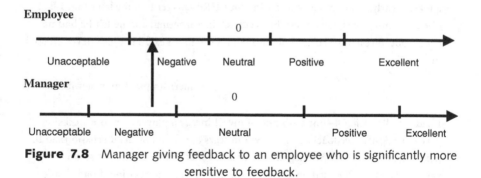

Figure 7.8 Manager giving feedback to an employee who is significantly more sensitive to feedback.

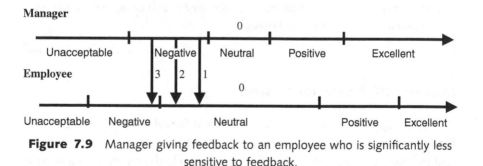

Figure 7.9 Manager giving feedback to an employee who is significantly less sensitive to feedback.

I almost got myself fired because I did not understand the feedback that my manager was giving me. It was worded so softly that I totally missed the point. In France, when you want to tell people not to walk on a patch of grass, you put a sign that says, "It is strictly forbidden to walk on the grass." In Canada, they put a sign that says, "Please keep off grass." To me, "Please keep off grass" means that I have a choice; yet the message is actually the same as when French people say, "It is strictly forbidden to walk on the grass." By the time I realized my manager was not happy with my behavior, he was ready to write me up.

—French engineer in Canada

The issue of giving and receiving feedback the way it was meant is compounded by the "feedback sandwich" approach commonly used in many North American organizations. Managers tend to give negative feedback using the pattern shown in Figure 7.10.

Position 1: A change in behavior is expected, but it is not a serious situation. Here, the North American manager will usually use the "feedback sandwich" approach. This starts with some positive comments (the first slice of bread), followed by negative comments (the "meat" of the sandwich), and ends with positive comments (the other slice of bread). This approach confuses some immigrants, who leave the meeting wondering what they should remember from this session. In their home countries, they received either positive feedback or negative feedback but never both in the same conversation. In such a situation, they need to remember that the key message is the negative feedback: You need to change your behavior, but it is not a big deal yet.

Position 2: This is more of a problem than in position 1, but it is still not a major problem. In this situation, you get an open-faced sandwich. North American managers will go directly into the negative feedback, but they still end on a positive note. When this happens, it means that the problem

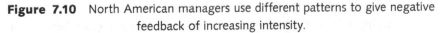

Figure 7.10 North American managers use different patterns to give negative feedback of increasing intensity.

mentioned is a real problem that requires prompt attention. To interpret this accurately in a North American setting, culturally different employees need to focus on the negative feedback and ignore the positive comments.

Position 3: This is a major problem. In this situation, North American managers only talk about the negative. There is no bread left. This usually means that managers have already mentioned this problem before and are starting to lose patience. If this is the first time they mention this problem, it clearly was a significant mistake in their minds. Either way, employees need to make a quick change in their behavior.

Position 4: The absence of strong corrective action will have major negative consequences. Here, managers are giving employees a double serving of meat. Whereas in position 1 they talk about inaccuracies, here they talk about blunders. They also use a much sterner tone of voice. This is really negative; the absence of very strong corrective action will likely lead to strong disciplinary action, such as putting employees on performance-improvement plans or terminating them.

Solution

Here are some suggestions that managers and employees who come from different cultural backgrounds may find useful when they work together.

- Refer to this text when discussing feedback with managers or employees. In particular, ask them to place their comments on the negative-feedback scale ("Is it a 1, 2, 3, or 4?") as a way to ensure that you understand how severe the problem is.
- Employees need to verify with their coach, buddy, or counselor whether their interpretation of the feedback provided by their managers is accurate and whether the action plan they have drafted will address sufficiently the issues described by their managers.
- When providing feedback to culturally different employees, managers should probably start from the same point as they usually would if their employees came from the same cultural backgrounds as theirs.
  - □ If they notice that their employees are not reacting to this feedback, this probably means that they are less sensitive to feedback. In that case, managers may want to restate their feedback more strongly, without taking the lack of reaction personally—employees are not trying to be difficult, they just did not get it. Managers can then escalate

the feedback until it registers and make a mental note of how negatively they need to state their feedback for their employees to register this feedback so that they can get to this point more quickly next time.

☐ If they notice that their employees react more strongly to this feedback than intended, they may want to state their feedback less strongly next time, until they find the right level.

Summary

Manager/employee relations can succeed only when the employee understands the expectations of the manager and is able to fulfill them. For newcomers that means making many adjustments in how they interact with their North American boss. The manager similarly must understand the employee and assist him or her to adjust to the corporate and national norms.

The goal of learning different cultural approaches to recruitment and retention topics is not so that we can always do things in the style of the other person. In most cases, it will be the corporate norms and the national environment that determine the appropriate standards. At the same time, by understanding the preferred or ingrained cultural approach of our coworker, we have a starting point for coaching and training. Making small adjustments to help the other person feel more comfortable can provide a good starting point.

As we have discussed, respect for position, ranking, making decisions and delegating, compensation, promotion process, and performance evaluation are all heavily affected by a culture's sense of hierarchy. Ideas for working with others who are different have been included in their respective sections.

8

Retention—Part 2: Teamwork

Being a "good team player" consistently ranks as one of the most important skills employers around the world look for in candidates. While there is consensus on the need to be "good team players," people coming from different cultural backgrounds often have very different ideas of what that means. Most people learn how to operate within teams by osmosis; few take courses on that topic. As a result, major issues often arise when culturally different people work together on the same team, because they assume that all teams operate according to the set of unwritten rules with which they are familiar. When team members come from different cultural backgrounds, this implicit assumption often leads to team breakdowns. This chapter examines some of the dynamics that may lead to such breakdowns.

This chapter also explores two key value differences that impact teamwork. The first and most prominent is a culture's and a person's sense of *individualism*. The second is their *risk orientation*. It concludes by examining the incompatibilities, the points of tension they create, and how people with differing views of teamwork might come to understand each other better and work together more effectively.

> In my first week of work I saw Americans eating food at their desks and at times eating food in front of me without offering any to me or other coworkers. I tried not to let this bother me. One day I offered some of my food to a couple of nearby coworkers to try to get them into the spirit of sharing. They turned down my offer politely and commented that it was my lunch and I should eat it. After I got over my shock, I realized that they weren't being rude; they were just following some very different social rules.
>
> —Asian in North American office

Individualism

One of the most striking differences related to teamwork is a culture's sense of how individualistically employees should behave or how much they should identify with their group. These two approaches are often incompatible. Whether greater prominence is placed on the individual or on the group can be a source of confusion and animosity among people trying to work together.

Individualism measures the importance a person assigns to his or her interests as an individual, as compared to those of the group to which he or she belongs. An individualistic society is one in which the interests of the individual are considered more important than those of the group and in which people are recognized by personal identities rather than by group characteristics. Adult members of this type of society are expected to be independent and are not encouraged to rely on a group.

An underlying belief of the individualist is that if people take care of themselves or their roles, then the larger group or organization will succeed. People ideally achieve alone and assume personal responsibility. Individual initiative is highly valued.

Canadians and Americans are among the most individualistic people in the world, as indicated in upcoming Figure 8.1. North Americans are more likely to move out of their parents' home to live on their own in early adulthood, choose a career based on personal interests, and feel they are responsible for their own career advancement. They more likely live by the motto "My life is what I make of it."

A group-oriented society considers the group to which a person belongs to be a vital part of his or her identity. Group loyalty is strong, and individuals contribute financially, practically, and psychologically to their parents, clan, or organization in exchange for protection, advice, and support. Identifying with a group means that the needs of the group either take precedence over individual needs or at least are seriously taken into consideration when a group member makes a decision. Some workplace and nonworkplace examples include the following.

- Mexicans typically take vacation all together, as a family. Several siblings, their spouses, their children, and their common parents will all go on vacation together. It is often difficult to reschedule such vacations because they involve so many people. When the VP of HR of the Mexican subsidiary of a multinational company was asked by the American head office to organize a visit for the CEO, he responded that he would organize it but would not be around to do the honors for the CEO, because he had already scheduled a vacation with his family at that time. He lost a significant exposure opportunity thereby.

- In North America, Somalis want to live near other members of their clan. They would rather live in the part of the city where other Somalis live and commute long distances than live in a house that might be near their work or other conveniences.

- An Ugandan couple living in Toronto mentioned that their relatives—first cousins, aunts, uncles, siblings, third cousins—in Uganda ask them at least once a month to send money to help them with a variety of problems (pay for the education of one child, repair a leaky roof, etc.). In virtually all cases, they send the money as requested, because not doing so would create major family issues.

- In Bhutan, the electoral system gives one vote to each family, not to each person.

- Menus in North America have many choices for one person. In France it is common to have choices for two people. One Mexican fast-food chain offers a deal for four, whereby a party of four can get a significant discount if all four order the same burger and the same two sides (contrast this North American fast-food companies, which encourage people to have their own). In China, groups of 8, 10, or 12 are common. Collective cultures are more likely to order together a variety of food and then share it among themselves. For example, Chinese people order food for the whole group and place it on a rotating tray in the center of the table; in that case, there is no such thing as "my dish"—everything is "our food."

- Popular beer commercials in North America often show a guy in his early 20s enjoying a beer by himself. For example, a young man climbs a mountain solo and can be seen sipping a beer at the top. In Asia, the message is likely to be misinterpreted as meaning that the guy is a loser who has no friends and is therefor drinking to forget how bad his life is. Advertising is often interpreted quite differently in collective cultures.

- On average, people from individualistic cultures invite fewer people to their wedding. Collective cultures, with strong extended family and friend relationships, will typically need and want to invite a very large number of people. If the average wedding size in the United States is 50 people, it is 300 in Italy and often exceeds 2,000 in India (Indian middle-class weddings usually have between 2,000 and 5,000 guests and last between 4 and

7 days). Indian employees will usually invite all the employees of the department or company they work for, regardless of the extent to which they collaborate, because they feel a sense of connection.

- Japanese hardly ever criticize the decisions made by their company. They will do what is in the best interest of their employer, even if that is, at times, against their own immediate best interest. If the company requires them to go overseas, they will go. This may now be slowly changing, though the tendency to a collective orientation remains strong.

I arrived in Canada in early January for a three-year assignment. It was really difficult for me, because I arrived at the beginning of the busy season—for several months, like all auditors, I did nothing but work. One month later, I received a call from my family saying that my mother had died in a car accident. I decided to stay and help my colleagues get through this busy season. I went back to Japan in August to pay my respects to my mother at a time when it did not inconvenience my teammates.

—Japanese auditor in Canada

The group with which people identify often depends on the country. Generally, Mexicans identify with their family (which North Americans call "extended family") and friends, while Japanese identify with their company, particularly those who work for one of the large corporations (e.g., Sony, Honda, Toyota) and Somalis identify with their clan.

It should be noted, however, that there seems to be a global trend moving away from group identity in non-Western societies. In Japan, for example, employee identification with the large corporations is weakening somewhat. In *Culture's Consequences*, Hofstede correlates individualism with national wealth: As nations become richer, the sense of individualism tends to increase. This does not imply that all developed nations are equally individualistic; among the G7 group of nations, Japan and the United States hold quite different views in this area, as Figure 8.1 indicates.

Individualism National Comparison Chart

The individualism chart in Figure 8.1 is adapted from Lionel Laroche's book *Managing Cultural Diversity in Technical Professions*, which, in turn, is adapted from the work of Dutch interculturalist Geert Hofstede. Hofstede's global study, first done in 1980 and since extended, lays important groundwork for studying individualism and how it affects teamwork relations.

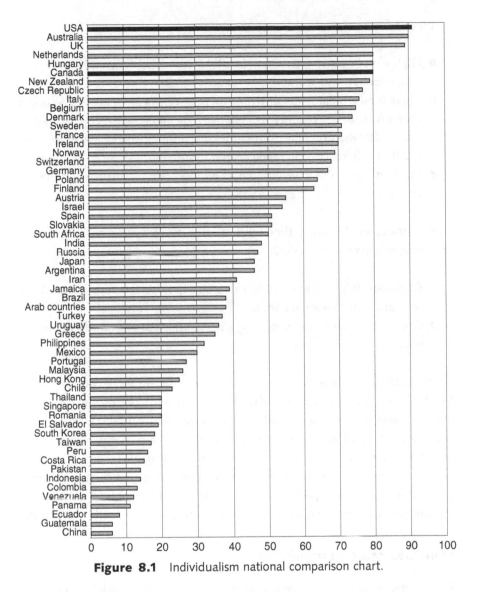

Figure 8.1 Individualism national comparison chart.

When looking at Figure 8.1, keep the following points in mind:

■ High scores correspond to individualistic countries. Conversely, collective countries have low scores on this chart.
■ There is no absolute right or wrong on this scale (a score of 80 is no better than a score of 20), but there is a relative right and wrong (people who have scores of 80 will experience difficulties in a country where the average score is 20). A difference of 10 is considered meaningful.
■ The implications of score differences on this scale are discussed in the following pages.

As in the case of hierarchy, the danger of using the data presented in this chart in a simplistic manner is twofold:

■ Each country's rank may not be exact, due to imperfect research methods or changes in a national culture.
■ One cannot assume when meeting a person that the person will follow the norm of his or her culture.

When meeting people who come from cultures that are more collective than North America (in essence, much of the rest of the world), one may assume a significant probability that these people have a more collective mindset. This knowledge should be used in a reactive manner rather than a proactive manner: It is meant to help identify collective behaviors so that, when one is confronted with such behaviors, one can avoid taking it personally, even when this behavior appears to be directed against oneself. Acting in a different way because one expects people to want that is a form of stereotype, which is usually not helpful.

Language and Communication

The language people use is often a good indicator of how individualistic or group oriented they are. The individualist will more commonly speak about individual initiatives, projects, achievements, and failures, whether about themselves or someone else.

People from individualistic cultures often don't know who is being referred to by *we* when it is used extensively by others. They find it confusing and evasive. In collective cultures, people quickly realize who *we* is; when they can't figure it out, not knowing who *we* represents is not a major impediment to the conversa-

Table 8.1 Determining Whether a Candidate or New Hire Is Individualistic or Collective

	Compared with collective people, individualistic people tend to:	Compared with individualistic people, collective people tend to:
Language	■ Use the word *I* extensively ■ Describe personal accomplishments ■ Make it clear if this was their idea	■ Use the word *we* extensively ■ Describe group (department/company) accomplishments ■ Present an idea with less concern for its source
Communication	■ Have a narrow distribution of information (short cc list)	■ Have a wide distribution of information (long cc list)

tion. Collective people often have a hard time using the term *I* repeatedly in conversation. They certainly don't want to be taking credit for something they think other people may have assisted with.

> I loved working in Mexico and found the Mexicans tremendously hard-working, perhaps even more dedicated than back home. But one thing I found strange and at first difficult to handle was that when I would ask my plant manager who was responsible for a particular portion of the project, I never got the name of an individual. It was always a group of people. I had been taught that a responsibility that is assigned to a group and not to one individual is no one's responsibility and will likely not get done. Eventually, I learned that the plant manager was not trying to protect an individual or avoid his responsibilities. Projects and portions of them were always the responsibility of a group. They still got done.
>
> —North American engineer in Mexico

When it comes to distribution lists in e-mail, the individualist is likely to be more specific about who he or she addresses it to, whereas the more collective person is more likely to copy a message to a wider audience. The collective person wants to make sure that everyone possibly affected by the content of the e-mail will be included in the loop.

If your colleagues are more individualistic with their language than you are, you can:

- Mirror the language of the other, using more individualistic language, such as *I*, *he*, *she*, and *you*.
- Make reference to individual responsibilities and accomplishments.
- Copy fewer people on e-mails.

If your colleagues are more collective with their language than you are, you can:

- Mirror the language of the other, using more collective language, such as *we* and *they*.
- Make reference to collective responsibilities and accomplishments.
- Copy all who may be affected on e-mails.

Office Layout

Table 8.2 compares how individualistic and collective people relate to office layout.

I didn't think a North American office would be that different from my office back home. In Ireland, there were no dividers that separated one employee from another.

Table 8.2 How Individualistic and Collective People Relate to Office Layout

Compared with collective people, individualistic people tend to:	Compared with individualistic people, collective people tend to:
■ Focus on individual space, even in open space environments (cubicles have virtual doors) ■ Focus on individual objects (labels, individual handouts) ■ Have their own individual network that cannot be shared with others ■ Have a stronger sense of privacy	■ Focus on sharing space ■ Focus on sharing objects (one copy for all) ■ Share their network with other members of their group ■ Have less of a sense of privacy

I could look around the room and see all my workmates, including my manager. I didn't realize how much I liked that environment until I moved here. Here, it's called an open office plan, but our cubicle walls are just high enough so that when I stand up I still cannot see whether anyone else is in the office. I feel so isolated. I don't feel I can just lean over and ask a quick question of my colleague. In fact it seems we are encouraged to send an e-mail even if the person is 10 feet away. I don't see any time saving in that. It feels cold and impersonal. I also feel as though I could goof around half the day and no one would notice, not that I would.

—Irish professional working in North America

As the Irish professional points out in his story, a person accustomed to a more collective style is apt to feel isolated and less productive when unable easily to make contact with other team members. A more individualistic person, on the other hand, likely appreciates the privacy and feels more productive because there are fewer interruptions. Sending an e-mail is considered more efficient for all concerned because no one is disturbed and the other person can reply at a convenient time.

One of the biggest challenges in multicultural offices comes from the different senses of privacy that people have in collective vs. individualistic cultures.

- In individualistic cultures, people have a strong sense of privacy. Looking at the documents left on someone's desk, looking over the shoulder of someone to see what is on his or her computer screen, or giving out someone's contact information all require asking this person's permission beforehand. In particular, if you want to give out the contact information for an individualistic person to someone else, this individualistic person expects you to ask for permission every time.
- In collective cultures, people have a much weaker sense of privacy. It is acceptable to look at the documents left on someone's desk, to look over the shoulder of someone to see what is on his or her computer screen, or to give out someone's contact information without asking permission first, if this person is part of one's group. Collective people often give members of their group carte blanche to pass on their information to anyone who might need it, as long as this action is clearly in the interest of the group to which they belong.

This difference often comes to a head in a multicultural office when someone finds a document left inadvertently on the glass of a photocopy machine or on a printer. What should this person do? The reaction will likely depend on whether this person is individualistic or collective.

- An individualistic person will usually either set the document aside without looking at it or look at the header to determine to whom this document belongs and put it in the mailbox that corresponds to him or her. The responsibility is on the person who found the document not to read it.
- A collective person will usually start reading the document. The responsibility is on the document owner not to make it available for others to read.

When individualistic people see collective people read documents that belong to them when they did not intend to share these documents with them, they often feel a tremendous sense of invasion of privacy. Since collective people do not have this strong sense of privacy, they do not apologize for reading this document; from an individualistic perspective, this is like adding insult to injury. Incidents like these often generate significant ill will.

If your colleague is more accustomed to an individualistic office layout, you could:

- Make a point of not interrupting more than is absolutely necessary.
- Ask permission before entering his or her space.
- Allow personal expression in work decorations (pictures of immediate family members or pets, drawings from children, etc.).
- Ask permission every time before communicating his or her contact information to others.
- Ask permission every time you want to use his or her equipment or documents.

If your colleague is more accustomed to a collective office layout, you can:

- Make a point of going to his or her desk rather than always sending an e-mail.
- Give permission to interrupt you.
- Offer to share your office items.
- Explain in which situations your colleague can give your contact information or use your documents or equipment without asking your permission first and in which situations he or she needs to ask permission first.

Working Together

In individualistic countries like Canada and the United States, team members are expected to focus on their own tasks and responsibilities. Roles are clearly defined, and the boundaries between the responsibilities of individual team members are sharp. The motto of such teams can be summarized as: "If we each take good care of our own area of responsibility and follow the plan, we will all achieve our objectives." Only one person is responsible for each task; in an individualistic country, "a responsibility that belongs to everybody belongs to nobody." (See Table 8.3.)

> I hired an Indian employee who had a great education, and good work experience and was a fine communicator. A colleague in a related department circulated a report among our group and asked for comment. The Indian not only made comment but basically rewrote the report, with suggestions that he thought would improve it greatly. The report's author was very offended that the guy had completely changed her report. She included none of his suggestions in her final document. When I mentioned to my Indian employee how the woman had reacted, he felt terrible and apologized profusely. He was only trying to help.
>
> —Financial director in Houston

This collective-culture Indian felt that to be a good team player he should make all the suggestions he could think of to improve the report of a coworker. The individualistic coworker, on the other hand, saw the extensive rework as an intrusion on her turf, tantamount to implying she was incompetent.

Table 8.3 How Individualistic and Collective People Differ Regarding Working Together

Compared with collective people, individualistic people tend to:	Compared with individualistic people, collective people tend to:
■ Follow the motto "Let's all do our own jobs" ■ Focus on one's role and responsibilities ■ Provide help only on request ■ Have their own, individual network that cannot be shared with others	■ Follow the motto: "One for all, all for one" ■ Keep track of what every team member is doing ■ Provide help when they consider that help is needed (even when no help has been requested) ■ Share their network with other members of their group

Individualistic and collective teams operate according to very different sets of unwritten rules; in many cases, these unwritten rules are actually mutually exclusive. Being a good team player by individualistic standards makes someone automatically a poor team player by collective standards, and vice versa.

Individualistic Teams

In an individualistic team, the first question that team members ask during their kickoff meeting is: "Who is responsible for what?" In essence, a key step in the progress of an individualistic team consists in breaking down something collective—the team objective—into individual roles and responsibilities. This is presented graphically in Figure 8.2: Individualistic team members have extensive discussions to determine where the boundaries of their respective roles and responsibilities are; they will usually be quite frustrated if the kickoff meeting ends without defining what they are responsible for.

In North America, team members share information on a need-to-know basis. They share information with specific people rather than the whole team. In addition, since team members see themselves as self-contained entities, they usually share information with the rest of the organization at a lower rate than they do with their teammates, but the difference between these two information flow rates is not major.

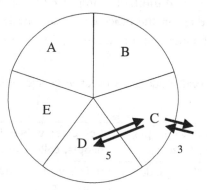

Figure 8.2   Schematic representation of an individualistic team. Each letter represents a team member. The arrows represent the flow of information between team members (here, C and D exchange information at a rate of 5) and between team members and the rest of the organization (here, C exchanges information with the rest of the organization at a rate of 3). All team members are assumed to be at similar hierarchical levels.

One key difference is the actions that a given team member would take if he or she considers that another team member is not performing a given task to specifications. For example, let's look at the situation where C is responsible for collecting technical data that B will use in his or her report to clients. Let's assume that B believes that C will not have the data ready on time. In this case, as in real life, it does not matter whether C has things under control or not; B's perception is B's reality. What should B do? Figure 8.3 presents graphically the approach B is likely to use if he or she comes from an individualistic culture.

- First, B goes and talks to C one on one (step 1 in Figure 8.3). B asks about C's progress and emphasizes the important of receiving the data on time in order to file the report on time. B talks about the impact of C's work on B's work but makes no comment on C's work, because such comments would be completely out of bounds by individualistic standards.
- If there is no visible change in C's data-gathering approach, B's next step consists in expressing concerns to the team leader by describing how C's progress will impact B's own deliverables (Step 2 in Figure 8.3). For example, B might say, "If I do not receive this data by the end of March, I will not be able to file the report by April 30." To an individualistic team leader, the message is clear: "I have concerns about this. I cannot do anything because it is outside my area of responsibility. Because you have overall responsibility for the project, I suggest you look into this—you and I know that the company will blame you if we are late." If the team

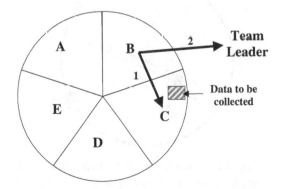

Figure 8.3   Schematic representation of the steps taken by an individualistic team member (B) who considers that another team member (C) is not completing a task properly. First, B talks to C one on one; if this does not yield the expected results, B talks to the team leader.

leader considers that C has everything under control, he or she will likely reassure B that everything is going according to plan and drop it. If the team leader considers that B may have a point, he or she may go and talk to C to find out how things are going and make sure that C truly has things under control.

Collective Teams

In collective countries (like China, India, and Mexico), the motto of teams is "One for all, and all for one." Team members have general areas of expertise; however, the boundaries between these areas are not as clearly delineated as they are in individualistic countries. Tasks are considered the responsibility not of an individual but of the team. For example, an American engineer working in China commented that, when he asked his Chinese colleagues, "Who is responsible for this task?" he would invariably hear, "This department" or "That team," as opposed to "Jiao" or "Jian." Figure 8.4 presents schematically a collective team. The lines or divisions separating individuals are less sharp and less defined than in Figure 8.2.

Collective team members are expected to provide support and to cover for one another. Being part of a team implies a significant amount of involvement and commitment to one's teammates, because each team member is expected to

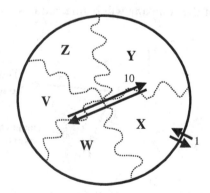

Figure 8.4 Schematic representation of a collective team. Each letter represents a team member. The arrows represent the flow of information within the team (here, information flows within the team at a rate of 10) and between the team and the rest of the organization (here, the team exchanges information with the rest of the organization at a rate of 1). All team members are assumed to be at similar hierarchical levels.

cover for all other team members. Therefore, one of the first questions that collective team members ask during their kickoff meeting is: "Who is part of the team? Who is not?" In essence, team members want to determine how far their commitment stretches.

Within collective teams, information flows more freely than in individualistic teams. As soon as one team member obtains a piece of information, he or she will pass it on to all other team members "in case they need it"—this is represented graphically in Figure 8.4 by the two arrows in the center of the diagram. By contrast, collective team members share only a limited amount of information with the rest of the organization. They "keep their dirty laundry in the family" and they "don't air their dirty laundry in public." This difference in the rate of flow of information is one of the reasons collective team members spend quite a bit of time figuring out upfront who is part of the team and who is not. If someone is considered part of the team, then he or she is provided all the information available to the team; if not, he or she receives far less information about what is happening in the team.

One key difference is the actions that a given team member would take if he or she considers that another team member is not performing a given task to specifications. For example, let's look at the same situation as in the previous section, i.e., X is responsible for collecting technical data that Z will use in his or her report to clients and Z believes that X will not have the data ready on time. Again, as in real life, it does not matter whether X has things under control or not; Z's perception is Z's reality. What should Z do? Figure 8.5 presents graphically the approach Z is likely to use if he or she comes from a collective culture.

- First, during a team meeting, Z brings up the topic of X's progress (step 1 in Figure 8.5). In front of the whole team, Z asks X how the data collection is going. Z and X discuss whether the data collection is moving along at a sufficient pace or not; the other team members (here, Y, W, and V) will act as panel discussion members, mediators, arbitrators, or judges, depending on the nature of the conversation.
- If there is no visible change in X's data-gathering approach, Z's next step consists of offering help to X with the data collection (Step 2 in Figure 8.5). Z might say to X, "I know you have a lot of work on your plate these days. Maybe I can help by taking care of this responsibility for you." If Z considers that the probability of X being late is very high, Z will jump in and help X, whether help has been requested or not (in some cases, Z will help even if X has explicitly declined help).

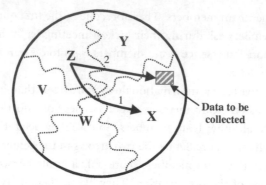

Figure 8.5 Schematic representation of the steps taken by a collective team member (Z) who considers that another team member (X) is not completing a task properly. First, Z talks to X during a team meeting; if this does not yield the expected results, Z jumps in and starts doing the task.

Mixed Teams

When a team includes both individualistic and collective members, sharing information becomes a major issue within the team, as Figure 8.6 demonstrates. Indeed, collective people send information at a rate of 10 and receive information at a rate of 5. This situation is interpreted negatively on both sides, and everyone thinks the others are very poor team players since:

- Individualistic people consider that their collective teammates are wasting their time copying them on memos, e-mails, and documents they do not need to know.
- Collective people consider that their individualistic teammates are hoarding information and keeping it away from them.

I had a major surprise when I moved from the Manila office of one of the Big Four accounting firms to the Toronto office of the same firm. After two weeks of training and preparation, I was assigned to a project and started to work on a team. I could not understand why my managers and colleagues were not copying me on their e-mail messages, particularly those exchanged with the client. When I discussed this point with my cross-cultural coach, he explained to me that this was totally normal. I was really wondering what I had done wrong to be excluded from the team in my first project.

—Filipino audit accountant in Canada

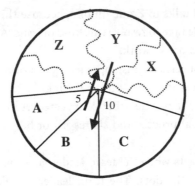

Figure 8.6 Schematic representation of a mixed team that includes three collective members (Z, Y, and X) and three individualistic members (A, B, and C). In this team, collective members send information at a rate of 10 while individualistic members send information at a rate of 5. All team members are assumed to be at similar hierarchical levels.

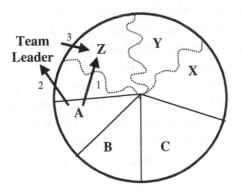

Figure 8.7 Schematic representation of a mixed team that includes three collective members (Z, Y, and X) and three individualistic members (A, B, and C). A considers that Z is not completing a task properly. Step 1: A talks to Z one on one. Step 2: A talks to the team leader. Step 3: The team leader talks to Z.

Team breakdown usually occurs when one member considers that another member is not doing what is needed for the team. Team breakdown is likely to occur when an individualistic team member (for example, A) considers that a collective team member (such as Z) is not taking care of a task for which he or she is responsible. The dynamic that leads to the team breakdown in this case unfolds in the following manner (see Figure 8.7).

- First A goes and talks to Z one on one, because this is the first step individualistic people take to resolve this kind of issue. A focuses on the impact that Z's work has on A's work.
- As far as Z is concerned, this approach does not make sense. Z responds to A: "Let's discuss this on Monday, during the team meeting."
- Since this is not the reaction that A expected, A moves to the second step of his or her usual process and shares his or her concerns with the team leader.
- The real issue starts when the team leader goes and talks to Z. He or she quickly connects the dots: The team leader is talking to me because A talked to the team leader. Z interprets A's action as a betrayal and feels that A stabbed him or her in the back, because Z feels that A made him or her lose face in front of the team leader. For collective people who are also hierarchical (which is the case for the majority of immigrants to North America these days), making someone lose face in front of his or her superiors is probably the worst thing one can do.
- In most cases, Z reacts in two ways:
  - ☐ In order to protect him- or herself, Z stops giving information to A. This way, A cannot report Z to the team leader.
  - ☐ Z has lunch with his or her collective teammates and they discuss the situation. Given the frustration they have regarding the lack of information provided by their individualistic teammates, it is easy for them to agree that working with individualistic people is really difficult, because they are so "selfish." Collective people perceive that individualistic people are members of a team only as far as it furthers their own best interests.

The same outcome is also likely to occur when a collective team member (X) considers that an individualistic team member (C) is not taking care of a task properly, as Figure 8.8 indicates. In this case, these are the steps that lead to team breakdown.

- First, X talks to C about the task during a team meeting. X expects all team members to join in the conversation in order to find a consensus.
- Individualistic team members do not join the conversation. In fact, C considers that this is not the right time and place to bring this point up. Since C is losing face in front of his or her teammates, C tends to feel quite

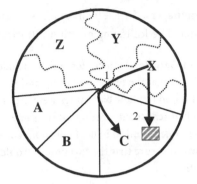

Figure 8.8 Schematic representation of a mixed team that includes three collective members (Z, Y, and X) and three individualistic members (A, B, and C). X considers that C is not taking care of a task properly. Step 1: X talks to C during a team meeting. Step 2: X jumps in and starts working on C's task.

defensive and responds something like, "Everything is under control; let's take this offline."

- This is not the reaction X expected, so X moves to the second step of the collective procedure to handle such situations and either offers to help C or jumps in and starts doing the task.

- As far as C is concerned, X has crossed the line. C interprets X's actions as telling him or her that he or she is incompetent, one of the strongest insults that can be leveled at an individualistic person. C reacts in two ways:

    □ In order to protect him- or herself, C stops giving information to X. This way, X cannot interfere with C's responsibilities and work.

    □ C has lunch or goes for a beer with his or her individualistic teammates and they discuss the situation. Given the frustration they have regarding the amount of information provided by their collective teammates, it is easy for them to agree that working with collective people is really difficult, because they are constantly meddling in other people's affairs. Individualistic people perceive that collective people have no idea how to work in teams.

Regardless of the starting point, the end result is the same: The team breaks down into two subteams. In the best cases, the two subteams completely ignore each other and work in parallel, with no interaction other than meetings mandated by senior managers. In the worst-case scenario, the two subteams compete with each other. The following examples illustrate both cases.

> I was the leader of a software development team that included people from many parts of the world. I knew that the team was not operating smoothly, but I was really shocked when I found out how bad things were. At one point, I realized that two parts of my team had scheduled meetings at the same time, though in different rooms, to work on the same technical issue. I ended up going back and forth between the two rooms to ensure that the two groups would not come up with entirely different solutions.

—Canadian software development manager

> I was the leader of a pharmaceutical research team that included people located in the United States and people located in Spain. Initially, everyone was really enthusiastic about the idea of working with different people. Quickly, the mood of the team deteriorated. The Americans started to make derogatory comments about the Spaniards, and vice versa. Instead of looking at the others as allies, they started looking at them as enemies and started to talk about sides. Eventually, things became so bad that, whenever one side completed some experiments and sent the results to the other side, the other side would redo the experiment to prove that the first side got it all wrong. I lost a lot of sleep during that time.

—American pharmaceutical research team manager

When subteams form, they are likely to start identifying themselves as such by giving themselves a name. For example, in one team made up of British and Latin American technical professionals, the British formed a group known as the "Brit pack." Members of the each subteam socialized together but did not socialize with members of the other subteam. As one British member of the Brit pack puts it: "Yes, we are all going to the pub this evening to watch the soccer game. Guess what? Only Brits are invited."

Solution

In order for multicultural teams to work well together, all team members need to feel that they are part of the *same* team and working toward the *same* goal. Since most people do not, by themselves, recognize the dynamics described in this section, many multicultural teams benefit from some cross-cultural training during the kickoff meeting and some facilitated discussions to come to a consensus on how the team will operate.

While the team is being formed, team members can observe and talk to one another in order to determine the extent to which they are collective or individualistic. Once they have identified whether their counterparts are more individualistic or more collective than they are, they can then choose to adapt their communication style to find a common approach. Here are some action steps that each individual team member can take to improve the effectiveness of his or her team.

If your counterpart is more individualistic than you are when it comes to working together, you may:

- Focus on your own role and responsibilities and let your counterpart take care of his or her own. Any attempt to influence or help is likely to be perceived as an intrusion. Wait until you are asked for help to provide it. If progress is not what you expect, talk to the team leader, focusing on how the lack of progress impacts your area of responsibilities. Do not comment on other people's work, particularly in their presence—defer to them for comments.
- Talk about your personal accomplishments. Learn to separate what the group did from what you did.
- Check whether you are providing too much information to that person. Ask yourself whether that person really needs to know what you are going to tell him or her. How will it help that person do his or her job better?
- Put forward your objections to your counterpart's decisions—do not expect him or her to know how these decisions affect your work.

If your counterpart is more collective than you are when it comes to working together, you may:

- Consider the impact of your actions and decisions on your counterpart. He or she expects that, when you make a decision, you balance the needs of the whole team.
- Talk about the team's accomplishments. Learn to put forward what the group did rather than what you did. Beware of taking credit for the work of the whole team. Avoid singling out individual accomplishments in public.
- Check whether or not you are providing enough information to that person. Ask yourself whether they would like to have more information on what you do. What additional information might they need?

■ Ask your counterpart how your decisions affect him or her. Do not expect him or her to volunteer this information.

Getting Down to Business vs. Getting to Know One Another

Hispanic, Asian, and Arab cultures tend to put more emphasis on developing relationships at the beginning of a shared project. Emphasis on task completion comes second. Conversely, North Americans prefer to focus initially on the task at hand and to let relationships develop naturally as they work on the task. Commitment to accomplishing the task and to valuing relationships is present in both approaches; however, the order is different.

> When I first moved to the United States, I was sure the other people in the office didn't like me. They didn't invite me for coffee, invite me for lunch, ask me about where I was from, or show any interest in me at all. I felt like I was being ignored and I felt very lonely. I wasn't sure I was going to survive the first year. Through the support of friends I made outside of work, I was able to get by. Much to my surprise, after a few months the people at work were warming up. Following a large and difficult project I was invited to go out for beers with the guys. It felt very natural. It turned out that they didn't dislike me; they were just private people who didn't normally socialize with workmates. Once they got to know me through working together, we would occasionally go for coffee or lunch.
>
> —Mexican engineer in the United States

North Americans will typically put work first while on the job. Little, if any, preamble is required prior to getting down to work. People unused to this style may find workmates to be cold, too businesslike, and uninterested in them. When North Americans used to a work-first approach encounter a relationship-first colleague, they may consider the person an unfocused, undisciplined worker.

Individualistic cultures tend to be work-first oriented, while relationship-first cultures tend to be more collective.

Solution

If your counterpart is more work-first oriented than you, you can allow the conversation to enter work topics more quickly than might be the norm for you.

If your counterpart is more relationship-first oriented than you, you can allow the workplace conversation to begin with "kitchen" or personal topics.

Decision Making

Individualist cultures are comfortable with the idea that, if each person makes good decisions respecting his or her own area, then the organization will do well. This may be seen as complementary with economist Adam Smith's belief that as individuals act in their own best interest, they contribute to the well-being of the whole system.

Group-oriented people tend to have less faith that individuals who each go their own way will add up to something good for the organization. Instead, they try to take into account the impact of their decisions on the whole organization. (See Table 8.4.)

Typically people coming new to North America, especially to the United States, find the business environment more individualistic than from where they have come. They may be unaccustomed to standing up to fight for their ideas and the interests of their work group. It seems selfish and narrow.

> The North Americans I worked with seemed only to think of themselves and their work. When they argued a point, and they often seemed to be arguing a point, it was sometimes hard to see how their company or our consortium would benefit. They would argue among themselves in front of us. I found that very confusing. I am completely loyal to my company and will be for life. What is good for the company is good for me.
>
> —Chinese National Petroleum Company oil worker

Table 8.4 How Individualistic and Collective People Differ on Decision Making

Compared with collective people, individualistic people tend to:	Compared with individualistic people, collective people tend to:
■ Make decisions based on the impact on their own areas of responsibility ■ Expect people responsible for other areas to speak up if their decisions affect them adversely ■ Speak up in meetings if they have a point to make and fight for their position	■ Make decisions based on the impact on the whole group ■ Expect everyone to take into consideration the impact of his or her decisions on everyone else ■ In meetings, will wait to be asked their opinion if the issue at hand relates to their work group

This Chinese oil worker had a hard time seeing how the North American approach was any more than a selfish pursuit of personal interest. In this case, the North American was seen as argumentative, narrow-minded, and disloyal. Collective people tend to believe that "two heads are better than one."

By contrast, individualistic people tend to think that "too many cooks spoil the broth" and that "an elephant is a mouse designed by a committee." The North American often becomes frustrated when people want to take into consideration how their decision might impact other groups in the company. It may be seen as a sorry waste of time in a marketplace where speed is highly valued. If others in the company will be negatively impacted by that decision, it is up to them to voice their concerns.

In his many books, American business guru Tom Peters suggests that readers forget about loyalty to a particular company and replace it with a self-motivated dedication to the work at hand. He recommends that employees consider that they are actually working for themselves rather than the company. This is task focused and individualistic.

Solution

One tool that helps flush out differences between individualistic and collective team members when decisions need to be made is the RACI matrix. This is a table where the names of the people who are involved in the decision-making process appear in one of the following categories:

Responsible: Who has the responsibility for ensuring that the right decision is made?
Agree: Who needs to agree with the decision made?
Consult: Who needs to be consulted?
Inform: Who needs to be informed?

Responsible	Agree	Consult	Inform

When collective and individualistic team members work together to complete this table, differences of opinion usually surface, in the sense that collective team members tend to push the names of people to the left relative to individualistic team members (collective team members think that someone needs to agree with the final decision, whereas individualistic team members think that he or she only needs to be consulted or informed). In particular, collective people might place several names in the Responsible category, whereas individualistic people tend to want to have only one name there.

If your counterpart is more collective than is the norm in your organization and business culture when it comes to making decisions, you may:

- Explain that making individual decisions is highly valued.
- Provide clear parameters of authority for making individual decisions.
- Provide close coaching and feedback, correcting where improvement is desired and rewarding when the employee gets it right.

If your counterpart is more individualistic than is the norm in your organization and business culture when it comes to making decisions, you may:

- Explain that a more collaborative approach is appreciated.
- Provide clear parameters of authority for making decisions.
- Provide close coaching and feedback, correcting where improvement is desired and rewarding when the employee gets it right.

Compensation

People from individualistic cultures such as Canada and the United States tend to prefer raises and bonuses based on their individual performance. The feeling is that one should be rewarded for extra effort and not penalized for the performance of others, which is assumed to be out of one's control.

The more collective approach consists of giving raises and bonuses based on group or team contributions. People work together to achieve corporate objectives and are correspondingly rewarded together. In recent years, the compensation norm in North America has moved from being purely individual based to having a component of team reward.

Solution

If your counterpart is more collective than is the norm in your organization and business culture when it comes to compensation, you may:

- Explain how individual compensation works and the rationale for it.
- Point out that working together with others is important, and explain how it is recognized in your organization.

If your counterpart is more individualistic than is the norm in your organization and business culture when it comes to compensation, you may:

- Explain how team-based compensation works and the rationale for it.
- Point out that individual performance is also important, and explain how it is recognized.

Hierarchy

Teams that include people at different levels in the organization's hierarchy can quickly become dysfunctional if they include members who have different notions of hierarchy.

- If a team includes egalitarian members who are in low positions in the organization and hierarchical members who are in high positions in the same organization, the egalitarian members often consider that their input is disregarded by higher-ranked team members while hierarchical people consider that they are not shown proper respect.
- If a team includes hierarchical members who are in low positions in the organization and egalitarian members who are in high positions in the same organization, the egalitarian members often consider that they are not challenged enough and that their hierarchical counterparts are not providing enough input, while hierarchical team members feel that they are placed in no-win situations when higher-ranked team members ask them for input in front of their direct managers.

We have seen these dynamics at play in two common situations:

- **In health and safety committees:** By law, these committees must include senior managers and rank-and-file employees. If the employee representatives have a strong sense of hierarchy, they will likely fall in line with senior managers as soon as senior managers express an opinion on any topic.
- **In teams that include people located in different parts of the world:** For example, many software development teams include people located in North America and in India, while manufacturing teams include people located in North America and in China, with management often (but not

always) being in North America. In many of these teams, managers consider that the non–North American team members do not provide enough input.

Solution

Changing someone's perspective on hierarchy often takes years; as a result, there is no quick fix to this problem. Here are some suggestions to help teams find common grounds more quickly.

If your teammate is more hierarchical than is the norm in your organization and business culture when it comes to teamwork, you may:

- Explain what initiative means to you.
- Explain when you expect to receive input and suggestions from your counterpart.
- Explain when you expect to be challenged by your counterparts.
- Ask your hierarchical counterparts who are in low-level positions to brainstorm on their own and provide their ideas separately.
- Remove yourself from the meeting if you want to get honest feedback on your ideas.

If your teammate is less hierarchical than is the norm in your organization and business culture when it comes to teamwork, you may:

- Describe the specific situations where his or her behavior is perceived as lacking respect.
- Point out the importance of following corporate protocol and procedures.
- Assign tasks to him or her that do not require close supervision by high-ranking team members.

Risk Tolerance

Risk tolerance measures the degree of discomfort experienced by members of a society when faced with unknown or uncertain situations. People from high risk-tolerant cultures cope well with risky situations where the outcome is unknown or difficult to predict. Organizations in these societies encourage individual employees to use their initiative and take risks. Employees have the freedom to do their own thing but are given little support if things go wrong.

People from low risk-tolerant cultures respond better when bound by rules, regulations, and controls. Institutions and organizations in these societies have clear structures, strong codes of behavior, and standardized management practices. They tolerate less deviation from these structures, but in return they tend to support their employees. More information is needed for people to make a decision and be comfortable that they are making the right decision in low risk-tolerant cultures.

Risk tolerance varies significantly from one culture to the next. When members of a team have different levels of risk tolerance, teams can easily and quickly fall apart.

Risk Tolerance National Comparison Chart

When looking at Figure 8.9, keep the following points in mind:

- High scores correspond to risk-tolerant countries. Conversely, risk-averse countries have low scores on this chart.
- There is no absolute right or wrong on this scale (a score of 80 is not better than a score of 20), but there is a relative right and wrong (people who have scores of 80 will experience difficulties in a country where the average score is 20). A difference of 10 is considered meaningful.
- The implications of score differences on this scale are discussed in the following pages.
- The same caveats mentioned in the case of hierarchy and individualism apply in the case of risk tolerance.

In Figure 8.9, some countries have negative scores. In the original study that G. Hofstede conducted with IBM subsidiaries, scores were normalized to fall in the range from 0 to 100. When the study was expanded to include more countries, some of the countries that were subsequently added ended up with negative scores on the risk tolerance scale.

Planning and Decisions

Figure 8.10 presents graphically the amount of information that people from two different cultures (such as Japanese and American) usually need to make a given

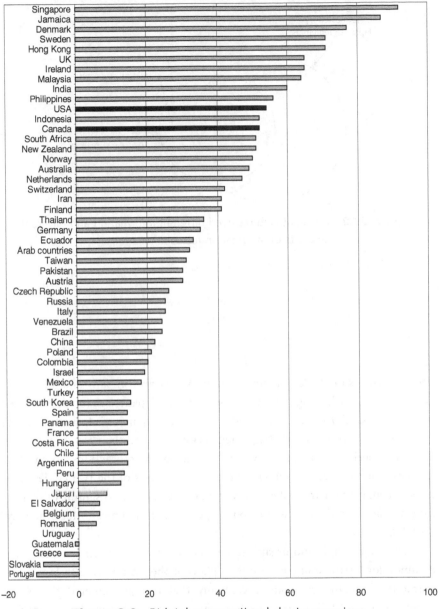

Figure 8.9 Risk tolerance national chart comparison.

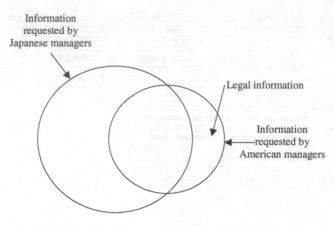

Figure 8.10 Different cultures need different information and different amounts of information to make decisions.

decision. For example, let's assume that an American company and a Japanese company are considering forming a joint venture. Japanese managers involved in such transactions are likely to gather significantly more information about their American counterparts (e.g., their technology and their reputation) than are the American managers involved in the same transactions about their Japanese counterparts, as shown by the different sizes of the two circles. This does not apply to all areas: American managers usually need significantly more information than their Japanese counterparts when it comes to legal matters. (See Table 8.5.)

Risk-averse people and organizations plan over much longer horizons. It is common for Japanese organizations to plan for the next 30 to 50 years. In its marketing brochure, a Japanese company that had just entered the North American market talked about its 100-year expansion plan in North America. By contrast, most North American organizations plan for the next two to three years, with a strong emphasis on quarterly results. The risk-averse approach can be summarized as "One ounce of prevention is worth a pound of cure," while risk-tolerant people often use the phrase "We will cross that bridge when we come to it."

Table 8.5 How Risk-Tolerant and Risk-Averse People Differ on Planning and Decisions

	Compared with risk-averse people, risk-tolerant people tend to:	Compared with risk-tolerant people, risk-averse people tend to:
Planning	■ Plan over a shorter time period ■ Plan in detail only the first few steps of a project, and examine only the most likely contingency scenarios ■ Have a "We will cross that bridge when we come to it" attitude	■ Plan over a longer time period ■ Plan over the entire life of a project and examine many contingencies ("What if?") ■ Have a "We can avoid a lot of rework through proper planning" attitude
Decisions	■ Ask that the team keeps moving ■ Want to avoid "collecting data for the sake of collecting data" ■ Focus on variables most likely to have an impact on the problem ■ Focus more on practice, rules of thumb, and empirical formulas ■ Use limited amount of data to support their points ■ Focus on the implications of their work for the future and for their colleagues	■ Ask for more data or information in order to have a "good grasp of the situation" and to make sure they are moving in the right direction ■ Do a thorough job and examine all possible variables ■ Focus more on theory and differential equations derived analytically ■ Use much data to support their points ■ Focus on convincing colleagues that they have looked at all possible aspects of the issue

Risk-averse and risk-tolerant people tackle team projects in completely different manners:

- Figure 8.11 presents the approach of risk-tolerant teams. Risk-tolerant team members usually spend very little time planning upfront. They quickly

Risk-Tolerant Team

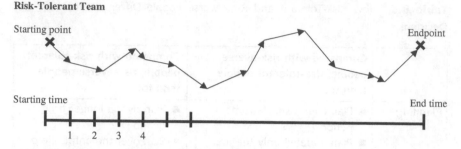

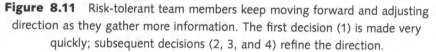

Figure 8.11   Risk-tolerant team members keep moving forward and adjusting direction as they gather more information. The first decision (1) is made very quickly; subsequent decisions (2, 3, and 4) refine the direction.

Risk-Averse Team

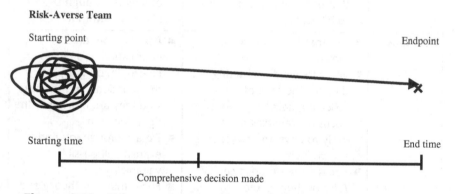

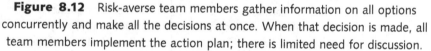

Comprehensive decision made

Figure 8.12   Risk-averse team members gather information on all options concurrently and make all the decisions at once. When that decision is made, all team members implement the action plan; there is limited need for discussion.

come up with a general direction and start moving in this direction while continually monitoring their progress. Over time, they keep adjusting direction until they reach their objectives. This approach requires several meetings: Team members need to meet on a regular basis to synchronize their progress and decide on the direction they will take after they have made each decision. Each decision is made in sequence; once it is made, that decision is considered as done and dealt with—the decision will not be reopened unless some really new and compelling evidence forces it, since this would be considered moving backwards rather than forwards.

■ Figure 8.12 presents the approach of risk-averse teams. Risk-averse team members usually start a project by gathering a lot of information in order to chart their complete course in detail. They will consider many options concurrently and gather information on all options in parallel. No decision is made until all the information is in for all the considered options. At that point, the team reviews all the options at the same time, using many criteria to determine which option is the overall winner. The option that is selected is then implemented; since each team member has already researched what he or she is expected to do when the decision is made, the implementation phase in the risk-averse approach is much shorter than the implementation phase in the risk-tolerant approach.

For example, compare the approach of a group of North Americans and a group of Japanese who have decided to take a trip together:

- A North American group that decides to take a vacation together will first decide what kind of vacation they want (e.g., fun in the sun, visiting some ancient ruins, ski trip). Once that is settled, they will discuss the location (since we have decided we are going on a ski trip, will we go to Aspen or Whistler? Lake Placid or Mont Tremblant?). A subsequent meeting will decide the type of accommodation, then the type of transportation, and so on.
- A Japanese group that decides to take a vacation together will examine all options together and gather information on all the sun resorts (like Hawaii and Bali), all the ski resorts, and all the ancient ruins it might consider visiting; it also gathers information on all the hotels, all the flight options, etc. for each option. Once they have all this information compiled, they examine all the options together using many simultaneous criteria (for example, they may assign a certain weight to cost and a certain number of points for cost difference) and determine which option is the best. At that point, the decision is made and everyone gets ready to go.

Note that one approach is not inherently better than the other. G7 countries have very different scores on this scale, going from 8 for Japan to 65 for the UK. What really matters is how good the team members are in putting these approaches in practice (Figure 8.9).

- Risk-tolerant people may start in the wrong direction. In that case, it takes them some time just to get back to square one.
- Risk-averse people may make a major move in the wrong direction. In that case, they have to go through the whole process again.

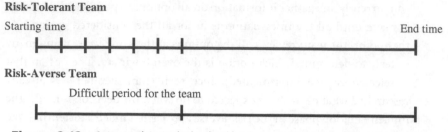

Figure 8.13 A team that includes both risk-averse and risk-tolerant members often experiences difficulties in the initial part of the project.

When risk-averse and risk-tolerant people work together on the same project, they usually experience significant frustration somewhere between the time by which risk-tolerant team members would have made their first decision if there were no risk-averse people in the team and the time by which risk-averse people make their comprehensive decision (see Figure 8.13).

- Risk-tolerant team members experience an increasing sense of urgency if no decision has been made by then. They think to themselves, "Come on! We have been talking for a long time. It is time to make a decision and get going. Our competitors are not sitting idle." Risk-tolerant team members see their risk-averse teammates as overly conservative.
- Risk-averse team members experience significant frustration if the team has already started to make decisions. They think to themselves, "We have started to move and we don't even know if we are on the right track. These premature decisions will close some opportunities for us." Risk-averse team members see their risk-tolerant teammates as "shooting constantly from the hip."

Most new immigrants come from countries that are more risk averse on average than North America. In planning, this creates the problem of too much time spent planning, with seemingly little action. North Americans take relatively little time planning and much time doing. Making mistakes on the way to discovering the best solution by trial and error is accepted. Time spent collecting too much information is considered wasted time or, worse, stalling. Slogans like "Just do it" epitomize the action orientation of North America.

Solution

Once you have identified whether your colleague is more risk tolerant or more risk averse than you, you can help to coach the person to adapt his or her style or adapt your own style to meet the other's expectations.

If your colleague is more risk tolerant in planning and decisions than is the norm for your organization and business culture, you may teach him or her to:

- Collect more data and information. The team may decide that more data and inf ormation is needed than he or she thinks.
- Demonstrate the value of moving ahead. If his or her colleagues think that more data is needed, they are unlikely to accept the idea of moving along. He or she will need to build a case for moving along. How much will the project gain by moving along? How much will the collection of additional data cost? How can the team gather data as it goes, rather than waiting until the data is collected?
- Stay the course. His or her risk-tolerant colleagues may change directions quickly. On some occasions, this may lead them to change course several times before coming back to the original course. Waiting for the "high-frequency noise" to die down may limit the amount of "spinning" he or she experience.

If your colleague is more risk averse in planning and decisions than is the norm for your organization and business culture, you may teach him or her how to:

- Forego some data collection. The team may decide to move along, even though he or she believes that a lot of uncertainty and risk remain.
- Demonstrate the value and necessity of the additional data he or she wants to collect. If his or her colleagues wants to move ahead, they are unlikely to accept the idea of stopping and waiting for the collection of some additional information. He or she will need to build a case and demonstrate the need for this information. How much uncertainty is there without additional data? How much does this uncertainty impact the possible direction of the project?
- Get used to changes in direction. A risk-averse employee is likely to need additional time to adjust to a sudden change (such as a new project direction or a new manager).

New immigrants often need to bring their planning approach in line with the North American approach, since this approach is so deeply ingrained in North Americans. When planning a task, North Americans spend approximately 5 percent of the time allocated to the whole project to create a first-draft plan, then discuss this plan with their colleagues and managers, gather their input, and start implementing their plan. Immigrants often need to adopt this approach in order to be perceived as effective team members by their North American colleagues.

When team members discuss among themselves the benefits of gathering additional data versus the benefits of moving forward, the team can make significant progress. By performing a cost/benefit analysis of data, the team can reach a consensus on what data is truly needed and reach an optimum in the balance between speed and risk minimization.

Career Management

Risk-averse and risk-tolerant employees tend to have fundamentally different objectives (see Table 8.6).

Table 8.6 How Risk-Tolerant and Risk-Averse People Differ on Compensation and Career Management

	Compared with risk-averse people, risk-tolerant people tend to:	Compared with risk-tolerant people, risk-averse people tend to:
Compensation	■ Be willing to take greater risk to get larger financial reward ■ Welcome compensation plans that include incentives based on performance	■ Willing to accept a lower but more stable income ■ Avoid performance-based compensation plans
Career management	■ Focus on shorter-term rewards ■ Plan over a shorter time horizon ■ Prefer smaller organizations	■ Focus on stability ■ Plan over a longer time horizon ■ Prefer large organizations, particularly those that offer job security (like government)

- Risk-averse employees are often motivated by security. One of their main career objectives is to avoid income fluctuation. They place a premium on predictability and will therefore prefer positions with lower income where employment is guaranteed over positions with higher but unpredictable income.
- Risk-tolerant employees are not motivated by security. While they may have a wide range of motivations, income tends to be a significant motivation for many North Americans. Risk-tolerant people prefer positions with higher actual and potential income to positions with lower but predictable income.

As a result, risk-averse and risk-tolerant employees tend to manage their careers in quite different manners.

- Risk-averse people look for positions where employment is stable and preferably guaranteed—government, governmental agencies, and large corporations. Risk-averse employees want to avoid pay-for-performance schemes, because they can plan their budget only based on the fixed part of their income, namely the part they are sure to receive. In risk-averse cultures, the government tends to control a much larger percentage of the economy than in risk-tolerant cultures, because employees and citizens appreciate the predictability that this approach provides.
  - □ In Japan, the graduates of the best universities often choose to work for the Japanese (federal) government. Working for one of the large multinational Japanese companies, which traditionally offered employment for life to their employees, is also considered very attractive.
  - □ The French and Greek governments control, respectively, directly and indirectly, a significant portion of the French and Greek economies. French civil servants have job security that is almost unmatched in North America, since both the Canadian and American federal governments have laid off people at times to reduce head count; in France, head-count reductions have only occurred through attrition. The only North American position that offers a level of job security comparable to the level of job security enjoyed by French civil servants is that of university professor.
- Risk-tolerant people, on the other hand, tend to prefer working for corporations. The more risk they enjoy, the smaller and more entrepreneurial the organization they prefer. People who thrive on risk will therefore either

work for start-up organizations or start their own. They enjoy pay-for-performance and stock option schemes, since these offer the opportunity to make more money if they perform at a superior level.

Risk-averse people tend to experience a high level of stress when they work in risk-tolerant organizations; the same is true in reverse.

- Risk-averse people who work in risk-tolerant organizations are often afraid of being laid off. Events seem to unfold at a pace such that they do not understand what is happening and feel a sense of helplessness. The approach to project planning and execution makes their heads spin—they have a feeling of complete lack of control and an unpredictability of their situation.
- Risk-tolerant people who work in risk-averse organizations are often frustrated by the lack of recognition of the risks they take and by what they consider a cumbersome decision-making process that prevents them from taking calculated risks.

One of the consequences of these major differences is that it is very difficult to create one compensation scheme that can be applied to all subsidiaries of a global organization, because a scheme that rewards risks, team work, and experience the same way everywhere around the globe, will likely miss the mark in many countries.

Solution

Not surprisingly, differences in career management and compensation preferences tend to show up during career management discussions, when culturally different employees examine their professional futures with their managers, coaches, or HR support professional.

If you are coaching employees who have a high tolerance for risk, relative to the rest of the organization, you may:

- Help them understand the impact of their approach on their colleagues.
- Discuss with them career paths that are likely to provide them with environments where they are more likely to thrive (such as sales) and be rewarded for their risk-taking approach.
- Explain to them the logic of the organization's compensation scheme.

If you are coaching employees who have a low tolerance for risk, relative to the rest of the organization, you may:

- Help them understand the impact of their approach on their colleagues.
- Discuss with them career paths that are likely to provide them with environments where they are more likely to thrive (such as corporate functions) and be rewarded for their long-term planning approach.
- Explain to them the logic of the organization's compensation scheme.

Other Topics on Risk Aversion (Table 8.7)

Risk-averse people tend to appreciate the order that rules and regulations bring. In this sense, North American society shows its more risk-averse side. North

Table 8.7 How Risk-Tolerant and Risk-Averse People Differ Regarding Rules and Regulations, Vacations, and Insurance and Investments

	Compared with risk-averse people, risk-tolerant people tend to:	Compared with risk-tolerant people, risk-averse people tend to:
Rules and regulations	<ul><li>Create few rules and regulations</li><li>Create rules that describe the "spirit of the law," leaving the "letter of the law" up to the people who implement and regulate the rules</li><li>Though fewer rules are in place, they follow a proportionally greater fraction of all the rules that are in place</li></ul>	<ul><li>Create many rules and regulations, which sometimes contradict one another</li><li>Create rules in a logical, step-by-step manner</li><li>Though more rules are in place, they follow a proportionally smaller fraction of all the rules that are in place (except possibly in Japan)</li></ul>
Vacations	<ul><li>Prefer spur-of-the-moment vacation plans</li></ul>	<ul><li>Plan vacations well in advance</li></ul>
Insurance and investments	<ul><li>Purchase less insurance</li><li>Purchase more stocks and volatile investments</li></ul>	<ul><li>Purchase more insurance</li><li>Purchase more low-risk, conservative investments</li></ul>

American society tends to be an early adopter of rules such as requiring the use of seat belts in cars, enforcing pedestrian crosswalk right-of-ways, restricting smoking, and requiring the use of helmets on motorcycles. As with the previous examples, the rules for corporations are many in the area of health and safety.

The more risk-averse tend to plan their vacations far in advance and like to have a pretty good idea of where they will be staying and what they will be doing. By contrast, risk-tolerant people may buy their plane tickets at the last minute and may not make any hotel reservation, with the idea that they will see where they feel like staying when they get there and discover what is available.

Solution

When discussing the topic of risk with your new employee:

- Explain the background to, and the reasoning behind, the rules that are in place.
- Be clear on the rules and regulations an employee needs to follow, no matter what, and in which instances the employee has some leeway.
- Explain the consequences of breaking regulations.
- Review how the compensation plan fits with the organization's objectives and expectations of employees.

Issues of Building Cross-Cultural Teams

Multicultural teams tend to experience many of these issues all at the same time, particularly if team members are located in different parts of the country or the world. As a result, the progress of most multicultural teams tends to be quite slow initially as compared with the progress of culturally homogeneous teams, because:

- Differences in communication style create many issues among team members.
- Hierarchy, individualism, and differences on risk tolerance often lead to issues that are recognized much later in the team's life and therefore lead to rework and/or missed deadlines.
- Many issues related to cross-cultural teams are perceived as performance issues by team members and the HR professionals who support them.

- Team-building approaches tend to be rooted in the culture of the HR professionals who provide this service. For example, many North American mingling events include people walking up to as many strangers as possible in a short period of time and asking them questions such as "Do you have a pet?" and "Have you traveled to more than three countries?" and then collecting the answers in order to have as many points as possible. This approach does not work in East Asia, where walking up to strangers to ask a personal question is culturally unacceptable. In East Asia, mingling often takes place in smaller groups over dinner.

Using the wrong team-building approach can significantly backfire, as the following examples illustrate.

We had a major team-building mishap in my organization. One member of the software development team in my corporation was not performing well, so the team leader decided to have a team-building activity. Since he came from Argentina, he decided to have a barbeque at his place. He wanted to treat his team, so he bought the best cut of meats. He just forgot one point: Half his team was Hindu and therefore vegetarian. Even though he ran to one of the local stores to get something they could eat, they felt completely left out of the event. The impact was so bad that the team was worse off afterwards than if he had not done anything.

—Canadian HR manager

I was the HR manager for the American subsidiary of a high-tech company that was split between France and the United States. One of the U.S.–French teams was not doing too well, so my French HR counterpart decided to organize a team-building event. She did not consult me, so I had no idea of what she had planned. When the American team members came back, they kept talking about how long one of their dinners was. Talking to them and to my French HR counterpart, I realized that this was the French idea of team building: Bring everyone to one of the fanciest restaurants in Paris and have a seven-course, four-hour dinner.

The next meeting was taking place in the United States, so the American team leader asked me to organize a team-building activity. He wanted something active, where people have a chance to work and accomplish something together. We ended up booking a go-kart place where small teams built their own go-karts and then raced them around a track; the whole event would conclude with a barbeque.

The French team members hated it. Whereas American team members showed up in jeans and T-shirts, the French showed up in slacks and turtlenecks. They did not want to get involved in the go-kart building, they did not seem to enjoy the race, and they kept talking to one another in French during the barbeque. I could not understand what they were saying, but their body language and tone of voice did not sound positive. When I asked my French HR counterparts how they liked our team-building event, she said that they could not wait for the whole thing to end.

My French HR counterpart and I realized in hindsight that we should probably consult each other before planning team-building sessions, to ensure that we organize events that work for everyone.

—American HR manager

Finding events that will work for everyone is an important part of a team-building event. The same applies to the working part of the team-building event: The way the sessions are laid out, the questions people debate, the way the questions are facilitated, and many other aspects of the event need to take cultural differences into account in order to ensure that everyone finds the event worthwhile and that it brings them closer together.

Solution

When you prepare team-building events for multicultural teams, you may want to:

- Ask people from various cultural groups to take a look at the social and work programs to ensure that what you have in mind will not alienate some team members.
- Learn what makes a team-building event effective in the various parts of the world from which team members come from.

Summary

In this chapter, we reviewed how a person's sense of individualism, hierarchy, and risk tolerance greatly influences his or her approach to teamwork. Recent immigrants will typically, but not always, be from more collective cultures. They will come with an understanding that teamwork means truly helping each other to accomplish mutual tasks. They will "jump in" to assist others and expect others to do the same for them. Many, but not all, recent immigrants will also tend to be more risk averse and more hierarchical than the average North American. They will expect more information in order to make decisions. They will take into consideration the ranks of the people who proposed an idea when evaluating that idea.

Knowing that these differences exist, you can assist your newcomers to adjust to North American workplace cultural systems by following the suggestions laid out in this chapter and by further developing your own strategies. Forewarned is forearmed, so sharing this information with the people within your organization who work closely with culturally different colleagues will help the organization as a whole.

Promotion

Failure to retain culturally different employees can have a negative impact on organizations.

- Companies miss their affirmative action targets (in the United States) or fail to make progress on their employment equity numbers (in Canada).
- Culturally different employees who feel their skills are not being fully used and rewarded may leave the company. These skills then are utilized by competitors or, in some cases, by the former employees as they create a competing organization.

The feeling of not being rewarded for one's efforts can stem from a combination of many cross-cultural dynamics located way "below the water line" (using the iceberg analogy presented in Chapter 1). These cultural dynamics are described in this chapter; suggestions on how to overcome the obstacles are presented at the end. The good news is that once your organization figures out how to execute the strategies for retention, culturally different employees will typically be among your most loyal. The orientation programs, coaching, and mentoring suggested in Chapter 5 are a great start to improving retention.

Rewards and Recognition

When hierarchical recent immigrants work in egalitarian North American organizations, they often feel their efforts are not recognized adequately.

- Even though they are working very hard, they are not given promotions. In the minds of their managers, they are not doing what it takes to be promoted. In their own minds, they are doing exactly what it takes to be promoted, so they do not understand why others, whom they perceive as not being as deserving as they are, get ahead of them. Since most do not expect differences in the promotion process, some interpret their lack of advancement as resulting from discrimination.

- Their managers may give them positive feedback in ways they do not understand because it is not worded strongly enough. Their home culture may praise much more lavishly for a job well done than we are used to in North America. Praise they receive from their new managers may be perceived as either neutral or less positive than intended (see Chapter 7 for more details on cross-cultural feedback issues). As a result, they feel their contributions are not receiving the proper recognition from management.

In Italy or France, if I did something worth praising, the praise that I received was unambiguous and quite lavish, by North American standards. When I think back to French managers I have had, when they complimented me for a job well done, they used language that Americans and Canadians use only when someone retires from the organization after many years of good service. When I started work in North America, I felt for many years that my work was not valued adequately since I never received the kind of praise I thought I deserved and was used to receiving.

—French national who has worked in France, Italy, the U.S., and Canada

- Recognition may also take forms that new hires are not familiar with. In hierarchical cultures, one of the most important measures of people's progress in their careers is the number of people who report to them directly or indirectly. Résumés of many recent immigrants often state the number of people they managed in each position. This information is listed as the first bullet point, since it is considered to reflect clearly their level of competence. In North America, recognition may come in ways that are much more subtle and not obvious to the new hire. Employees within a work group may seem on the surface to have equal benefits. However, if one employee develops a good "reputation" or rapport, this individual may receive special perks. His or her opinions may have more weight than the opinions of others, and some of these employees may be given advantages that others may not have (see the next example).

I worked in a research center where all researchers were at the same level and had the same title. There were very few lab and area managers, and most of them had been in their positions for a while, so there were very few opportunities for career growth. Initially, I thought that every researcher was considered to be on par with every other researcher—for example, we all had the same computers and we all had the opportunity to attend one conference every year. It took me awhile to realize how managers were showing their appreciation for someone's work. I realized that, while everyone was entitled to one conference per year, you had to have a good reputation to go to a conference in Hawaii, Europe, or Asia. Recognition also came in the form of equipment purchase: If you had a good reputation, it was much easier to get a new equipment purchase approved than if you did not.

—French researcher in Canada

Promotions

Retention and promotion tend to be two sides of the same coin, in the sense that most of the people who leave organizations voluntarily, do so because they feel their efforts are not sufficiently appreciated and rewarded and that they will probably not obtain the kind of promotion they had hoped for.

Promotions Drive Retention for Culturally Different People

This is particularly true in the case of culturally different employees, since they tend to come from cultures that are significantly more hierarchical than North America. In their home cultures, the key motivators for employees tend to be titles and the number of people who report to them either directly or indirectly. The HR systems in other cultures reflect these preferences, as the following example illustrates.

Our organization has about 6,000 employees and operates in 20+ countries. We took over a Chinese organization of 100 people based in Shanghai and operating in China only. When we looked at the details of their HR policies, we realized that they had twice as many levels from top to bottom in their organizations as we did. One of the first actions we took to integrate them into our organization was to have them use the same levels as the rest of the organization.

—Canadian organizational development specialist

Compared with the rest of the world, North Americans tend to be much more strongly motivated by increases in responsibilities and the corresponding increases in income that usually follow. As a result, it is often difficult for hierarchical people to understand how egalitarian people can operate large organizations with so few levels, while egalitarian people have difficulty grasping the benefits that hierarchical people derive from the many levels they use.

> Part of our expansion plans into India included the creation of a technical center that would do software development and customer support for much of the organization around the world. We planned to hire a total of 200 people in this tech center. We started by hiring three: the general manager, the controller, and an HR specialist. The HR specialist insisted on being called HR manager, even though she did not manage anyone and there was no plan that she would (her main role would be hiring and training new recruits). When she came over to Canada, we presented to her the compensation and benefit system we used. From entry level to CEO, we had seven levels in a 15,000-employee company. She remained silent throughout the presentation; at the end, she looked at us in shock and said that there was no way our system would work in India. If she did not have the ability to promote people every year, the attrition rate would be horrendous.
>
> —Canadian compensation and benefit specialist

Egalitarian and hierarchical people use very different approaches when it comes to promotions. What people need to do in order to be promoted is quite different in hierarchical and in egalitarian cultures.

The Promotion Process in Egalitarian Cultures

In egalitarian countries (in particular, the United States and Canada), the promotion process is usually fairly gradual. People start taking on more responsibilities that are usually associated with a higher hierarchical level than their current level. In order to be able to focus on higher-level responsibilities and tasks, they need to shed some of the responsibilities that are on the low end of their current level. How they take these tasks off their to-do list is up to them: They may delegate these tasks to someone below them who is also trying to be promoted, subcontract them, hire someone to do them, reorganize their area to eliminate or streamline them, work longer hours, etc. The key is that they free themselves to take on tasks and activities at the next level.

Progressively, over time, they take on more and more responsibilities at the higher level, up to a point where they operate entirely at that level. In the United States and Canada, "you need to be able to do the job without the title" (and without the money) in order to get a promotion to that level. Once someone has operated successfully at the level above his or her current title for a little while, he or she is likely to be offered a position at the next level when such a position becomes available. Figure 9.1 presents this process schematically.

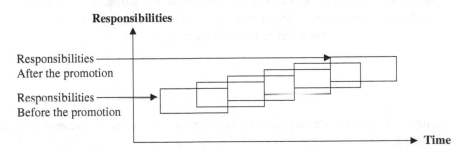

Responsibilities

Responsibilities —
After the promotion

Responsibilities —
Before the promotion

Time

Figure 9.1: Schematic representation of the promotion process in egalitarian cultures: The employee takes on gradually more responsibilities at the next level while passing on to others the responsibilities at the low end of his or her initial level. The promotion can take place when he or she operates entirely at the next level.

Promotion Process in Hierarchical Cultures

In hierarchical countries, people are promoted by focusing on their current responsibilities and by doing them very well. Once people have demonstrated that they can fulfill their current responsibilities without a glitch, they are likely to be offered a position at the next level when one becomes available.

In hierarchical cultures, promotions tend to be step changes in responsibilities rather than gradual increases. While the announcement of a promotion tends to make official something that already exists in practice in egalitarian corporations, the announcement of a promotion in hierarchical cultures really marks the passage from one level to the next. Someone who has been promoted trades one set of responsibilities for another set, which is often quite different from the first set. In many cases, he or she may also start wearing different

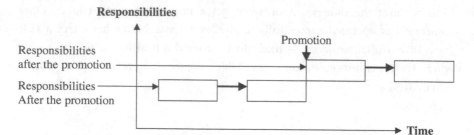
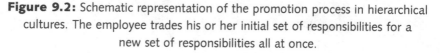

Figure 9.2: Schematic representation of the promotion process in hierarchical cultures. The employee trades his or her initial set of responsibilities for a new set of responsibilities all at once.

clothes. The promotion process in hierarchical countries is presented in Figure 9.2.

Comparing These Two Approaches

When egalitarian HR professionals examine hierarchical organizations, they often perceive the hierarchical approach to promotions as being fraught with significant risk, since it requires people to move into positions for which they have not been prepared. Because hierarchical organizations have significantly more levels than egalitarian organizations, the step from one position to the next in a hierarchical organization is not nearly as large as the step from one level to the next one in an egalitarian organization. For example, each level in an American or Canadian organization often corresponds to three levels in an Indian organization (junior, intermediate, and senior).

As a result, the gradual increase from one level to the next that is expected in Canadian and American organizations (see Figure 9.3a) is replaced by three separate step changes in an Indian organization (see Figure 9.3b). In this schematic, the solid-line boxes represent the responsibilities of an individual who is moving from one level of an egalitarian organization to the next within an egalitarian organization. This individual gradually takes on responsibilities at higher and higher levels in the organization. Someone who is moving from the same starting point to the same endpoint in a hierarchical organization will experience three step changes in responsibilities, as indicated by the dashed-line boxes.

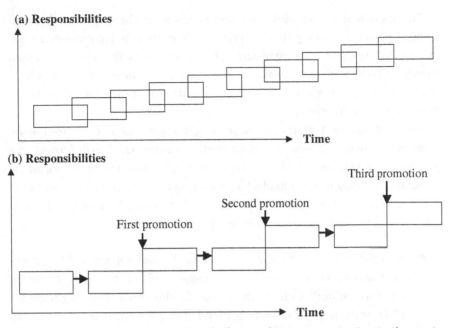

Figure 9.3a: Moving from one level of an egalitarian organization to the next in an egalitarian organization. **b:** Moving from the same level of an egalitarian organization to the next corresponds to three separate promotions in a hierarchical organization.

Mixing These Two Approaches

These two promotion processes are not easily mixed. When egalitarian people operate within a hierarchical organization and try to take on responsibilities at the next level in order to be promoted, they are often perceived by their hierarchical managers as being insubordinate, because they are trying to work on tasks for which they do not have enough authority. For example, Americans working in Japanese corporations or Canadians working in Korean organizations need to pay attention not to overstep their authority if they do not want to be perceived as "loose cannons," which would immediately curtail all their career opportunities within these organizations. In other words, the very actions they would take to get to the next level in their career are likely to prevent them from being promoted.

The opposite situation results in a similar outcome: The very thing that hierarchical people do to be promoted prevents them from being promoted when they work in an egalitarian organization. In order to focus on taking care of their current responsibilities very well, they often turn down some of the responsibilities their managers might offer them to demonstrate that they have what it takes to move to the next level.

For example, an American manager might suggest to a recent immigrant employee, "There is a new task force starting next week. It will look at that problem. Are you interested in being part of it?" And the employee might respond something like, "Actually, I have a lot on my plate right now and I want to make sure that I complete the projects and tasks you have assigned me on time, so I would rather not join this task force."

- From the employee's perspective, joining this task force will dilute his or her efforts. He or she perceives the manager's offer as stretching his or her box of responsibilities through the top. To him or her, shedding responsibilities at the low end of his or her level of responsibility would be equivalent to "passing the buck;" it would be tantamount to professional suicide in his or her home country.
- From the manager's perspective, this employee is clearly not management material. He or she just turned down an opportunity to operate at a higher level and interact with other people in the organization—clearly, this employee has limited ambition.

One important challenge that hierarchical employees experience in egalitarian organizations is that they are asked to take on tasks at higher levels without getting a raise—the raise is expected to follow good performance at higher levels rather than coincide with the increase in responsibility. This leads people from hierarchical cultures to turn down career growth opportunities, as the following story describes.

> I own four pharmacies, and I take on new students and interns on a regular basis since there has been a shortage of pharmacists in Ontario for the last few years. I came in contact with one pharmacist intern who was originally from Egypt. He seemed to have what it takes, so I was glad when he accepted my offer. I had high hopes for him—he was technically solid, his communication skills were good, and I thought he could become a store manager for me within a couple of years. I don't remember whether I told him in these words, but I know I clearly hinted at that fact, because he certainly saw himself as getting such a position one day.

I asked him to run our clinics the following year, to see how he would handle it. I gave him the schedule of these clinics and asked him to take care of them. When the first clinic came up, I asked him a few questions, just to see how prepared he was. It quickly became apparent that he had not done any of the necessary prework. He told me that he had been very busy—it was flu season, so we had been really busy, and I decided to drop it.

The same scenario was repeated during the next three clinics—he had not prepared and gave me some excuses as to why he had not had a chance to prepare. After the fourth time, I called him into my office and read him the riot act. I told him that he could never become a store manager if he did not take more initiative and responsibilities. He told me that he would be glad to take on more responsibilities, but he wanted to be compensated for these additional responsibilities. To which I responded that this was part of his job, particularly if he intended to become a store manager.

He felt insulted and quit. He went to work for a chain and did not like it, so he came back a few months later and asked me to take him back. Now he is filling scheduling gaps, working one or two days a week. He still pictures himself as a store manager; I certainly don't see him managing any of my stores, and I doubt that anyone else would offer him such a position.

—Canadian pharmacy owner

Relative Importance of Technical Skills and Soft Skills

Another major difference between North American and hierarchical organizations relates to the skills one needs to have and cultivate in order to move up and get to the top of the organization. In all cultures, a mix of technical skills and soft skills is required, but the optimum mix differs significantly from culture to culture, as portrayed in Figure 9.4.

Technical Skills

The relative weight placed on technical skills in hierarchical corporations is much higher than the relative weight placed on them in egalitarian cultures. For example, in Russia, the relative weight of technical skills might be 90 percent while the relative weight of soft skills is 10 percent. By contrast, the average relative weight of technical skills in Canada and in the United States is only 60 percent versus 40 percent for soft skills. In Sweden, the relative weight placed on technical skills is significantly lower (20 percent) and the relative weight placed on soft skills is significantly higher (80 percent).

The relative differences are presented graphically in Figure 9.4. (below). Three lines represent the preferred skill set mix for managers in Russia, North America, and Sweden. Managers are perceived to be of equal value if they possess the mix of skills represented by any point on their respective country line.

In Russia, managers with good technical skills are highly valued regardless of whether they have low, medium, or high soft skills. Therefore, the Russian line on the graph is virtually flat.

In North America, a manager could have high technical skills and low soft skills, medium technical skills and medium–high soft skills, or medium–high technical skills and very high soft skills and be considered of equal value to the organization. The North American line is on a significant angle.

In Sweden, the line is almost vertical with high soft skills being essential for success as a manager. It does not matter as much whether his or her technical skills are low, medium, or high, as long as the soft skills are high.

These differences come from the expectations placed on managers in these three different environments.

- In Russia, managers are expected to know how to solve problems. A good Russian manager is someone who can tell his or her employees, in detail, what steps to follow in order to get to the solution. Soft skills are not par-

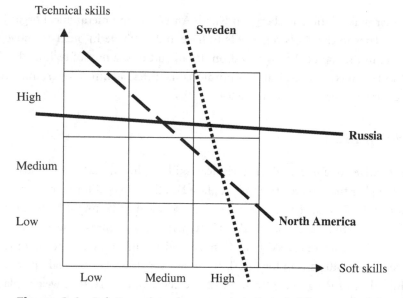

Figure 9.4 Relative value of manager's technical skills vs. soft skills.

ticularly important in Russia, since Russian managers are not expected to convince employees; employees will follow the direction set by their manager because he or she is the manager.

- In North America, managers are expected to set the direction for their employees but are not expected to tell them how to do their jobs. Managers need enough technical skills to set reasonable directions, but they also need soft skills to convince their employees to go in the direction they recommend.

- In Sweden, managers are expected to ensure that the initiatives taken by various employees add to something cohesive rather than detract from organizational goals. Swedish managers have limited disciplinary tools at their disposal to force employees to follow the directions they would set; they need good soft skills to create consensus and ensure that employees' efforts are congruent.

Soft Skills

In North American organizations, the relative weight of soft skills increases as one moves up in the organization. For example, the weight of technical skills for individual programmers might be 80 percent, while the weight placed on their soft skills is only 20 percent. They need to know the latest programming languages but do not need to have extensive conflict-resolution skills. By contrast, technical skills are not nearly as important to a chief information officer (CIO); however, soft skills become critical to the success of people in high-level positions: A CIO needs to be able to convince the CFO, the CEO, and the Board that a new IT system is needed or that the company could save significant amounts of money by investing in new technologies. So the relative weight placed on soft skills increases as one moves up in egalitarian corporations.

Recent immigrants who come from hierarchical cultures often have difficulty understanding the importance of soft skills in North America, at least at the beginning of their North American careers. Initially, many are placed in the top left square of Figure 9.4. Indeed, they have excellent technical skills—they would not be able to get through the immigration process without that. On the other hand, their soft skills are considered low by North American standards, primarily because the standards of soft skills are so cultural in nature. Someone who has good soft skills by Indian or Polish standards will often be considered as having poor soft skills in North America because he or she is likely to give feedback in a way that is considered too blunt and destructive in North America.

In addition, many culturally different employees had good soft skills by their home country standards before they immigrated to North America, so they need to redevelop their soft skills. This is a complex process, since it requires that they:

1. **Identify where the differences and gaps are.** In many cases, this happens the hard way: They do something in North America that, back home, would have yielded the results they wanted. Here, they find that the result is very different. In some cases, nothing happens; in others, very negative results occur.

2. **Determine what the preferred action should be.** Once you know there is a difference, you know what you should not do. However, knowing that you should not go north does not tell you in which direction you should go. The next step is to find out what should be done instead to achieve your goals. This may require asking coworkers, asking your boss, talking to a cultural coach, or talking to someone from your own culture who has been through the transitional experience and may be able to shed some light on the situation.

3. **Practice the soft skills in a North American context over and over again.** It often takes time and the application of the same skill in a wide range of situations to develop the level of confidence and expertise in the skill that is required to get to the top.

The soft skills that most culturally different employees need to redevelop in the North American context include the following.

- **Communication skills:** There are major cultural differences related to presentations and executive summaries:
  - ☐ As discussed in Chapter 8, a good presentation in North America focuses on the *impact of the content* of the work performed by the presenter and his or her team on the audience; the key question that a presentation needs to answer in North America is "What's in it for me?" This approach usually makes good North American presentations appear empty by Japanese standards. Japanese presentations aim to demonstrate that the presenter and his or her team have turned absolutely every stone to come to the conclusion they have reached. As a result, culturally different employees often need to study how to make presentations and work on understanding what in their work is of interest to their audiences in

order to reach the point where their presentations are considered better than average by North American standards.

□ The concept of an "executive summary" does not translate easily in many other cultures, because hierarchical and risk-averse senior managers there expect to be given all the details so that they can ensure that their employees have collected the right data and interpreted it in the appropriate manner. As a result, reports tend to be quite comprehensive, and culturally different employees often struggle when having to condense all their thoughts to one page.

■ **Management skills:** Culturally different employees need to learn how to manage people, projects, and time the North American way.

■ **Conflict resolution/negotiation:** The way one negotiates an agreement or a contract or resolves a conflict is highly cultural. Do you go through an intermediate or do you deal direct? Do you bring it out in the open or do you keep it quiet? Therefore, culturally different employees also need to learn the North American version of these skills.

■ **Leadership:** The skills and attributes of a good leader differ significantly from one culture to the next. The easiest way to see the differences here is to compare the political leaders of the United States and Canada. If the 2000 or 2004 U.S. presidential elections had been held in Canada, President Bush would have been soundly defeated in both cases (polls made in Canada at the time gave his opponents a 60–40+ lead). Conversely, Jean Chrétien, the Canadian Prime Minister from 1993 to 2003, would never have become president in the United States—his speech impediment (his face is partially paralyzed) would have prevented him from even being on the ballot. So culturally different employees need to understand what makes someone a good leader in Canada or in the United States, depending on where they live and work.

Other Factors

In many hierarchical cultures, having good technical skills is not the only factor required to reach the top. Family background, education, gender, country of origin, and seniority are expected to play, at most, a limited role in promotions in North America. They, however, may play an important role in hierarchical cultures. People who come from the best backgrounds are expected to achieve more and will therefore more often be given the "high-profile" projects and assignments. This, in turn, makes them more likely to achieve and to rise more quickly through the ranks. Having the "right" degree from the "right" university will also make a major difference in people's careers in hierarchical cultures.

In Japan, for example, many employees of the famous MITI (Ministry of Industry) are graduates of the University of Tokyo. Japanese teenagers have been known to commit suicide when they fail to be accepted by the university of their choice, making suicide for this reason one of the leading causes of death among Japanese teenagers. In France, over half of the executives of the large French corporations are graduates of the École Polytechnique de Paris. Here is the experience of a retired French engineer who worked for a large French corporation.

> I graduated from what French people would consider a "third-rate engineering school." I joined this organization 30 years ago. Past a certain level in this organization, you only find graduates of the École Polytechnique de Paris. I was determined to break this "educational glass ceiling." Over time, I rose through the ranks and came to the point where I was one promotion away from "breaking through." At that point, new rungs started to appear on the ladder: The organizational chart would change, and new levels appeared between this glass ceiling and my current level. In this manner, I could be promoted to the next level without breaking through. This took place a couple of times until I finally made it. Then I could retire.
>
> —French engineer working in France

Another major difference between North America and the cultures from which most immigrants come is related to the sense of individualism. Indeed, collective people emphasize interactions between people, teams, and departments. By contrast, individualistic people focus on their own role and responsibilities.

- In individualistic organizations, the people who reach the top of organizations often come from the part of the organization that is considered critical to the success of the organization. Many CEOs of oil and gas companies often have engineering backgrounds, since the success of these organizations often comes from understanding the technical risks encountered in new ventures. By contrast, CEOs in pharmaceutical companies need to understand the results of clinical trials and are often medical doctors. In many North American organizations, sales is the most important function in the organization, and CEOs often come from sales. North American organizations tend to prefer specialists over generalists.

- In collective organizations, the people who reach the top of organizations are often people who are able to see the interactions between the various parts of the organization. Just like the Japanese "on-boarding" process aims to create an understanding of the connections between the various parts of the organization (see Chapter 5), Japanese organizations value people who can see how their decisions and initiatives will impact the whole organization. Japanese organizations tend to prefer generalists over specialists.

Who Is Responsible for Your Career?

Retention and promotion issues are compounded by the following facts.

- In North America, people are brought up to believe that they are individually responsible for their own careers. Other people (coaches, their direct managers, HR, senior managers, etc.) are there to provide feedback, encouragement, support, and advice. However, in the end, everyone is responsible for his or her own career in North America.
- In hierarchical cultures, people do not consider themselves directly responsible for their own careers. They consider that their managers, their HR Director, their senior management, their alumni association, or their older relatives are responsible for promoting their interests to others, while their responsibility is to not let these people down and to make sure they are always doing a good job and being loyal to them.

The following experience illustrates this difference.

It took me about 12 years to understand what Americans and Canadians mean by "You are responsible for your career." I attended a number of career management workshops and every one of them started with the facilitator's asking the rhetorical question "Who is responsible for your career?" Everyone, including me, answered in unison: "I am." However, it took me a long time to stop blaming others when something did not happen the way I wanted it (for example, when someone got a promotion I thought I deserved).

—French engineer working in Canada

When hierarchical people come to North America, they often find that they have to make a significant mental shift in order to manage their careers effectively. Some have difficulties making this switch.

> One difficult situation involved a Vietnamese pharmacy intern whom I was mentoring for her two-month hospital rotation. She was very shy but very book smart. She wanted expectations spelled out precisely. The area that was of most concern to me was patient counseling. Despite demonstration by me, coaching, and reflection, she never did master this skill over the two months that she was my student. My first reaction was one of surprise since she had just completed two months in a community pharmacy setting and I expected that her counseling skills would be good. My next response was to work harder at improving her performance. By the end of the two months, when improved performance at this activity did not occur, I felt that I had put far too much energy into the task.
>
> In her final evaluation of the rotation, she thought I was a good teacher but that I did not do everything I said I would do within the time frame I had originally set out. She was completely unconcerned about her poor patient-counseling skills. Her written reports and small projects conducted during the rotation were excellently done. Discussions using a question-and-answer format were tedious sessions generally.
>
> On reflection, her goals for the rotation were different than mine. She had no interest/motivation to improve in this area. I did not pick up on this at all. Near the end of the two months, she told me that her parents and her boyfriend had encouraged her to go into pharmacy after obtaining a four-year biochemistry degree. She followed that advice, but had yet to own this decision. She hoped to find a work setting with little patient contact.
>
> —Canadian hospital pharmacist

It Is Not "What You Know," but "Who You Know" and, More Importantly, "Who Knows You"

Networking is often a critical component for most North American professionals. At some point or another, they happened to meet the right person at the right time, or someone who knew the quality of their work put their name forward for a major opportunity. While this happens all around the world, the dynamics of networking are very different in different countries. When culturally different employees attempt to network according to the networking approach used in their home country, this approach may lead them nowhere or, in some cases, may even produce negative results.

For example, Mexicans tend to network along family and friendship ties. The equivalent of the annual conference of one's professional association in North America is the annual ball of, for example, the Hernandez family, if this family includes people who are in important positions within Mexican society. In the case of upper-class-family events, this may take place in a large villa with large grounds and involve from a few hundred to a few thousand people.

During my last trip to Mexico, I talked to my Mexican counterpart, who is also an HR consultant, about the job search of her daughter. I asked her what her daughter was doing to find a job. She answered that her daughter was talking to all her family members. She said that she has something like 120 cousins, plus their spouses and relatives, so someone within that group was bound to know someone who needed someone who had her daughter's qualifications and who came from a good family.

—Canadian HR consultant

In France and Japan, people network within alumni associations. For example, a graduate from the École Polytechnique de Paris who works as a chemical engineer is closer to another graduate of the École Polytechnique de Paris who works as a banking executive than to a graduate of the École Centrale de Paris who works as a chemical engineer. French professional associations usually have far fewer members than their North American counterparts. Alumni association events tend to play the role that the annual conferences of professional associations play in North America: The Annual Ball of the École Polytechnique de Paris takes place at the Opera (the alumni association books the entire place for this event) and is attended by more than 5,000 people. The Bicentennial Ball (which took place at the Palace of Versailles in 1989) gathered about 20,000 people.

By contrast, one of the most important avenues for networking in North America is to be active in professional associations. As a result, North American professional associations have developed into large organizations with significant memberships. There are far more professional associations in North America than in many other countries. Both membership and active participation in these associations are often mentioned on North American résumés. Participating in these events gives North American professionals the opportunity to:

- Talk shop and gather qualitative information and knowledge that is not available through other means (in particular, on the Internet).

- Get new ideas on how to solve the problems they are currently facing, whether these problems are technical or career related.
- Demonstrate their skills to their peers, i.e., people who can really appreciate these skills for what they are. This applies to both technical skills (through formal presentations or informal discussions of their work) and nontechnical skills (by participating in the organization of the events, making presentations, leading panel discussions, etc.).
- Obtain information on where they might go next for their career. Many North American professionals make connections during professional association meetings that eventually result in new job opportunities.
- Get suggestions from other people regarding who could help them to solve the technical or organizational problems they are currently facing. North Americans place a lot of weight on these top-of-mind suggestions. If someone tells them, "If you have this kind of problem, call Sally at this number and she will take care of it for you," there is a very high probability that Sally will get a call, and this call will likely lead to a contract.

Many culturally different employees underestimate the importance of networking through professional associations. As a result, they often miss out on the opportunities that these associations can generate.

- They participate in fewer events than North Americans, so they are not as well known within their industry as their North American counterparts. As a result, people do not put their names forward when others ask them who could help them solve this or that problem.
- They focus on the technical part of their work and skip all the social/networking parts of the conference program, thereby missing out on the networking opportunities. They end up being perceived as people who are only interested in technical matters—this means that they are not management material by North American standards.
- They may socialize extensively within their cultural group, which limits their opportunities to network with top decision makers, because these decision makers often do not belong to their cultural group.
- They do not put their skills and accomplishment forward as much as their North American counterparts; this makes them look like second best in the minds of North Americans.

In addition to these differences, there are differences between collective and individualistic cultures in what can be expected from one's network.

- In individualistic cultures, your network is your personal responsibility and property, and you cannot share your network with others, even your spouse or close friends. When you access the network of an individualistic person, what you can expect to retrieve is usually a name, a phone number, and an e-mail address. The best the person whose network is accessed can do for you is tell the person you plan to contact that he or she should expect a call from you.

- In collective cultures, all members of your group have access to your network, and vice versa. When you access the network of collective people, they are likely to make the introduction themselves rather than letting you introduce yourself. In this process, they often put their reputation on the line: In essence, they lend credibility to both sides; making an introduction suggests implicitly that both sides should have something in common and that it should be worth their while to get to know one another.

I was in the office of my Mexican counterpart when she received a phone call from one of her friends. This friend had just been laid off and was contacting everyone in her network in order to find leads for a new job. My Mexican counterparts told her friend, "Send me your résumé. I know a few companies that are likely to need people with your expertise. I will call my contacts there to find out if they are hiring. If they are, I will pass on your résumé and set up an interview for you."

—American engineer in Mexico

In hierarchical cultures, people in senior managerial positions can modify the rules of hierarchical organization to a much greater extent than their counterparts in egalitarian organizations. In particular, they can often create positions for people they know. It is usually expected by others that they do so—if not, they will be perceived as having less power than others thought. They are also expected to "weigh in" significantly on the recruiting process (this is the reason why hierarchical people send their résumés to the people at the top of the organization—see Chapter 2 for more details). Some immigrants transfer this expectation to the North American workplace, as the following experience of this Romanian engineer indicates.

I had a good relationship with one of my neighbors, who is also Romanian. When he found out that I had a managerial position, he asked me to give his daughter a job. When I explained to him that I could not do that but that I would be happy to take her résumé to the HR department and put in a good word for her, he was quite upset. He thought I was letting him down.

—Romanian engineer in the United States

As a result, people who come from hierarchical cultures often focus their networking efforts on people in very senior positions, even though, by North American standards, these people cannot influence their career because there is too much of a gap between their level and these senior managers' levels.

Glass Ceiling

The misunderstandings resulting from the differences in the promotion process, in the skills that are required to reach the top, and in the ownership of someone's career all combine to slow down significantly the careers of many culturally diverse employees. These issues are compounded by the fact that, in most cases, neither egalitarian nor hierarchical people suspect that there might be a difference. They contribute significantly to the feeling of a "glass ceiling" that many culturally different people have when they look up in their organizations. Indeed, many North American organizations have large percentages of immigrants in their workforce, up to a certain level; past that level, the percentage of immigrants drops very rapidly. Here is an example of this.

I joined a large consumer product company shortly after graduating from an American university. At that time, this corporation was trying really hard to attract women and visible minorities, and these efforts were really paying off in terms of recruitment: More than half of the people who were hired that year were either women or visible minorities (sometimes both). After a few months, I realized that there were few women and even fewer visible minorities in middle and senior management ranks. The corporation was losing women and visible minorities almost as fast as it would hire them: Many of them would leave within the first two years. They would look up the organization and realize that it was going to be extremely difficult for them to get there, so they looked for other organizations where they would have better odds. I did the same—I left after four years.

—Indian engineer in the United States

This feeling of a glass ceiling and of a lack of a future within the organization leads many culturally different employees to leave their organizations prematurely. In many cases, they move on to competing organizations (sometimes in

North America, sometimes in their home countries), which may result in a loss of knowledge and talent for the original organization and in a boost to their competitors. More damaging potentially is the situation where culturally different employees leave the organization and start a competing organization, thereby increasing the competitiveness of the sector in which the organization they left operates. This threat is particularly important in the case of professional service organizations, where the threshold to market entry is quite low.

How Can Culturally Different People Reach Their Professional Objectives in North American Organizations?

What can individual recent immigrants do to ensure that they reach their full professional potential in a North American organization? Several approaches can be used, and it is important for each individual to find the steps that best fit his or her own situation and personality.

- **Realize, and help your counterparts realize, that cultural differences go much deeper than most people realize.** Operating in a culturally different environment means that people play by different rules, and you need to understand these rules well in order to compete on a level playing field. You need to ask your North American counterparts to explain these rules, often using specific examples and going into detail to make sure you have understood how these unwritten rules apply in several different situations.
- **Observe extensively how your North American counterparts behave in a wide range of situations.** Find out who is considered to be a really good leader/negotiator/presenter (depending on the soft skill you are trying to learn), and watch this person in action. Ask others what makes him or her stand out in this area. Go into specifics to make sure you understand what you need to change in your approach in order to improve.
- **Take initiative and ownership of your career.** While coming from a culturally different part of the world means that you have to overcome additional challenges and work harder than your North American colleagues to get to the same point, you will get limited sympathy from your North American colleagues if you complain about that. Focus on the things that you can do and that you can either control or influence in order to make things better for yourself.

- **Read books and watch movies that describe the lives of North Americans, and compare them with the lives of people in your home country.** For example, the comic strip "For Better or For Worse" describes the life of a North American family. Read these comic books and, when you do so, keep asking yourself the following questions: Would these issues/situations arise in my home country? If not, why? If so, how would they be resolved? If it is different from the approach used in North America, why is it different? Similarly, read books about the history of the country in which you live and work—understanding how it became what it is will help you understand why it operates the way it does.

- **Read books or watch movies about famous people in your new country.** When you do, keep asking yourself these questions: Why is this person considered great? What makes him or her stand out? Would his or her accomplishments be considered more important or less important in my home country? For example, New Canadians can watch the CBC series *The Greatest Canadian* as a way to understand what traits and characteristics Canadians admire in people.

- **Solicit feedback.** Most culturally different employees experience significant difficulties understanding the feedback they are given the way it was meant, so soliciting feedback more often than you would if you were dealing with people from the same cultural background helps reduce the frequency and magnitude of misunderstandings. Making people aware that you are actively trying to understand the culture makes them more inclined to help you in your quest.

- **Learn the soft skills that are practiced in North America.** This is usually done through a combination of classroom training, books, experiential learning (through organizations like Toast Masters or by volunteering in nonprofit organizations and professional associations), and individual coaching. You need to understand the standards of soft skills by which you are evaluated; you also need to develop these soft skills in order to get to the top.

- **Find a coach/mentor/counselor** who will help translate the career management challenges you experience into concepts that you understand and who will teach you how to apply these concepts to your everyday professional environment. When it comes to cultural differences, discussions in theory often result in limited progress, since it is very easy to obtain an agreement in principle while having vast disagreement on the application of these principles.

- **If you have children, follow their education, particularly on the soft skill side.** What are they learning? How are they learning it? The educational system in every country is set up to teach children what people in that country consider important to know in order to become productive members of this country. Your children are learning North American soft skills through the educational system—observe what they are learning, and try to transfer this information to your workplace.

- **Learn to network—North American style.** Become an active member of the professional association that corresponds to your expertise and the direction you want your career to take. The best time to create a network is when you do *not* need one. You need to help people and contribute to their well-being (by contributing to a professional association, by volunteering time or advice, etc.) so that you can call on these people when you need something from them.

- **Attend high-potential-development programs**—events where people who are identified as having high potential come together for a few days to mingle and gather information on the organization, its goals, and its successes. These programs are very helpful to culturally different employees when they provide information on what is valued within the organization and offer networking opportunities that would be difficult to obtain independent of such programs. When attending such programs, it is important for culturally different employees to keep in mind that being asked to attend such a program does not imply that a promotion will automatically follow—it just means that the organization provides an opportunity that each participant is expected to seize in his or her own way.

- **Be patient.** It usually takes anywhere between 6 and 12 years for immigrants to reach the point where they feel that the position they have in North American society is equivalent to, or better than, the position they had in their home society.

- **Beware of relying excessively on people who come from the same part of the world as you do.** While it is really tempting to socialize with people who are like you, with whom you can use your own language and your own sense of humor without being afraid of offending others, there are limitations to these interactions; you can get into a situation where "the blind are leading the blind." People who come from the same part of the world have the same perspective as you on North America, and their interpretations of the challenges you are experiencing are likely to come from the same vantage point. When this vantage point does not match the vantage point of North Americans, their advice may create more of a problem than it solves, as the following anecdote illustrates.

I worked for several years in a research center. I experienced a lot of difficulties there when working in teams; somehow, I felt like I was not getting enough information from my teammates, and they were visibly annoyed by my behavior. There was another French researcher in this center, and she started working there 10 years before me, so I would go and meet with her whenever I was having difficulties with my American teammates. Usually, we would agree that Americans have no idea how to work in teams, and she would give me advice on how to improve myself as a team player that made perfect sense to me. After a while, I realized that the advice she was giving me was rooted in the French definition of teamwork. The more I followed her advice, the more I irritated my American teammates.

Things started to get better when I started asking Americans for advice on how to improve the situation. While their advice made no sense to me initially, I could see that my American teammates seemed to appreciate my new approach.

—French researcher in the United States

How Can North American Organizations Help Their Culturally Different Employees Reach Their Professional Objectives?

One critical point is the extent to which North American organizations need to adapt to their culturally different employees versus the extent to which their culturally different employees need to adapt to their new environment. When asked this question during workshops, participants usually agree on the following.

- Culturally different employees need to make 80 percent of the adaptation, while North American organizations need to make 20 percent of the adaptation.
- Immigrants need to make the first step. North Americans will be glad to reciprocate, but they will not initiate this process.
- The time scale on which immigrants need to adapt is much shorter than the time scale over which North Americans need to adapt. Immigrants will

quickly end up on social assistance if they do not quickly adapt to their new environment; issues created in North American organizations by the lack of adaptation will take much longer to surface.

For this reason, the resources applied by organizations to alleviate these issues should be split in the same manner, i.e., 80 percent of the resources applied to solving these issues should be aimed at helping culturally different employees understand their environment, while the remaining 20 percent are applied to helping the organization adapt to this category of employees.

Since immigrants are expected, and generally expect themselves, to make the first step, it is usually best to design programs to help culturally different employees from a support perspective. The authors' experience with programs used in different organizations operating in very similar sectors indicates that investing 80 percent of the resources on the immigrant side and 20 percent on the organization side yields significantly better results in terms of recruitment and retention.

Here are some steps that North American organizations can take to help culturally different employees integrate more quickly and more effectively.

- Provide coaching and/or mentoring and/or orientations and/or training right from the start, when the person has just joined the organization. It is often much more difficult to turn around a situation that has gone sour than to prevent it from going downhill in the first place (see Chapter 5 for more details).
- Organize high-potential-development events to give people some form of recognition. Emphasize that participation in these events does not imply that one will be automatically promoted.
- Create and provide career management courses that are specifically geared to the needs and situations of the culturally different employees in your organization. Make sure the culturally different employees in your organization attend this course by making it mandatory.
- Provide more comprehensive and more frequent feedback to culturally different employees than you would to other employees so that they have a chance to understand exactly the performance evaluation criteria used in your organization and how these criteria apply to them.
- Encourage culturally different employees to become active members in the professional associations that are relevant to their activities and career directions. Discuss with them what this participation means and what

approaches, actions, behaviors, and attitudes they may consider during professional association meetings.

- Emphasize the importance of networking in North American careers through one-on-one discussions (coaching/performance-appraisal discussions) and career management training courses.

- Provide training and development opportunities to culturally different employees, particularly on the soft skill side. Suggest books and activities that may help them develop the soft skills they need or will soon need in their career.

- Provide support to the managers of culturally different employees. This can take the form of one-on-one coaching on an as-needed basis, of classroom training, of discussions at management retreats, etc. Since managers have so much impact on the careers of the people who report to them directly, it is usually helpful for them to understand the challenges their culturally different employees face in adapting to the organization and in navigating their careers within it.

10

Conclusions

Jack Welsh, the former leader of GE, repeatedly stressed it was the company's diversity that was its greatest strength. By diversity he referred to both its varied business divisions and its multicultural employees. While the popular management thinking of the 1980s and 1990s was to focus on a core business and "stick to the knitting," Jack Welsh helped the multifocused conglomerate GE to thrive. He did it, in part, by taking best practices from one division, reworking them, and applying them to other divisions in the company. As with diverse corporate divisions, so with multinational employees—take the differing and often-conflicting ideas, work them, and come up with something better.

The two biggest reasons immigrants are a growing segment of North American workforces are simply that qualified immigrants are showing up in greater numbers with a desire to work, and there is not an overabundance, locally, of qualified people to draw on. As a result, our workplaces become more culturally diverse.

Cultural differences are a source of both challenges and opportunities. In most cases, the challenges come first and the opportunities later. To make it beyond the early challenges and to reap the rewards requires preparation, patience, and persistence, as do most good things in life.

In our Prologue, we listed common negative statements that you perhaps have heard from others in your organization regarding the employment of recent immigrants. Under stress, and without preparation or support, it is common for multicultural teams to display some of the worst traits of each culture represented. Just throwing people together and expecting them to work it out doesn't usually bring the best results. To bring out the best traits in cultures and individuals takes a bit of work.

In this book, we don't spend much time discussing the pros and cons of a culturally diverse workforce. This is because most workforces *are* culturally diverse now to some extent, and those that aren't will be soon. That's just the reality. So the question we have tried to address is not *why* but *how*. Since available workforce candidates are culturally diverse, how best do we work with that reality and prosper from it?

It is our hope and expectation that you have found some advice in this book that will help you persevere, improve the situation in your organization, and reap the rewards possible from a culturally diverse organization. That being said, we would like to mention what we see as the potential benefits of having a well-run culturally diverse workforce.

Individual Employee and Manager Benefits

We see two primary benefits for your staff to be working with recent immigrants. First, your employees are learning to work with a wider range of situations and people. They are becoming worldlier without leaving the office. The skills employees learn in order to interact successfully with their diverse coworkers are the same skills that are required to interact successfully with diverse clients. North American clients are becoming more diverse as our general population becomes less homogeneous.

Second, employees learn to work with people who present ideas differently. Rather than succumbing to the temptation to dismiss an immigrant's idea outright, the experienced member of a multicultural work group is able to pick out new and useful ideas like "diamonds in the rough." He or she is able to work with recent immigrants to build on these gems in order to satisfy their work objectives in creative new ways.

Companies find that the learning and stretching their employees experience by integrating recent immigrant employees better prepares them for working with other forms of change and diversity. Employees have come to better understand their own values and behaviors, to understand a different set of values and behaviors in others, and to learn new ways to integrate these differences. They are stronger and made more resilient in dealing with other forms of change or difference.

I was part of an IT team of network specialists that manages the entire IT system of all the American operations of a large multinational corporation, except the United States. Our computer network spanned all of the Americas, from Nunavut to Tierra del Fuego, except the 48 states of our American friends. I really learned a lot from working with my Latin American colleagues. In particular, I learned from my Latin American colleagues to "go with the flow" more. When something unexpected came down the pipe from headquarters, I often reacted with some impatience, since it was not part of my plan. My Latin American colleagues would take it as if it was a normal part of their days.

One of the situations where we truly benefited from being a multicultural team was when we had to do a major systems upgrade. This would require taking down all the computers for several days. Given people's strong reactions when the system was down for just one hour, I dreaded the time we would send the e-mail to everyone saying that the system would be down for several days. I was trying to find ways of doing this change incrementally—upgrade some computers while keeping others running, for example. It did not look like it would work easily, because the new system was not really compatible with the old one.

My Latin American colleagues came to the rescue and said, "Look, we are now in late May. This year, July 1 is on Friday and July 4 is on Monday. If we prepare everything for that weekend, we can take the system down on Thursday night and bring it back up during the weekend. We will have some time to work out the bugs in the new operating system and nobody will notice: Americans and Canadians will be off and Latin Americans will go, 'Que sera sera!' What do you say?"

That was a great idea! It meant that I would lose my long weekend, but I knew that this was far preferable to having the company down at any other time. I ran this idea by my boss, who was really impressed. We implemented my colleagues' plan and it worked like a charm. My boss gave me a major bonus for this one and it was one of the points he put forward when I was up for promotion.

—Canadian IT network manager

The individual benefits complement and lead into the company benefits of having a culturally diverse workforce.

Company Benefits

A reason sometimes given for hiring a recent immigrant is to have that person return to his or her country of origin as a representative of the company. Perhaps the person is being hired as a sales representative. The problem here is that the employee is being hired on the basis of nationality and not on experience and skills in the job function. It may take years to properly train someone to be an effective sales representative in the domestic or international office. There are a number of good reasons for hiring recent immigrants, but this is not usually one of them.

As individuals gain capacity to deal with a wider range of change, so the organization increases its capacity as well. Canadians, as a rule, prefer incremental changes over large-scale change. This may blind them to the potential value of rapid and drastic change in certain circumstances. Americans, by contrast, are more open to disruptive change. Mixing Canadians and Americans in a work group can provide the benefit of both approaches.

An organization containing people with different tendencies toward risk tolerance can move the company forward with better-informed decisions. Risk-averse employees will do a detailed cost–benefit analysis and still ask for the collection of more data. The risk takers will recommend forging ahead quickly and "striking while the iron is hot." As these employees gain experience with each other, they sort out which type of decisions they do want more detailed background information on and for which decisions they can move forward quickly and effectively.

More and more companies would like to be able to offer services to different client ethnicities through people of the same ethnicity. It doesn't mean that the Muslim woman entering a bank will necessarily be served by a Muslim woman. However, the female Muslim client may feel significantly more comfortable if she sees a Muslim woman working somewhere in the office. The Filipino client will likely be very impressed if he or she is able to make an appointment to speak with a client representative in his or her native language.

> A large department store takes advantage of a government-sponsored bridging program that helps immigrants find jobs. A department store senior executive and her team meet the interns and use them as a focus group. They learn about shopping preferences, with the intention of expanding their potential clientele.
>
> A multinational consumer-products company hires students in American universities who are originally from other countries. It trains them in company practices and corporate culture and posts them back in their home countries as managers. They are responsible for bringing new products and work methods from head office to the local subsidiaries.

The following example illustrates a situation where one organization benefited strongly from cultural differences.

> I worked for a multinational chemical company at the time. I wanted to hire a technician, but I did not have any budget for that, so I contacted one of the nonprofit agencies that help immigrants find jobs in Canada. I learned that I could have someone work for me essentially for free, as long as I helped the person in his or her job search. I liked that idea and decided to bring in some candidates for interviews.

At the same time, one of my fellow chemical engineers was also looking for a technician. We talked about it and decided to interview the candidates I brought in the same day. One of these candidates was Mohammed. Mohammed was from Somalia; he had fled the country as a result of the civil war. I interviewed Mohammed and thought that he was really wonderful; he had dedication, commitment, and initiative, everything I was looking for. His chemistry was a bit rusty, since he had not worked as a chemist for several years. During the civil war, he had acted as a translator for the United Nations and he started a shrimp import–export business, but he did not do much chemistry.

At the end of the day, my colleague and I compared notes. I asked him what he thought of Mohammed. He answered, "His bachelor's in chemistry is not worth a Canadian high school diploma." I thought that this was a harsh statement. I decided to hire Mohammed anyway.

Mohammed was really good. He went from an unpaid internship, to a three-month contract, to a one-year contract, to a permanent position, to a company award. Our organization would have missed out on a great resource if I had followed my colleague's assessment of Mohammed's skills.

I know that Mohammed obtained a bachelor's in chemistry and that he studied roughly the same subjects as Canadian undergraduate students, because my wife had a bachelor's degree in chemistry from a Canadian university. She had lent me her organic synthesis book. One day, Mohammed came into my office while I was on the phone, so I gestured that he should sit down while I finished my call. He looked at the books on my shelf; when I hung up, he pointed to the book my wife had lent me and said, "We studied the same book in Somalia."

When Mohammed started working for me, I remember watching him doing an experiment for me. The last of the experiment was, as usual, "washing the dishes"— taking some soap, scrubbing the glassware to remove all traces of chemicals, then rinsing thoroughly with distilled water, and finally drying all the glassware in an oven. The first time I watched Mohammed do this, he was taking a small amount of distilled water, then moving the beaker in many directions in order to have that little bit of water cover every area of the beaker.

After a while, I asked him, "Mohammed, why do you do it this way?" He answered that distilled water was at a premium in Somalia since there is little water and little energy. I understood his perspective and told him that, in Canada, water and energy are no issue—the resource that is always in short supply is time. So I told him to rinse his glassware under running distilled water (we had distilled water on tap in this research center). In essence, I told him to be as quick and wasteful as every other technician. He agreed and started being as quick and wasteful as everyone else in the center.

A year later, our research team had come up with a new formulation for one of our products that was truly superior to anything on the market at the time. We had demonstrated the feasibility of the process at small scale and we were now looking at scaling up to full production. Our company's process for that included a project review meeting. This meeting included people from all over the company (sales, marketing, engineering, production, etc.), all trying to anticipate the issues that may arise as we try to commercialize this product.

During this meeting, our research team presented its results. Since this product was so much better than anything on the market, we were really proud of ourselves. At one point, one of the production engineers from our midwestern plant raised his hand and asked, "How much water do you use to wash the product at the end of the process?" We had never thought of that point. At small scale, it did not matter. We answered straight: "1,100 kg of water per kg of product." The plant engineer made a calculation in his mind and came back quickly with, "We are going to have to divert the Mississippi into the plant in order to wash this product."

At that point, we realized we had a major problem on our hands. That is when Mohammed's experience in washing and rinsing things and knowing that they were well washed came in really handy. He helped us get through this difficult problem.

—Canadian chemical engineer

Making a connection with other cultural groups is particularly important when one considers the growth of purchasing power among culturally diverse people. A 2005 study by the University of Georgia's Selig Center for Economic Growth gives the projected rate of increase of the buying power, by race, for the period 1990–2009 in the United States. The projected percentage increases are shown in Figure 10.1.[1]

A 2003 Canadian government survey titled "The Impact of Employment Equity on Corporate Success in Canada" revealed that corporate leaders felt the employment equity program showed greatest impact in the following areas (with percentage of respondents agreeing with the statement in parentheses):

- Creating a work culture tolerant of diversity (51 percent).
- Improving the corporate image (39 percent).
- Improving recruitment efforts (37 percent).
- Enhancing creativity in decision making (29 percent).
- Increasing employee commitment (27 percent).[2]

[1]http://www.selig.uga.edu/
[2]http://www.hrsdc.gc.ca/asp/gateway.asp?hr=/en/lp/lo/lswe/we/special_projects/
RacismFreeInitiative/ConferenceBoard.shtml&

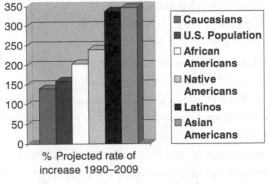

Figure 10.1 Buying power, by race.

The bottom-line results support the commitment to diversity. Examined over a 10-year period, The 2006 Diversity Inc. magazine Top 50 Companies for Diversity Index outperformed the Nasdaq by 28.2 percent, the Standard & Poor's 500 by 24.8 percent, and the Dow Jones Industrial Average by 22.4 percent. Results for one-, three-, and five-year performance were competitive as well.[3]

If a company's workforce is becoming more diverse simply because there is a short-term shortage of labor, the organization should recognize that. The more successful companies will be those that are able to connect the firm's overall strategies and its human resources practices, such as the recruitment of a culturally diverse workforce. Rather than asking, "Why are we seeing more diverse cultures in our workforce?," company leaders will ask, "How can we best integrate cultural diversity in our workforce?"

Final Words of Advice

Here are a few final words of advice when working with people of other cultures.

- Admit that you don't know when you don't know.
- Suspend judgment.
- Use empathy.
- Systematically check your assumptions.

[3]http://www.diversityinc.com/public/21000.cfm

- Become comfortable with ambiguity.
- Celebrate and benefit from cultural diversity.

The skills necessary to be successful in recruiting and retaining culturally diverse employees are the same as those required for excellence in individuals and organizations of the future. It's challenging and at times frustrating, but the greatest leverage for future success for most of us is our ability to work successfully with people who are different from us.

Successfully incorporating recent immigrants into the workplace requires, and in turn fosters, a dynamic environment that will benefit future recruitment, products and services, customer service, and financial performance. These are the benefits for companies that prepare themselves.

Appendix: Global and North American Migration Demographics

Table A.1 Percentage of Foreign Born in Major North American Cities

U.S. American cities	% Foreign born (2004)[a]
Miami	58.7
Los Angeles	40.4
San Francisco	37.3
New York City	35.9
San Diego	27.1
Houston	27.0
Boston	26.8
Dallas	26.6
Chicago	21.3
Denver	18.4
Minneapolis	16.6
Philadelphia	11.4
Canadian cities	**% Foreign born (2001)[b]**
Toronto	43.7
Vancouver	37.5
Calgary	20.9
Montreal	18.5
Ottawa-Hull	17.6

[a] http://factfinder.census.gov/servlet/GRTTable?_bm=y&-geo_id=01000US&-_box_head_nbr=R0501&-ds_name=ACS_2004_EST_G00_&-redoLog=false&-mt_name=ACS_2004_EST_G00_R0501_US30&-format=US-32
[b] http://www12.statcan.ca/english/census01/products/analytic/companion/etoimm/subprovs.cfm

Table A.2 Percentage of Foreign Born in Major International Cities

City	% Foreign born (2004)[a]
Singapore	33
Sydney	31
London	28
Paris	23
[a] http://hdr.undp.org/reports/global/2004/pdf/hdr04_chapter_5.pdf#page=3	

Table A.3 Top 10 Countries, by Share of Migrant Population

Country	% Foreign born (2000)[a]
United Arab Emirates	68
Kuwait	49
Jordan	39
Israel	37
Singapore	34
Oman	26
Switzerland	25
Australia	25
Saudi Arabia	24
New Zealand	22
[a] http://hdr.undp.org/reports/global/2004/pdf/hdr04_chapter_5.pdf#page=3	

Table A.4 Foreign-Born Population, by Country

Country	% Foreign born (2000)[a]
Luxembourg	32.6
Australia	23.0
Switzerland	22.4
New Zealand	19.5
Canada	19.5
Germany	12.5
Sweden	12.0
Ireland	10.4
Netherlands	10.1
France	10.0
United Kingdom	8.3
Spain	5.3
[a] http://www.oecd.org/dataoecd/61/37/34607274.pdf	

Table A.5 Country of Origin of the Largest Percentage of Foreign Born, from Total Immigrants

United States—five largest foreign-born groups	Percentage % (2000)[a]
Mexico	29.5
Philippines	4.4
India	3.3
China	3.2
Vietnam	3.2
Canada—five largest foreign-born groups	**Percentage % (2001)[b]**
United Kingdom	10.9
China	6.1
India	5.7
Italy	5.6
United States	4.6
[a] http://www.migrationinformation.org/DataTools/migrant_stock_groups.cfm [b] http://www.migrationinformation.org/DataTools/migrant_stock_groups.cfm	

Table A.6 Country of Origin of the Largest Percentage of Foreign Born, from Recent Immigrants (2004)

To United States[a]	To Canada[b]
Mexico	China
India	India
Philippines	Pakistan
China	Philippines
Vietnam	United States

[a] http://uscis.gov/graphics/shared/statistics/yearbook/2004/table3.xls
[b] http://www.cic.gc.ca/english/monitor/issue06/01-highlights.html

Bibliography/Recommended Reading List

Axtell RE, Fornwald M. *Gestures: The Do's and Taboos of Body Language Around the World*. New York, John Wiley & Sons, 1997.

Hall ET. *Beyond Culture*. Anchor, New York, 1977.

Harris PR, Moran RT. *Managing Cultural Differences—Leadership Strategies for a New World of Business*, 6th ed. Woburn, MA, Butterworth-Heinemann, 2004.

Hofstede G. *Culture's Consequences: Comparing Values, Behaviors, Institutions, and Organizations Across Nations*, 2nd ed. Newbury Park, CA, Sage Publications, 2003.

Hofstede G. *Culture and Organizations: Software of the Mind*, 2nd ed. New York, McGraw-Hill, 2004.

Laroche LF. *Managing Cultural Diversity in Technical Professions*. Woburn, MA, Butterworth-Heinemann, 2002.

Morrison T, Conaway WA. *Kiss, Bow or Shake Hands, 2nd Edition: The Best-Selling Guide to Doing Business in More Than 60 Countries*. Adams Media, Cincinnati, OH, 2006.

Murphy M, Burgio-Murphy A. *The Deadly Sins of Employee Retention*. BookSurge, North Charleston, SC, 2006.

Storti C. *Figuring Foreigners Out: A Practical Guide*. Yarmouth, MA, Intercultural Press, 1998.

Thomas DC, Inkson K. *Cultural Intelligence: People Skills for Global Business*. Berrett-Koehler, San Francisco, 2004.

Trompenaars F, Hampden-Turner C. *Riding the Waves of Culture—Understanding Diversity in Global Business*, 2nd ed. New York, McGraw-Hill, 1998.

Trompenaars F, Hampden-Turner C. *Managing People Across Cultures.* Capstone, Oxford UK, 2004.

Web Sites

Diversity Inc. magazine	http://www.diversityinc.com/
Intercultural Communication Institute	http://www.intercultural.org/
Society for Human Resource Management	http://www.shrm.org/
Statistics Canada	http://www.statcan.ca/
U.S. Immigration Statistics	http://www.uscis.gov/ graphics/shared/statistics/

Index